UK Eyes Alpha

Mark Urban was the Defence Correspondent of the *Independent* for more than three years. As a foreign affairs and defence specialist for BBC2's *Newsnight* he covered the Gulf War and the coup in the Soviet Union. During 1994 he worked as the BBC's Middle East correspondent based in Israel, and then returned to *Newsnight*. He is also the presenter of the BBC's *Leviathan*, a history and current affairs programme. Mark Urban is the author of *Soviet Land Power*, *War in Afghanistan* and, for Faber, *Big Boys' Rules*.

By the same author

Big Boys' Rules: The SAS and the
secret struggle against the IRA

UK Eyes Alpha

Inside British Intelligence

Mark Urban

faber and faber

LONDON · BOSTON

For Ruth and Edwin

First published in 1996
by Faber and Faber Limited
3 Queen Square London WC1N 3AU
This paperback edition published in 1997

Typeset by Faber and Faber Ltd
Printed in England by Mackays of Chatham plc,
Chatham, Kent

A CIP record for this book is available from the British
Library

ISBN 0-571-19068-5

10 9 8 7 6 5 4 3 2 1

Contents

Introduction

How good is British intelligence? What kind of a return do ministers and officials get for the hundreds of millions of pounds spent on espionage each year? How does this secret establishment find direction and purpose in an age when old certainties have evaporated? Very few people, even in Whitehall, would feel confident enough to answer these questions. So the time is right, I think, to explore the matter publicly.

The aim of this book is firstly to examine the performance of the British intelligence services during the last years of the Cold War, as they finally came to terms with the fact that this historic clash of ideologies was over, and secondly to examine the relevance of those services in the 1990s and beyond. In researching this book, I have had many revelations: about the effectiveness of those agencies, about their relationship with the USA, about how much government ministers knew, and many other matters.

This book takes the coming to power of Mikhail Gorbachev in 1985 as its starting point. The publication in February 1996 of the Scott Report on the 'arms to Iraq' affair marks its conclusion. It is not a study of the broad sweep of world events during those tumultuous years, but rather an examination of how well British intelligence understood them, whether its product was particularly useful to those in power or to Britain's allies, and how the agencies are now trying to remain relevant in an age where many no longer believe there is any direct threat to the security of the United Kingdom. I have tried to provide just enough information about events to answer these questions, but by necessity this is not a history book.

In trying to address these questions, I have been helped by the change of climate brought about by John Major's premiership, which has allowed a freer discussion of intelligence issues. Several years ago I was tempted to start a similar book, but the idea soon ran aground because so few people were prepared to talk. In writing this one, I was able to interview key officials and politicians: I therefore believe it is the first account of the subject to draw on a truly authoritative cast of players. Another sign of the changed climate is that access to many key people is not dependent on an unquestioning or 'sympathetic' journalistic approach – so I have also sought to scrutinize areas that people in power or those giving Whitehall briefings often prefer not to discuss.

It might be argued that now is too early to look at such recent history. But there are important differences between the examination of intelligence matters and the wider business of government. Despite changes in the procedures for declassifying government papers, those concerning the sources of secret intelligence are likely to remain hidden from public view for decades, perhaps for as long as a hundred years. Given the present willingness of so many people who have been involved in this field to talk, my imperative was to interview them as soon as possible, before memories fade.

Many in the intelligence agencies would still like to cloak everything they do in secrecy: this may be necessary to protect the life of an agent, or it may simply be useful to those who are guilty of overspending. Even in the changed atmosphere of the mid-1990s, the writer on intelligence matters must respect certain requirements of secrecy. I do not reveal the names of serving intelligence officers (unless already publicly identified), the identity of any current agent, the precise location of buildings where not previously publicized, or the specific signals intelligence techniques used against any current target.

This book was not cleared, in its entirety, before publication by any arm of government nor by the Defence Press and Broadcasting Committee, better known as the D-notice committee, the joint press/official liaison body which has been in existence since 1912. Instead a few chapters were shown to officials of GCHQ, MI6 and MI5 in instances where I had specific concerns about endangering their sources or operations. I agreed to a small number of changes on these operational grounds. After the hardback edition of *UK Eyes Alpha* was published I was told that senior officials at the Cabinet Office had asked the Ministry of Defence to ensure that no future book of this kind would be brought out without prior clearance. In the age of the internet and fax, I believe this simply shows how outdated many mandarins are in their attitudes to secrecy.

Now the Cold War is over, my personal view is that the time has come to scrap the D-notice committee and the system of so-called 'voluntary' consultation between journalists and Whitehall which goes with it. This type of self-censorship belongs to an era when many believed the UK might be involved in total war with as little as four minutes warning. Since defence and intelligence planning in this country is now predicated on the assumption that it would take months or years for a new threat to emerge, the restoration of arrangements like the D-notice system can now safely be added to some unspecified future time of tension when war clouds are gathering – just as they were in 1912.

Would the ending of this cooperative system affect national security? I do not believe it would in the slightest. Having reviewed the D-notice committee's papers at the Public Record Office and talked to many people about the past workings of the system, I do not believe there has ever been an occasion when a journalist has tried to name an active agent of MI5 or MI6 or perhaps to reveal the operation of particular eavesdropping techniques – the real secrets which the agencies are entitled to protect – let alone one where this system has stopped such a disclosure happening. Peter Wright began the destruction of old attitudes to secrecy with the publication of *Spycatcher*. The D-notice system has been widely ignored in recent years, be it by tabloids revealing Stella Rimington's address, television journalists compiling timely reports on counter-terrorist operations or by the recent book-writing of former members of the Special Air Service.

Only a fool would forget that the government may still choose to take legal action against a former employee for breach of confidentiality or a journalist for damaging national security. I think it would be better for all sides if the intelligence agencies named press officers and made their telephone numbers widely available (as I understand MI5 is planning to do at the time of writing). That way the journalist with concerns about a story will know where to find them. Who knows, the agencies might well find that, by undermining further cloak-and-dagger mystique, such a step would work in their interests too.

In addressing the effectiveness of British intelligence collection, I targeted the two principal centres of analysis: the Cabinet Office Joint Intelligence Committee staff and the Defence Intelligence Staff. These compile the assessments sent to ministers, using publicly-available information as well as that produced by British and allied agencies. They usually know how good signal intelligence or agent reports were on any given subject and how great a role British collectors of intelligence played. In examining the work of the analysts themselves, I have asked the ministers or officials who received such reports to say whether they were useful or not.

Despite the atmosphere of greater openness, those in the principal collection agencies – MI6, MI5 and GCHQ – remain very reluctant to be quoted. I have however had many briefings from intelligence officials since 1990, although the terms of strict non-attributability on which they were provided prevent me from referring to them in any specific way. Although they formed part of my general background knowledge, these interviews did not play a major role in this study. Even when available, such interviews tend to be governed by strict briefing terms, so I sought my own interviews with individuals who had been involved with these three organizations; it was something of a relief not to be bound by any deals with the agencies. About twenty people who had worked for MI5, MI6 or GCHQ helped on condition that I did not use their names; for this reason they do not appear in the list of interviewees below. About the same number of people in the Foreign Office, other government departments, the armed forces and industry also provided non-attributable information.

I would like to thank the following people who have helped me with this study: Julian Loose, my editor; Nick Menzies, for valuable research help; Jean-Claude Racape who kindly allowed me to live in seclusion at the Manoir des Mauvaises Lignes while writing the book; Jonathan Lloyd, my agent; Peter Horrocks, editor of Newsnight, for putting up with a correspondent distracted by book production; and most of all, my wife Hilary for her patience in supporting me through the project.

The list of source interviews uses titles or ranks current at the time of publication. In the interests of brevity, I have avoided mentioning knighthoods or peerages in the text. In a couple of cases, quotations in the text have come from previously unpublished sections of BBC interviews that I conducted during the production of reports on intelligence matters. However, the great majority of the people listed below were interviewed specifically for this book.

Morton Abramowitz Assistant Secretary for Intelligence and Research (INR), US State Department, 1985–9

Air Chief Marshal Sir Michael Armitage Chief of Defence Intelligence, 1982–5

Derrick Averre University of Birmingham

David Bickford Legal Adviser to DG of the Security Service, 1987–95

General Sir Peter de la Billière Commander of British Forces Middle East, 1990–1

Lieutenant-General Sir Derek Boorman Chief of Defence Intelligence 1985–8

Sir Rodric Braithwaite, Chairman Joint Intelligence Committee 1992–3

Yigal Carmon Director of Counter Terrorism (Israel), 1988–92

George Churchill Coleman Commander of the Metropolitan Police Anti-Terrorist Unit, 1985–92

Captain Jonathan Cooke Director of Intelligence for Eurasia, DIS, 1993–5

Sir Percy Cradock Chairman of Joint Intelligence Committee, 1985–92

Gary Crocker US State Department (INR)

Sir Brian Cubbon Permanent Under Secretary, Home Office, 1979–88

Dwayne Day, George Washington University, USA

Sir Anthony Duff Chairman of JIC, 1982–5, Director General of Security Service 1985–7

Robert Gates Director of the CIA, 1991–3

Mikhail Gorbachev General Secretary of the Communist Party of the Soviet Union, 1985–91

Oleg Gordievsky KGB, 1962–85

John Gordon Head of Nuclear Energy Department, FCO, 1986–8

Michael Herman, GCHQ, 1952–87

Mark Higson Iraq Desk, FCO, 1988–90

Lord Howe of Aberavon Foreign Secretary, 1983–9

Oleg Kalugin KGB, 1957–89

Richard Kellaway Chief Investigating Officer, HM Customs and Excise

Tom King MP Defence Secretary 1989–92

Owen Lewis formerly Ministry of Defence (Army)

Pierre Marion, Head of DGSE (France), 1981–5

David Mellor Minister of State at Home and Foreign Offices, 1986–90

Martin Morland Chief of Assessments Staff, JIC, 1984–6

Lieutenant-General William Odom Director of US National Security Agency, 1985–8

Peter Pigden Deputy Chief Investigating Officer, HM Customs and Excise, 1989–95

Sir Charles Powell Private Secretary to the Prime Minister, 1984–91

Julian Perry Robinson University of Sussex

William Taylor Assistant Commissioner for Special Operations, Metropolitan Police, 1991–5

Air Marshal Sir John Walker Chief of Defence Intelligence, 1991–4

Lieutenant-General Norman Wood director of US intelligence community programmes, 1990–2

Part One

Chapter 1

1985 The Coming Earthquake

The Central Committee vote of 11 March 1985 was, in the manner of all important votes by the Communist Party of the Soviet Union, a foregone conclusion. Foreign Minister Andrei Gromyko, the inscrutable hard man of the Politburo, stepped up to the rostrum in the role of kingmaker. Gromyko, a top official since the days of Stalin, proposed that Mikhail Sergeyevich Gorbachev be appointed General Secretary, and the vote was carried unanimously. The three hundred or so members of the élite who gathered in conclave behind the fortress walls of Moscow's ancient imperial citadel had watched the dynamic progress of the man from Stavropol. Although the ageing party bosses had for the most part themselves come to power under Brezhnev, they recognized that new life was needed to galvanize their system, to save it from stagnation.

Throughout the previous months, while serving as deputy to Konstantin Chernenko, the party leader who had come to power in 1983, Gorbachev had used his youth and dynamic manner to sell himself as the apostle of change. In a speech three months before Chernenko's death, he had discussed various reforms in the fields of manufacturing and technology, and said, 'There is no alternative'. This phrase had become his unofficial campaign slogan.

In the days that followed his appointment, Gorbachev set about trying to make it clear publicly that he stood for something new. He conducted walkabouts, meeting a people hitherto used to seeing their leaders only in glimpses through the curtains of their Zil limousines or in retouched official photographs. He spoke frankly about the problems of the economy. Then he sent a signal to the West.

After less than a month in office, the new General Secretary announced he was freezing deployments of new nuclear weapons in the so-called INF (Intermediate Nuclear Forces) category. In a classic episode of the Cold War arms race, Moscow's decision to field these weapons, most famously the SS-20 missile – most of which were targeted on western Europe – had caused alarm in London, Bonn and Washington. It had prompted the Nato powers, amid public protests and political ferment, to come up with an answer: hundreds of Cruise and Pershing missiles to be based across Europe from Greenham Common in England to Sigonella in Italy.

On the second floor of the Cabinet Office in Whitehall, the best and brightest of British intelligence would gather each Thursday to mull over developments in Moscow and elsewhere at the meetings of the JIC, the Joint Intelligence Committee. When the gathering came to a view about some topical development, as it usually did several times during each meeting, this was duly minuted and circulated throughout government as the highest agreed position of the nation's intelligence gatherers and analysts. Chairmanship of the JIC carried with it many duties, including organizing the espionage community and overseeing the work of the Assessments Staff, a body of twenty-five to thirty analysts which stood at the hub of national intelligence output.

Percy Cradock, a Foreign Office diplomat, had taken over as the new Chairman of JIC early in 1985. With his starred first-class degree from Cambridge, Cradock's clipped speech, great care in his choice of words and reputation for not suffering fools, reinforced the impression that he was among the brightest of men. Between 1971 and 1975 he had served in the Joint Intelligence Committee as Chief of Assessments, later becoming ambassador to Peking and a key figure in the government's negotiations with China over Hong Kong. China and intelligence were Cradock's driving passions: it was the quality of his work on China that led the Prime Minister to want him working close to her, as foreign policy advisor and in charge of intelligence.

Cradock took charge of JIC at almost the same time as Gorbachev took the reins of Soviet communism. An analyst at the Assessments Staff who watched Cradock's arrival recalls, 'His intelligence was intimidating. He was a powerful man in terms of influence, and he completely dominated the intelligence community by sheer force of intellect.' Geoffrey Howe, then Foreign Secretary, had been a contemporary of Cradock's at Cambridge, and knew him as a 'debating star' at the Union. Although a part of the inner Cabinet team, Howe felt a sense of anticipation bordering on trepidation at Cradock's appointment; as he noted in his memoirs, 'My five years' experience as a senior Cabinet minister gave me (I like to think) the confidence to match his far from diffident intellect.'

As Chairman, Cradock was, in the words of a government brochure released several years later, 'specifically charged with ensuring that the Committee's warning and monitoring role is discharged effectively'. He later wrote of this job, 'It was a crisis post with the impossible task of foreseeing and warning against every international contingency affecting British interests.' The colleagues from different information-gathering agencies who sat on the JIC with him – the Director of the Government Communications Headquarters (GCHQ), the Chief of the Secret Intelligence Service (SIS or MI6), the Chief of the Defence Intelligence Staff (DIS) and the Director General of the Security Service (MI5) – might have employed thousands of people, and since 1945 spent billions of pounds, but they did not individually have responsibility for the overall picture of what was going on in the Soviet Union, and indeed the rest of the world. Putting that jigsaw together rested with the Chairman and his staff of analysts.

Gorbachev's accession did not cause ripples of anticipation among the mandarins of British intelligence. Martin Morland, the JIC Chief of Assessments at the time, recalls that there were no special studies of what the new Soviet leader might do, or how he might differ from his predecessors. 'The received wisdom at the Cabinet Office was that, as you would expect, the Cold War would go on for ever.'

The great majority of the intelligence flowing into London was signals intelligence, or 'sigint', gathered by GCHQ. The eavesdropping specialists had a network of stations scooping up fragments of electronic energy from the world's skies.

GCHQ had 7,000 civilian employees, augmented by another 3,000 or so serving in the armed forces. Its J Division, responsible for gathering Soviet Bloc sigint, had huge resources: more people worked for it, directly and indirectly, than for the whole of MI5. GCHQ's annual budget was greater than that of MI6 and MI5 combined. Much of the take of the US sigint organization, the National Security Agency (NSA), also flowed through Britain's eavesdropping centre in Cheltenham. NSA had resources of a higher order still, most importantly the satellites which hoovered up thousands of conversations and data transmissions around the world every day. Under a secret treaty signed in 1947, GCHQ, NSA and the sigint organizations of Canada, Australia and New Zealand divided up their global operations and exchanged the product. 'The special relationship in sigint was as special as it could possibly be,' says one former JIC staff member.

There were however some crucial limitations to what GCHQ, and its sigint partners, were delivering. Martin Morland, the Chief of Assessments at JIC, remembers, 'People called it "farm gate intelligence". You picked it up from the end of the drive at Cheltenham in a completely raw form . . . there wasn't a proper mechanism for digesting it.' Almost every day, vans bearing sacks of intercept reports fresh from the 'farm gate' would arrive at the Cabinet Office. A great deal of work was required to piece together disparate fragments.

Sigint was protected by the highest secrecy, a system of vetting those allowed to see it and of code words for the material itself. Within the Whitehall 'ring of secrecy', those with access to the most sensitive product of GCHQ knew a disturbing truth: the vast majority of it was barely relevant to what would become the central question – what is Gorbachev up to? In 1985 the Soviet Union was almost completely successful at protecting its strategic communications from eavesdropping. Geoffrey Prime, a British agent of the KGB arrested in 1982 after years working in Cheltenham, had helped them do it. A senior GCHQ officer reveals that 'on the political side, there was a time up until the mid-1970s when we used to get useful political and high-level military communications, but that dried up, partly as a result of Prime. We never ever had the Soviet diplomatic traffic.'

Instead, the allied sigint machine focused its activities on the Soviet military machine and on easier targets elsewhere. Codes tend to be weaker or non-existent at the lower levels of military command, and it was there that GCHQ made its principal contribution, by piecing together the order of battle: the deployment and structure of Moscow's armed forces. The ability to give warning of a surprise military attack on the West was, after all, one of GCHQ's primary purposes.

The Secret Intelligence Service – often referred to as MI6 or, within the espionage world, as Box 850 or 'the Friends' – was the other principal gatherer of foreign intelligence. MI6 had about 2,400 staff in 1985 and its task is to gather human intelligence: getting people to betray their country in the UK's interest. The Service relies on a network of foreign stations, with officers posted under 'light cover' in embassies and London-based 'deep cover' operatives who travelled in and out of other countries and often ran the most sensitive 'cases' or agents.

Forty years of Cold War and hundreds of man-years of effort by station officers had produced just a handful of good Soviet agents. SIS had scores of contacts or sources around the world, providing information to its officers, but good-quality agents – defined by the spymasters as people prepared actively to seek out secrets on MI6's orders – were another matter. But early in 1985, SIS had every reason to feel pleased with itself. Its best agent, an officer of the KGB First Chief Directorate, the key organization for overseas spying, named Oleg Gordievsky, had been designated as the *rezident* or chief of station in London. As well as providing information on Soviet efforts against the UK, Gordievsky's long career as a political intelligence officer meant that he was party to Moscow's foreign policy process. Gordievsky's reports were kept on the tightest possible distribution: even the Foreign Secretary had to read them in the presence of a senior civil servant, without taking notes. For Geoffrey Howe, the reports from SIS's top source were an 'invaluable commentary on thinking within the Kremlin . . . an important part in shaping our own strategy'.

The Defence Intelligence Staff (DIS) also gathered foreign intelligence, although its main function was as a centre for analysis of the military information which would be needed if Nato and the Warsaw Pact went to war. Its head, Chief of Defence Intelligence (CDI) Air Marshal Michael Armitage, also had the role of Deputy Chairman of the Joint Intelligence Committee. His organization of 800 people, many times the size of JIC's Assessment Staff, had the capability to exploit GCHQ's sigint to build a really detailed picture of the Soviet Army and to chart the development of its new weapons, giving early warning so that defence chiefs could start lobbying for new technology of their own. DIS applied 75 to 80 per cent of its analytical effort to the Warsaw Pact.

The last leg of the intelligence structure was the Security Service or MI5, the counter-intelligence arm charged with protecting the UK from foreign espionage, subversion and terrorism. Anthony Duff, its Director General, had preceded Cradock as JIC Chairman. The Prime Minister and Robert Armstrong, the Civil Service head, had sent him to MI5 headquarters in Gower Street to rebuild the Service. Commenting on his arrival there, Duff told me, 'In the past there had been an over-autocratic system of management, with unhappiness

7

among people who didn't know how the Service was being managed.' The Service had for years been structured to deal with the Soviet threat, having two principal branches: K Branch, Counter Espionage, and F Branch, Counter Subversion. Although K Branch tried to recruit discontented members of the Soviet diplomatic corps in London, it had no agents of worth in 1985. Instead, its contributions to JIC's estimates of what was going on inside the Soviet system consisted mostly of trying to measure the scale of KGB and GRU (Soviet military intelligence) operations against Britain.

Each of these four elements produced their own bulletins: GCHQ had its digest of sigint reports known as the Blue Book; SIS turned out its Weekly Summary of Intelligence, usually referred to in Whitehall as CX or the CX Book, the initials being a long-standing MI6 code for agent reports; the Ministry of Defence had its Defence Weekly Intelligence Summary (DWIS); and MI5 circulated its information in the form of memos to the Home Secretary and other key officials. Although each agency was therefore in a position to select the reports that it provided to intelligence operatives and certain decision-makers, the Whitehall system invested ultimate authority in the weekly minutes of the Joint Intelligence Committee with attached papers. This document, circulated after each Thursday's session in the Cabinet Office, was sometimes called 'current intelligence', known officially as the Weekly Survey of Intelligence but referred to by almost everybody in government by the colour of its cover – the Red Book. Unlike the individual agency reports, the Red Book goes to all principal ministries and to some other bodies, such as the Bank of England. As events in Moscow unfolded, Cradock and his Assessments Staff were, according to the official arrangements at least, the intelligence high priesthood and the Red Book was their writ.

Britain's spymasters generally felt that this system had great strengths compared with, for example, the situation in Washington, where different agencies supplied competing views and the decision-makers were left to make up their own minds. According to Michael Armitage, 'The Americans would use us as a sounding board – the conflicting views produced by the American system resulted in them coming to us, with our single view, to try to resolve some of these questions.'

Conversely, there were others who felt that the Red Book's wide distribution meant that it was sanitized lest GCHQ's methods or MI6's agents be endangered, and that the JIC's deliberations represented a kind of bureaucratic lowest common denominator, devoid of imagination. Martin Morland reflects on his years as Chief of Assessments: 'Some of the raw intelligence was quite interesting, but by the time the differences involving the Foreign Office and intelligence services were resolved and the non-intelligence input added, it was pretty bloody bland ... I found it a frustrating job and I think many others do. I had interminable series of meetings trying to get a view together.'

In theory, the Foreign Office – whence Morland had come and to which he would return in 1986 – was the principal customer for political intelligence, but many diplomats, who after all were part of a completely separate system for gathering reports on the wider world, were deeply sceptical about whether the JIC or the agencies had anything useful to say to them. David Mellor, who served as a Minister of State both at the Home and Foreign Office, regularly consumed the Red Book and concluded, 'Very rarely were those reports telling us something better than one could read in the quality newspapers.' It was the very blandness of this 'assessed intelligence' that often led the small number of people who had access to raw GCHQ and SIS reports to consult them in search of a clearer picture.

The limitations of the Red Book were implicitly recognized by the intelligence system, which provided a Rolls-Royce service to a handful of individuals – people who would receive personal briefings and access to the most highly classified one-off reports as well as the Red Book. This inner circle included Margaret Thatcher, Geoffrey Howe, his Foreign Office Minister of State, Robert Armstrong in his capacity as Cabinet Secretary, the Permanent Under Secretaries or top civil servants in several government departments, and a small number of key Downing Street and Cabinet Office officials.

None of those initiated into the cherished mysteries of this cult of information consumed the reports with greater relish than the Prime Minister herself. The work of what she often called the 'secret services' fascinated Thatcher. Nigel Lawson, then Chancellor of the Exchequer, comments in his memoirs, 'Margaret, an avid reader of the works of Frederick Forsyth, was positively besotted by them.'

The paragon of provincial Conservatism was suspicious of the patrician Foreign Office élite, having been influenced by a number of right-wing thinkers to believe that the bureaucrats of King Charles Street put their own conception of diplomatic tranquillity ahead of Britain's real interests. A senior mandarin recalls, 'Mrs Thatcher was a devotee of intelligence. She liked it, she respected it, she believed it gave her the truth as the Foreign Office reports wouldn't.'

The Prime Minister's attitude often puzzled Charles Powell, the diplomat seconded to Downing Street as Private Secretary who became part of her inner circle. 'She had an institutional, deep-rooted, long-standing aversion to the Foreign Office, a deep-seated belief that the Foreign Office was there to give things away to foreigners. Then there were the Foreign Office people – almost all of those she worked with she liked. She didn't seem to connect the people and the institution.'

When Thatcher, mindful of the limitations of the JIC's weekly Red Book, departed for weekends at Chequers, the rural prime minister-ial retreat, she would also take the sigint Blue Book and MI6's CX Book. Intelligence was like a hobby, something she often saved for the moments that other people would have called free time. Each Fri-day, Charles Powell marked up these reports to highlight points of interest. The papers would return on Monday, often covered with annotations requesting more information or directing a particular course of action.

'I was never sure who read the stuff,' says Martin Morland, 'but there was evidence the Prime Minister read it, and that was a great encouragement.' As events unfolded in Moscow, those involved at least knew that the Prime Minister would digest their reports, unlike many of her predecessors and contemporary Cabinet ministers.

Perhaps the most important consequence of the Prime Minister's love affair with the agencies was financial. Charles Powell notes, 'She increased their funding and supported them in ways which no Prime Minister since the Second World War had done.' During her years at Number 10, the money spent by the agencies more than doubled.

Britain's failure to predict the Argentine invasion of the Falklands in 1982 has produced a spending spree in intelligence. In Latin Amer-ica, for example, there had been only one SIS officer at the time of the invasion. By the mid-1980s there were three stations there. The num-bers of UK-based officers able to be sent abroad on specific missions had also been increased; they had, for example, been involved in covert assistance to the Afghan resistance.

For GCHQ, which had also experienced financial constraints dur-ing the Labour governments of the 1970s, the Thatcher era marked a period of substantial spending. Large sums went on new computer technology and research into better ways of intercepting emerging forms of communications, notably satellites.

Intelligence spending plans were worked on by a committee of permanent secretaries, known within Whitehall by its acronym PSIS. The plans were then referred to the Prime Minister for final approval. One Whitehall mandarin confirms that one year she did so 'on the nod', without inspecting the figures. Mrs Thatcher did not ask MI6 why its 2,400 employees and more than £100 million budget could only produce one top-grade Soviet agent, or why GCHQ, with its even greater resources, could not crack Russian codes. She took the intelligence world at its word, trusting that it was composed of honourable, professional people who did their best to pit their wits against the immeasurably greater resources of a superpower. Nigel Lawson, who as Chancellor pursued with vigour the Tory quest to cut government spending, later concluded that the intelligence services were 'one of the very few areas of public life virtually untouched by the rigours of the Thatcher era'.

While allowing the agencies considerable budgetary room for manoeuvre, the Prime Minister was careful to construct her own view of events in Moscow quite distinct from that of Percy Cradock and the Joint Intelligence Committee. Her appetite for information was colossal: in addition to the Red, Blue and CX books, she read almost all significant telegrams from the British ambassador in Moscow and received verbatim texts of many of Gorbachev's speeches. One senior intelligence analyst remembers, 'The Prime Minister arrived at a meeting full of vigour and said, "Have you read Gorbachev's speech to the Central Committee Plenum?" There was an awkward silence as we all looked down at the desk.'

Most importantly, the Prime Minister had invested personal political capital in the new leader. She had famously declared Gorbachev to be 'a man we can do business with' during his visit to London in December 1984. That meeting made diplomatic and intelligence history as the only Anglo-Soviet summit in which the same official, Oleg Gordievsky – then a KGB lieutenant-colonel in the London embassy – had briefed both leaders. With Gorbachev's elevation to General Secretary in March, she felt she had backed a winner. David Mellor notes, 'Mrs Thatcher, to her credit, took to Gorbachev and did her best to sell him . . . her openness of mind towards him was quite surprising, given her view of leftists and socialists in general.'

During Gorbachev's early years, as Cabinet Office analysts wrestled with the question of whether he could be taken at face value, Thatcher would have several meetings with him, often of two or three hours at a time, in which to form her own view. The General Secretary often seemed to use her to debate new ideas, to see how the West would respond. Charles Powell, often the only British official present at these meetings, observes, 'For him, it was a chance to test his new ideas to destruction. If some new plan of his took account of her view, it was more likely to survive.' It is in this context that the intelligence community's input into the substantial menu of information and experience in front of the Prime Minister must be placed.

At the beginning of July 1985 the new Soviet leader elbowed aside Andrei Gromyko, Foreign Minister since 1957, and replaced him with a Georgian party boss, Eduard Shevardnadze. In the foreign ministries and espionage organizations of Nato countries, many were puzzled about why the new leader had done this to the man who had put him forward for the leadership in March. In fact, Gromyko's tough line on arms control, which had kept superpower talks going around in circles for more than ten years, was no longer acceptable. It would have been an excellent moment for SIS to have consulted Colonel Gordievsky, but their principal Soviet asset was in Moscow, fighting for his life.

Chapter 2

1985 A Dark and Curious Shadow

Colonel Oleg Gordievsky had been summoned back to Moscow on 22 May 1985. 'When they took me back,' he would later recount, 'I thought it was all over, that I would die.' In fact, Gordievsky's KGB superiors subjected him to lengthy interviews in which they tried to get him to confess to espionage on behalf of a foreign power.

Gordievsky's career as an agent of Britain's Secret Intelligence Service (or MI6) had begun in 1974, during a posting to Copenhagen. The British had learned that he had been unhappy with his work since the Soviet invasion of Czechoslovakia in 1968. He had been marked down as a target for cultivation and watched for years by SIS. The first contact was made on a badminton court early one morning in 1973 by an MI6 officer from the Copenhagen embassy. In his memoirs Gordievsky, who referred to that MI6 man only as 'Dick', recalled, 'I went over and he simply said it would be nice to meet.' After a few initial meetings, the SIS officer did not contact the KGB officer for a year, at which point he invited Gordievsky for another meal and made a play for his services as an agent. A London-based officer then took over the case, SIS having made one of its most important recruitments of the Cold War. The Russian continued to provide information for years, and his usefulness to SIS soared when in 1982 he was appointed to the KGB *rezidentura* in London, with overall responsibility for political intelligence-gathering.

MI6 analysts were to conclude later that Aldrich Ames, the CIA officer who began working for the Russians in 1985, was probably responsible for their man's downfall. 'It was almost certainly him, but it isn't possible to prove it absolutely,' says one SIS man. During Ames's trial, though, it was stated that the names of Western agents were not handed over until June 1985, after Gordievsky's recall to Moscow. Furthermore, it is known that Sergei Motorin and Valeri

Martinov, two KGB officers recruited in the Washington *rezidentura* as American agents and betrayed by Ames in June 1985, were incarcerated and then executed on their return to Moscow.

Colonel Gordievsky, on the other hand, was allowed to return to his flat. In June he was joined by his wife Leila and their two children. She had been brought back from London, and he was told that he would never be allowed to serve abroad again. The KGB had its suspicions, but was clearly not sufficiently confident of them to execute such a senior officer. He believes that he remained under surveillance but, despite this, managed to contact SIS officers and tell them what had happened.

SIS put together a plan to rescue their prize agent from the heart of Moscow. Clearly, much could have gone wrong with this ambitious undertaking, and it was referred for approval to Geoffrey Howe, the Foreign Secretary. On 19 July 1985 Gordievsky left his wife and children to go jogging. After taking a train towards the Finnish border, Gordievsky was met by MI6 operatives driving embassy cars. They put him in the boot of one and smuggled him into Finland. The next day he arrived in Norway, from where he was flown to Britain.

Rescuing Gordievsky had been a remarkable operation, one that earned SIS the admiration of the CIA and other allied services. However, one SIS officer in the counter-intelligence division, a man whom the Russian describes as 'professionally suspicious', felt it had all been a little *too* easy. Other British officials shared his puzzlement that Gordievsky had not been shot after his recall.

On his arrival in England, the KGB man was taken to Fort Monkton near Gosport. 'The Fort', as it is known throughout the British intelligence community, is used for SIS induction courses and for conferences. It offers seclusion and security. Gordievsky was told that he was being held in isolation there for his own safety, as the KGB might try to assassinate him, but it was also evident that, initially at least, SIS wanted to make quite sure it had not been the victim of some complex, long-term KGB plot.

Less than a fortnight after Gordievsky's escape, Colonel Vitaly Yurchenko, deputy head of the KGB North American division, defected to the CIA in Rome. Yurchenko's motives were complex: he had apparently come to believe that he had cancer and could only get the best treatment in the West. Yurchenko had also become infatuated with the wife of a Russian serving at the embassy in Ottawa. US doctors subsequently told Yurchenko that his cancer fears were groundless, and the lady of his dreams spurned his offers of elope-ment. Disillusioned, Yurchenko re-defected in November, but not before he had given CIA officers large amounts of information, including assurances that Gordievsky had been a bona fide agent and defector.

Most senior SIS officers needed no convincing of Gordievsky's credentials; his track record of passing information to Britain for more than ten years was sufficient. But it was a hangover from an ear-lier era – when James Jesus Angleton, the CIA's chief spy-hunter, had contended that the West was penetrated with Soviet agents and that some defectors were fakes – and perhaps from the kind of Cold War mind-games embodied in novels like John Le Carré's Smiley series that, for one or two officers, some small element of doubt could never be extinguished.

It is clear that British intelligence, rocked in the 1950s and 1960s by the treachery of Guy Burgess, Kim Philby, Donald Maclean, Anthony Blunt and John Cairncross, viewed Gordievsky's ability to give a clean bill of health to their own organizations as one of his prin-cipal virtues. Those most closely involved in his early debriefings at the Fort included Gerry Warner, Director of Counter Intelligence and Security (the number three post in SIS), and John Deverell, Director of K Branch, the counter-espionage arm of the Security Ser-vice (or MI5). They were able to satisfy themselves that the KGB's First Chief Directorate, its main foreign spying element, had for years been unable to recruit agents in any significant department of British government. Gordievsky told them that Roger Hollis, a former Director General of MI5, had never been a Soviet asset. In fact, it seemed that the only real success the KGB had enjoyed in Britain in the 1980s was to find one or two members of parliament and jour-nalists prepared to accept Moscow's hospitality and push various political lines which Moscow hoped would undermine Western unity; the success or failure of such 'active measures' was a highly subjective matter.

As a political intelligence operator who had defected at a critical juncture in East–West relations, Gordievsky was often puzzled by SIS's preoccupation with the KGB's modest operational successes. To some extent he shared the view of some Foreign Office diplomats and Assessments Staff members that MI6 and MI5 were, as one puts it, 'obsessed with fighting the opposing intelligence service rather than putting more effort into finding out more about the wider world'.

Early in his career as an MI6 agent, Gordievsky says, 'the Service had wasted so much time asking questions about agents and penetrations and so on. They didn't ask me elementary questions about politics. I assumed it was because they knew about these issues, but they didn't. Sometimes I would see really important political telegrams or notes and brief my handlers on some trivial operational details. I would wonder why they didn't ever ask me about the really important things.'

Although Gordievsky says that his SIS handlers became less pre-occupied with the spy versus spy battle during his career as an agent, even during his debriefing at the Fort he felt that his British colleagues could not fit Soviet espionage into its proper context: 'There was a lot of exaggeration of the role of the KGB. The Party was more the boss. The KGB was the servant, particularly in foreign affairs.'

Happily for both the Service and its prize catch, most of the debriefing was done by someone who exploited to the full the political aspects of the information he acquired. Gordon Barrass, a softly-spoken Sovbloc analyst from SIS, spent weeks cloistered with Gordievsky in the Fort, mining away in the dimmest recesses of the KGB man's extraordinary memory. Gordievsky says that Barrass was 'practically the only person who understood all the implications of my information. When I was tired or depressed, I would forget things which he could remember. He was like the doctor and I the patient.'

Barrass's methodical approach was vital, not only because of the depth of the agent's information but also because of his sense of guilt and frustration at having to leave his wife and children behind in Moscow. Gordievsky remembers, 'I was so depressed as a result of losing my family that I needed a distraction. I asked them to continue the debriefing on Saturdays. They couldn't do it on Sundays, so instead I was taken on excursions, for example to nearby churches.'

Another of Gordievsky's early visitors at the Fort was Major-General Derek Boorman, who had taken over from Air Marshal Armitage as Chief of Defence Intelligence (CDI). Boorman did not fit the mould of a spymaster: a compact soldier who'd spent most of his career 'east of Suez' rather than in Nato, he had little time for the conventional view of the 'Soviet threat'. Boorman recalls that he was introduced to Gordievsky by an SIS man who, struggling to explain the general's function, described him as the head of 'our GRU'. The Russian stood to attention, but Major-General Boorman told him to sit because those days were over.

This intense period was not without its moments of light relief.

During his early days at the Fort, Gordievsky went jogging in the surrounding lanes. At that time local naval bases were on alert as part of a Ministry of Defence exercise designed to improve security against Soviet saboteurs and *spetsnaz* commandos. An armed Ministry of Defence policeman stopped Gordievsky and asked him what he was doing so close to the base. Gordievsky recalls that his reply was delivered 'in a terrible Russian accent'. An MI5 minder who had been following the jogger on a bicycle appeared, to be informed by Gordievsky that he had told the policeman he was a KGB colonel. The incident passed off with laughter all round. As the story was retold among intelligence officers, a new, apocryphal ending was added in which the policeman telephoned the Fort and said, 'We've got a man here who says he's a colonel in the KGB and that you can vouch for him.' Word of SIS's new catch was spreading in the intelligence community, and legends were attaching themselves to his name.

MI6 officers suggest Gordievsky's recall was quite extraordinary, allowing Barrass and others to produce thousands of reports ranging from titbits of one or two sentences, perhaps some detail of a KGB officer who had operated in the West, to full analyses of Soviet policies. The analyst's most important paper was a highly-classified study of how the Kremlin made foreign policy, setting the role of the Communist Party, KGB and Foreign Ministry into their proper context; it was to be a vital primer for many Foreign Office and SIS experts in the months ahead.

The intelligence gleaned from Gordievsky also gave a full explanation of Operation RYAN, a joint KGB–GRU initiative launched in 1981 amid Kremlin fears that the West was preparing a surprise nuclear attack. RYAN was to involve thousands of Soviet intelligence officers around the world in a daily search for signs, ranging from how many lights were on late at night in Nato defence ministries to mysterious disappearances of Western leaders as possible indicators of an impending nuclear catastrophe. Even while their agent was still in place, the intelligence received about RYAN had led Margaret Thatcher to send reassuring signals to the Kremlin leadership and to urge President Ronald Reagan to moderate his 'evil empire' rhetoric. For Major-General Boorman, learning the full scope of RYAN 'really was a shock to us. An example of the lack of sensible assessment on both sides of the intelligence battle. We asked ourselves, do we really understand this animal? How could they seriously have thought that the West could initiate a nuclear war?'

The Gordievsky 'take' was a famous victory for SIS within White-hall. The running of Soviet sources had been elevated into a matter of professional esteem within the organization. It had the drama to be expected of an activity for which the penalty for failure was often death. SIS has a rigid pecking order: officers are divided into General Service and Intelligence Branch, the latter representing the high fly-ers. Within the Intelligence Branch, the *crème de la crème* tradition-ally served in the Soviet Bloc area, generally referred to within MI6 as Sovbloc. One SIS officer refers to Sovbloc officers as 'the master race', and a former MI6 man notes, 'They were very special and kept themselves to themselves. It was the route to the top.'

Just as Soviet communications security severely restricted the sig-int that GCHQ could gather on political matters, so the existence of an army of around 100,000 KGB counter-intelligence operatives within the Soviet Union limited what SIS could do from its heavily-watched Moscow Station. Instead, up and coming Sovbloc officers, including the Chief, Colin Figures, and his successor but one, Colin McColl, served in cities like Warsaw or in places like New York, Vienna and Geneva (where Christopher Curwen, who would suc-ceed Figures, had worked) where the presence of large international organizations produced a healthy supply of Soviet citizens ripe for suborning.

However, SIS officers serving in favoured Sovbloc hunting grounds outside Moscow still had to beware of large numbers of War-saw Pact operatives who might be conducting surveillance of them or their sources. For this reason, running agents of this kind required MI6 operatives to be highly proficient in 'tradecraft', the spy tech-niques that ranged from efficient counter-surveillance drills to choos-ing the best locations for 'dead-letter boxes', the hidy-holes where agents left secret material. An SIS officer explains, 'Sovbloc became such an élite thing because of the difficulties of running agents in Moscow, Warsaw or Prague. They had such a huge effort that there had to be a real reliance on tradecraft – something you couldn't say for our people operating in much of the rest of the world.'

SIS had been determined to pay the KGB back for Philby and the other traitors. The successful rescue of Gordievsky created a real feel-ing of victory within the Service and triggered a wave of paranoia in Moscow.

The KGB did not know for sure what had happened to Gordievsky, but suspected the worst. As part of their damage-limitation exercise, three long-term 'illegals' (agents with false identities) were ordered out of West Germany. On 6 August 1985 a woman known as Sonja Lüneberg – in fact, an illegal agent who had been working for the chairman of one of Bonn's ruling political parties for twelve years – disappeared. A few weeks later another illegal, known as Ursula Richter and also working as a secretary in a political organization, and one Lorenz Betzing, a defence ministry messenger, also fled. After these agents had spent years successfully living in the West, the KGB had abandoned the operations because of fears that Gordievsky might know who they were. The British agent had worked in the S Directorate of the KGB, the one dealing with illegals, from 1962 to 1965, creating false identities for people being sent into West Germany. In fact, Gordievsky says he had forgotten both the real names and the aliases of those he helped to infiltrate Germany so many years before.

On the fifth floor of MI5's HQ in London's Gower Street, the Director of Counter Espionage or chief molehunter, John Deverell, had given his list of the KGB and GRU staff at the London embassy to Anthony Duff, the Director General of the Security Service, for action. Gordievsky suggests there were twenty-three KGB and fifteen GRU people working there. There is no doubt that MI5 pushed hard for expulsions. Deverell's subsequent obituary in *The Times*, written by an officer of the agency, noted that the expulsions had been 'at the Service's instigation'. Duff had established a good working rapport with Thatcher during his earlier stint as Chairman of the Joint Intelligence Committee, and had little trouble convincing her that there should be a large-scale expulsion of personnel from the embassy in Kensington Gardens.

On 12 September 1985 the Foreign Office declared that twenty-five of them were *persona non grata* because of activities incompatible with their diplomatic status. At the same time the government confirmed publicly that Gordievsky was in Britain and had been a long-term agent. Two days later the Kremlin responded by expelling the same number of British diplomats, journalists and businessmen. On 16 September the UK expelled a further six from London, to which Moscow predictably answered by evicting six more Britons on 18 September.

Foreign Secretary Geoffrey Howe, aware of the strict limits on the number of UK citizens allowed to work in Moscow, sometimes doubted the wisdom of these moves and remarked later in his memoirs that 'our own tough policy was now beginning to hurt us more than it hurt them'. He added that the spying battle and its resulting expulsions cast 'a dark and curious shadow over relations with the Soviet Union'. But the Prime Minister did not intend to let her good personal relations with the General Secretary prevent her from protecting what she regarded as the national interest.

With hindsight, it might be asked whether the expulsions were advisable, since British intelligence knew from Gordievsky exactly who all the main players were in the KGB and GRU, and indeed how limited their success had been in penetrating British institutions. Would not the best action simply have been to enjoy the Kremlin's discomfort at Gordievsky's escape and to allow its compromised staff to continue in their ineffective labours? A former intelligence mandarin replies, 'It is hard to overestimate how difficult it is for a minister to say no when approached with hard evidence of espionage by security officials seeking expulsions. Would you take the responsibility of ignoring their advice?'

What officers like MI5's John Deverell and Gerry Warner of SIS must have known in September 1985 was that the KGB and GRU were reeling from a series of disasters. In addition to Colonels Gordievsky and Yurchenko, two other, less well-known officers of the same rank had defected during the previous few months. One, Colonel Piguzov, had been a CIA agent, according to Yuri Shvets, a Washington-based KGB officer who later wrote a book. The other, Colonel Kutergin – whose existence has not been publicly revealed before – had defected to West Germany late in 1984. Kutergin, according to Gordievsky, had been an agent of the Bundesnachrichtendienst (BND), Germany's Federal Intelligence Service, for seventeen years. Colonel Kutergin apparently felt strongly that he wanted to slip into obscurity, and for this reason the BND was never able to publicize his defection, even though in the coming months, rocked by allegations of Eastern Bloc penetration of the highest political circles in Bonn, it would be sorely in need of a success story to give the German public. In addition to these four KGB men, the GRU deputy station chief in Athens, Lieutenant-Colonel Sergei Bokhan, had defected to the CIA in May 1984.

SIS already knew from Vladimir Kuzichkin, a KGB officer who defected to them in Tehran in 1982, that morale and efficiency in the Soviet intelligence services were poor. In his subsequent memoirs Kuzichkin described the activities of his bloated Tehran *rezidentura*, which operated on the principle that 'he who does nothing never gets caught'.

Kuzichkin's job in Tehran had been as an S Directorate officer, supporting illegals. When he heard that two of them had been decorated he was angry because, as he later wrote, 'the question of obtaining intelligence was to all intents and purposes never raised. Illegals were cherished like children. Each of them was surrounded by the care and efforts of dozens of S Directorate officers.'

According to Kuzichkin, the KGB in Tehran had only one really good agent, an Iranian Army brigadier who was caught and executed. The entire embassy had succumbed to corruption of various forms, and individual officers and diplomats were largely interested in staying on in order to make money out of various scams. The GRU, the military intelligence service, remained more of a closed book to MI6 and the CIA, but Kuzichkin confirms that 'their Residency had everything: drunkenness, corruption, loose living and more than enough operational failures. All in all, right in the Soviet vein.'

Shortly after Gordievsky's defection, Yuri Shvets began working in the Washington *rezidentura*. He also subsequently wrote about his experiences; unlike Kuzichkin and Gordievsky, he was not a defector, although several years after leaving government service he did go to live in the USA. Shvets confirms that 'bluff was king in the intelligence service . . . in the lively metaphor of the KGB resident in Rome, "Where there are no birds, even an asshole sounds like a nightingale".'

In Washington, as in Tehran several years earlier, most KGB and GRU staff did nothing because they did not want to get expelled. 'The beaten path promised an easy life, an enviable career and material success', Shvets wrote. When he did try to cultivate an American for possible recruitment as an agent, the station chief (*rezident*) 'was clearly disgusted with me . . . the intelligence brass was unanimous in its loud demands for a strenuous recruitment effort, but as soon as any real action was required, they would invariably find a thousand excuses for nipping it in the bud.'

Under such circumstances, the only people who were likely to become agents of Soviet intelligence were those who offered themselves. One such 'walk-in' was Michael Bettaney, an MI5 officer and aspiring traitor who pushed an envelope of classified papers through the letter-box of the Soviet embassy in Kensington Gardens in 1983. Arkady Gouk, the London *rezident*, was so timid that he did not respond, so losing his chance to recruit an agent of extraordinary potential inside the Security Service. In any case, Gordievsky told his handlers about the would-be agent, and Bettaney was subsequently arrested and convicted. Gordievsky suggests in his memoirs that the management of MI5 were initially reluctant to believe that an officer of the Service was intent on betrayal – an example of the complacency which had provoked the damning Security Commission report and the later appointment of Duff as DGSS.

Ever since 1971, when 105 Soviet diplomats had been kicked out of the UK in a move appropriately code-named Operation FOOT by MI5, its experts in K Branch had regarded KGB and GRU operations in London as considerably disrupted. They told ministers that, whereas before FOOT about one-third of the embassy staff had been involved in spying, afterwards they had not put the proportion of espionage operatives higher than one-quarter.

It was not in the institutional interests of British intelligence to tell ministers or officials what they knew about the inefficiency of the KGB and GRU. Perhaps it was for this reason that Vladimir Kuzichkin was not shown to a stream of Whitehall visitors in the way that Gordievsky was to be. But it can equally be said in defence of the agencies that the events of 1985 had shown that in the world of counter intelligence – sometimes characterized as a 'wilderness of mirrors' – there were few certainties, and it was often impossible to quantify the risks.

The survival of Colonel Kutergin as an agent of the BND seemed extraordinary to SIS officers who knew about it, because the German services had such a bad record of penetration by their eastern cousins and the Russians. This was underlined by the flight to the east of Hans-Joachim Tiedge, a senior counter-intelligence official, in August 1985. But the strict compartmentalization of intelligence within professional agencies, which had saved Colonel Kutergin from betrayal by Tiedge, also meant that MI5 and MI6 could not take Gordievsky's assertion that Britain was free from serious penetrations as a complete guarantee.

Just as the West Germans' Russian agent had survived the treacherous Tiedge, so Geoffrey Prime, the KGB's man inside GCHQ, had operated for several years after Gordievsky started working for SIS. Gordievsky had not known about Prime because the GCHQ man was being run by a different arm of the KGB, which had successfully, and in the event wisely, argued that the case should not be transferred to the First Chief Directorate, where Gordievsky worked, because it had been penetrated by Western agents. Therefore John Deverell of MI5 could only rely on Gordievsky's information to a limited extent; other departments of the KGB and much of what the GRU did were beyond the ken of their star defector. Deverell also knew that his agency's over-confidence in the wake of Operation FOOT had helped create the preconditions for Michael Bettaney's treachery.

Gordievsky's escape coincided with a trial in London that underlined another fear common to counter espionage officers. Many in K Branch felt that since 1971 the KGB and GRU had shifted their recruitment efforts to Britons to foreign countries. In June 1985 the trial opened at the Old Bailey of seven servicemen accused of giving documents, including sigint transcripts, to foreign agents. The accused had worked at 9 Signals Regiment, stationed at Ayios Nikolayos in Cyprus, GCHQ's principal eavesdropping post for the Middle East. Many in the sigint community were concerned about the case going ahead at all; after the Prime case it seemed to represent a further breach of security in this most sensitive area of UK–US intelligence collaboration.

The prosecution claimed that the members of the spy ring had been blackmailed after being lured into sex sessions by Arab men, probably acting on behalf of the KGB. They estimated that two thousand sigint documents marked Secret or Top Secret had been passed over by the servicemen. Michael Wright, the prosecution barrister, told the court during one of its few open sessions that 'the damage caused by the passing of such material to foreign agents is quite incalculable.' The 9 Signal Regiment trial added to MI5's desire to hit back at Moscow with expulsions of its London-based spies.

Lurid details of 'splash parties' involving gay and heterosexual couplings among the accused and their wives ensured that the trial received maximum publicity. Ultimately, though, the Crown's case rested solely on confessions extracted from the men by RAF Police investigators. A few weeks after the Gordievsky expulsions from London, the trial collapsed. After 115 days and a process costing £5 million, the jurors acquitted the accused. The jury regarded the confessions with suspicion, believing unreasonable pressure had been applied.

Although the Army and RAF personnel accused of espionage were not found guilty of any crime, many in the counter espionage community refused to accept their innocence. Some suggest that certain evidence was held back (despite the fact that much of the trial was held *in camera*); others say, conspiratorially, that the case was allowed to fail to prevent further damage to the relationship with the Americans.

On 3 October 1985, with the prospect of a superpower summit later that month, Mikhail Gorbachev tried to prepare the ground by offering a 50 per cent cut in strategic nuclear weapons if President Reagan would stop his Strategic Defence Initiative, commonly known as Star Wars. The Western powers needed good information on whether such offers were sincere and what Gorbachev's real agenda was. Sensing its moment, SIS offered Bill Casey, Director of the CIA, the opportunity to talk to Gordievsky. The meeting went well, and was much appreciated by the Americans. Derek Boorman, then Chief of Defence Intelligence, says, 'We were always conscious that we had to trade for this incredible relationship with the US. With Gordievsky, we were able to exploit everything that he meant in terms of exerting sensible leverage from the CIA.'

In the coming months, SIS would parade Gordievsky as a star turn on the international intelligence lecture circuit. The case had impressed Thatcher and other ministers too. Gordievsky's message was to be highly useful to SIS. Unlike some other defectors, he was not cynical about the Soviet threat. Instead, he was articulate about the power of the Communist system – a walking advertisement for the need for good intelligence. Although Gordievsky helped boost the careers of many in MI6, it is worth recording that the SIS station officer in Copenhagen who had actually cultivated him in 1974, received no decoration. His story illustrates the perils of working in the secret world.

In March 1975, on leaving Denmark, the man Gordievsky called 'Dick' was posted to the SIS staff in Northern Ireland. Seven months later he was removed from the posting, and shortly after that he left the Service at the age of forty-eight. His brief tour in Ulster coincided with MI6 losing an acrimonious battle with MI5 over who should gather intelligence in Ireland. The Security Service had won, taking control of SIS agents. The SIS man's employers were reduced to a limited liaison role, and by the mid-1980s would have withdrawn their Ulster-based staff altogether. It appears that the MI6 officer had little appetite for this inter-service spat. Someone who knew him suggests that he asked to be transferred, and that on returning to London was told by SIS management that this request had blighted his chances of further promotion. Cultivating a star KGB agent, the SIS officer's friend suggests, counted for less with MI6 managers than the smooth running of the personnel posting system.

Ultimately, SIS would have been happier had Gordievsky remained undetected and carried on delivering intelligence about the inner workings of the Kremlin foreign policy process. But Aldrich Ames, the KGB's new agent in the CIA, was busy delivering the USA's agents in the Soviet Union to jail and the firing squad. SIS officers express surprise at the fact that the KGB moved against its traitors with such speed, viciousness and finality, rather than trying to turn them and use them to send false information back to Washington. It may be that the Soviet action was a panic response in a year in which several senior officers had defected and several more had been revealed as agents. After his conviction for espionage Ames said, 'In '85, '86, as a result of the information I sold to the Soviets, it was as if neon lights and searchlights lit up all over the Kremlin, shone all the way across the Atlantic Ocean, saying "There is a penetration".' Ames feared these Soviet actions would result in his exposure, but that was not to happen for a further eight years.

A senior officer of the CIA's Directorate of Operations wrote in an internal memo in 1987, 'I am not aware of any Soviet case we have left that is producing anything worthwhile.' Later examinations would conclude that Ames had frustrated more than a hundred operations by the CIA and allied services aimed at finding new sources.

As President Reagan and General Secretary Gorbachev headed for Geneva and their summit on 19 November 1985, SIS was not in a position to repeat its feat of eleven months before, when the Prime Minister met the Russian leader in London after having been briefed with high-grade human intelligence. SIS, like the CIA, had no quality Soviet agents left.

Chapter 3

1985/6 The Charm Offensive

The November 1985 superpower summit in Geneva, complete with its fireside chat between the US and Soviet leaders, served to mark a change in the climate of international relations. After the meetings had finished, Mikhail Gorbachev did something previously unheard-of for a Soviet leader: he held a two-hour press conference. President Reagan's version of events did not emerge until later, as he had gone to Brussels to brief Nato on the summit. Gorbachev's press conference began a sort of love-affair with the Western media that was to last for years; in fact, until long after he had become unpopular with the great majority of his own people. The evident excitement of the journalists, for whom summits normally consisted of recycling briefings, mostly from the US side, rather than having extended conversations with the Russian participant, touched a nerve amongst those in British intelligence who regarded Gorbachev as a committed Marxist-Leninist who was putting a public-relations gloss on what were, in their view, traditional Kremlin policies.

Summitry was intimately connected with issues of security. Much of the superpower agenda was given over to an arms-control process that had yielded no results since the détente of the early 1970s – the very impasse which Gorbachev was trying to break. However, those watching the proceedings for signs of change were often the people most closely associated with the defence and intelligence world, an inward-looking caste which for decades had been locked with its Soviet opposite numbers in a frigid embrace of insecurity and distrust.

To the security hawks in Washington or London, little of conse-quence emerged from the summit, but it was becoming evident to some people, notably diplomats, that the Russian leader was inter-ested in breathing life back into the arms-control process. The Krem-lin's fear of Reagan's Star Wars programme, which Moscow believed was simply a plan to protect the USA so it could wage nuclear war against the Soviet Union with near-impunity, had previously led them to link any progress on strategic arms or on dismantling the Intermediate Nuclear Forces (such as the SS-20 missiles) to a US commitment to scrap the Strategic Defence Initiative. Some US diplomats sensed that, with the replacement of the tough old Foreign Minister Andrei Gromyko, Gorbachev's freeze on new INF weapons and the language used in Geneva, the new Russian ruler was trying to move away from linking these themes and so restart progress towards arms-control agreements. Of all the senior figures in the Western world, George Shultz, the US Secretary of State, was the earliest to become convinced of the sincerity of Gorbachev as an apostle of reform. In the meantime, the President continued to push his plan for a system to shoot down Soviet ballistic missiles. On 6 December 1985, the UK signed a Memorandum of Understanding with the US government which would bring a small slice of the Star Wars research budget to Britain in the shape of joint projects.

On 15 January 1986 Gorbachev launched an initiative for a nuclear-free world. His call did not propose a practical programme, but was rather an attempt to convince the wider world that the USSR no longer thought that it could acquire security through endless production of nuclear weapons and that cuts were required. What Western governments did not know (it was revealed years later by a Soviet energy minister) was that about the time of this initiative Moscow's nuclear arsenal had reached its peak – an extraordinary 45,000 devices, or twice what the USA had. About one-third of these Russian nuclear weapons were old and no longer operational, and it was in 1986 that they began secretly to reduce this huge stockpile.

That February, the USA decided to test its hunch about Gorbachev's new flexibility on INF weapons with a public offer by President Reagan to scrap them within three years. Nato was in the process of deploying Pershing 2 missiles to West Germany and Tomahawk ground-launched cruise missiles to Britain, Belgium and Italy. Even so, the planned Nato deployment would still fall far below the destructive potential of the Soviet INF arsenal, believed at the time by intelligence analysts to include 112 old SS-4 missiles and 440 SS-20s, each of the latter with three nuclear warheads and all but ninety of them aimed at western Europe. But the Kremlin was determined to stop the new Nato deployments, so there was something for both sides in scrapping INF.

There was no immediate answer from Moscow to Washington's offer, but two days later the key players gathered for the 27th Congress of the Communist Party of the Soviet Union. The Congress, held only every five years or so, was an important event for the ideologists. Up to five thousand delegates would gather inside the Kremlin walls in the specially-built Palace of Congresses, an ugly concrete block that sat uncomfortably next to the classical lines of the tsarist arsenal, for set-piece votes that would endorse the Party's domestic and foreign policy for the coming five years. Interesting debates did sometimes take place at congresses, but they were traditionally held in closed session.

Gorbachev's speech to the Congress on 25 February 1986 was his chance to reveal many of the new political ideas that he hoped would galvanize his country and improve international relations. To prepare the delegates for the tough medicine he was prescribing, he used the old-established general secretary's ploy of quoting Lenin's statement that 'our strength is in stating the truth'. Economic productivity, he told them, had 'fallen seriously' and previous attempts to find a way forward had 'aggravated the problem'. The answer, he said, lay in convincing people of 'the correctness of the chosen path'. This was the basis of his later idea that the demoralized Soviet worker needed to be inspired through *glasnost*, or openness, before there could be real *perestroika* or reconstruction of the economy. He also suggested changes in the system of prices and a move away from supporting uneconomic factories – small gestures in the direction of what some would have seen as capitalism, and therefore potentially divisive within the party.

He tried to make it quite clear that he did not believe the Soviet Union could win a nuclear war – partly because it was the consistent view of the Pentagon and its Defence Intelligence Agency that this was precisely what the Kremlin leadership was planning. 'The struggle against the nuclear danger and the arms race . . . will remain in future the main trend of the party's activity in the world arena,' he said, adding his unofficial slogan, 'There is no alternative.' This was not a new line: Soviet leaders since Brezhnev had protested that they did not think nuclear war was winnable, but the Western defence and intelligence community had simply not believed them because of the scale of Soviet preparations in certain military fields. So Gorbachev sought to elaborate a new strategic concept: 'The present-day world has become too small for wars and policies of force . . . it is in fact impossible to win the arms race . . . it is essential above all to reduce considerably the level of military confrontation.' He added that real security 'is guaranteed not by the highest possible but by the lowest possible level of the strategic balance'. As in economic matters, Gorbachev had set out the bones of his new ideas: that force could not solve international problems and that there could be 'reasonable sufficiency' in defence, meaning greater security with far fewer weapons. These ideas would form the basis of most of his dramatic foreign policy and military initiatives in the coming years.

That Gorbachev's 27th Congress speech contained new and fascinating signals was not in doubt to many of the diplomats and journalists based in Moscow. There were to be differences of interpretation, however, based on different views of the sincerity of his words.

How were these events viewed by the Joint Intelligence Committee in London? The structure and personalities at work in the JIC's Assessments Staff were central to this question.

The twenty-five to thirty people under Martin Morland, Chief of Assessments, came from a variety of government departments and backgrounds: 'I had a brigadier working for me who called me "sir" and a Cabinet Office clerk who called me "matey" – it was that strange mix of traditions.' Morland's two deputies each chaired several Current Intelligence Groups or CIGs. In 1986 these were Middle East, Far East, Western Europe, Northern Ireland, South and Central America, Sub-Saharan Africa and of course the Soviet Bloc. There were also functional CIGs covering Terrorism and Proliferation, and an Economic Section. Each of the groups functioned in the same way, usually chaired by a Deputy Chief of Assessments with one member of the staff there as note-taker and representatives of each of the intelligence agencies dealing with that geographic area or topic. In the Soviet Bloc CIG, for example, this would include the Head of J Division from GCHQ (this Division, also known as Special Sigint, dealt with the Warsaw Pact nations) and SIS's Controller Sovbloc. The CIG considered a question, usually on the basis of a paper prepared by the Assessments Staff desk officer for the subject under discussion, by a section of the Defence Intelligence Staff or one of the other agencies, and drew up an agreed memo that would then either be circulated in the next Red Book or put forward to the JIC itself for further discussion during one of its Thursday meetings.

The official who chaired the Soviet Bloc CIG was Harry Burke, a senior GCHQ officer brought into the Cabinet Office by Anthony Duff. Because of Burke's sigint background, his superior Martin Morland found him extraordinarily adept at sifting through the sacks of intercepts which poured in from Cheltenham and piecing together a fuller picture. Intelligence analysts, like journalists or politicians, often sort information in ways which validate their own ideas, and Burke is remembered as someone who took the toughest view possible of the Soviet threat. His attitude chimed well with that of his ultimate boss Percy Cradock, the JIC Chairman, who felt a deep scepticism about the 'Gorbymania' that was to sweep the West.

Lieutenant-General Derek Boorman, by this time promoted in his role as Chief of Defence Intelligence (CDI), was one of the few senior figures in this Whitehall group who was truly pragmatic on Soviet questions. He felt 'there was evidence even pre-Gorbachev that certain developments were taking place in the Soviet Union which could have allowed us to reduce our military posture and so reduced the level of risk'.

In March 1986, with Gorbachev's 27th Congress speech still fresh in people's minds, SIS held a conference on developments in the Soviet Union at Century House, its headquarters in London. Key officials from the Foreign Office and MI6's sister intelligence agencies were there; ministers were not invited. The conference was the Service's first chance to parade Gordievsky in front of a wider audience. The former KGB man remembers, 'I suggested a cautious attitude. I knew he [Gorbachev] was young and had ideas, but they were so basic – there was nothing revolutionary.' Others present say that Gordievsky described Gorbachev as a typical party *apparatchik* from whom radical new developments could not be expected. Gordievsky recalls, 'My colleagues in SIS said, "Good, good, you've got them eating out of your hand."'

Lieutenant-General Boorman and others with a basically benign view of the new Soviet leader recognized the impact of Gordievsky's views on his listeners and the genuine fear which details of Operation RYAN, the KGB–GRU plan to monitor Western countries for signs of a possible nuclear first strike, engendered. The RYAN intelligence in particular 'had a pretty profound effect', he says; 'It set back the "wets" a long way.'

The Century House conference was followed by a turn at the Chiefs of Staff seminar, an annual event put on by SIS at the Fort. The Chief of Defence Staff, Britain's top serving military officer, and the chiefs of each of the three service staffs were flown from a barracks in central London to the MI6 base on the south coast by RAF helicopters. Once more, ministers were not present. Gordievsky was produced as 'one of the after-dinner delights', says one of the people there. During the two-day event SIS put its reading of what was going on in Moscow and the world to the nation's top military officers. The seminar, says one Whitehall mandarin, 'was part of the skill which SIS have at selling themselves'.

JIC's view of the Gorbachev speech in February and of other statements that soon followed was, according to someone party to the Assessments Staff papers of the time, that they were 'a pragmatic way of approaching a disastrous economic situation, putting on a different face to the West while not reducing his conventional military capability'. The notion of Gorbachev as two-faced came frequently from Harry Burke and other prominent officials. These views, and those of intelligence officers on the other side of the Atlantic, were reflected that spring in two annually-produced documents: the Pentagon's *Soviet Military Power* and Britain's Statement on the Defence Estimates, or Defence White Paper.

The 1986 *Soviet Military Power* commented: 'None of these proposed measures is new, nor do they represent a wholesale restructuring of the Soviet Union's economic system. What is new is Gorbachev's forceful style.' Even if Gorbachev did revive the economy, it said, 'the Soviet military has a strong long-term interest in the success of initiatives designed to stimulate the economy'.

Quoting from the Pentagon brochure or the JIC's views in these months is not an unfair use of hindsight; it is worth recalling the views of others as well – for example Martin Walker, the *Guardian* correspondent in Moscow. In a book he wrote that summer, Walker took the speech and other signs that the new General Secretary was being influenced by a radical group of economists to mean 'that the new Soviet leadership has already started to make the hard choices which will impose strict limits on military spending', adding prophetically that 'he and the armed forces are set on a collision course over the defence budget'. More conservative commentators, like those at the London-based International Institute for Strategic Studies, took a cautious line in their review of the year, but even they acknowledged that 'the battle over reform has clearly entered a crucial stage'.

Soviet Military Power, which had first appeared in 1981 at the height of President Reagan's anti-Soviet campaigning, was a glossy annual that helped Caspar Weinberger, the US Secretary of Defence, to justify the substantial increases in military spending he was requesting at the time. It was distributed to Congressional staffers and journalists, and from embassies overseas, and was an extensively-illustrated, unclassified version of what might previously have been a secret briefing. Its tone throughout the mid-1980s was markedly harsher than that of the British Statement on the Defence Estimates, which contained a section on the balance of forces between Nato and the Warsaw Pact. Much of the Pentagon document was geared to helping US service chiefs get funding for their own projects.

In 1985, for example, *Soviet Military Power* said that a new Soviet gunship helicopter code-named Havoc was 'expected to be deployed in the near future'. Britain's Defence White Paper simply said that Havoc was 'likely to enter service in the later 1980s'. In fact, at the time of writing this chapter, ten years later, Havoc has still not gone into service. However, the US Army successfully used the threat of the new Soviet helicopter to get the administration and Congress to provide funds for hundreds of additional Apache gunships of its own. This single example of what was a broad Pentagon approach helps to explain why British intelligence considered the Americans to be more politically-influenced and procurement-orientated. One British former intelligence chief concludes that *Soviet Military Power* was 'an absurd document, but it worked on the Hill all right. It got them their money.'

Although British analysts took what might be called a less commercial view of the Soviet threat, there were pressures on the Defence Intelligence Staff to provide as much information as possible to assist service chiefs in making the case for their own projects and to provide a rationale for the annual cycle of Nato exercises. Lieutenant-General Boorman remembers, 'We would draw attention to the threat every April so as to give meaning to the forthcoming training season.'

The March–April period was important in the alliance's intelligence calendar because it saw the compilation of a document classified Nato Top Secret and called MC/161. This paper (MC stood for Nato's Military Committee) was an extended, multinational version of *Soviet Military Power*. Nato did not have its own intelligence collection staff or facilities, so it relied on individual countries to contribute it. The vast majority of what went into MC/161 came from sigint collected by the three English-speaking Nato countries – a group known as Canukus, an acronym from Canada, UK, US. The annual Nato intelligence procedure was therefore a chance for the sigint allies to hand their view of what was happening inside the Warsaw Pact to nations like Denmark or Portugal that had minimal intelligence services of their own. A British intelligence officer involved in the MC/161 process says, 'The bulk of the input came from the Canukus team, although the Germans had a role with their special knowledge of East Germany. The very sensitive stuff would be kept quiet by Canukus, and it would be watered down if it was going to appear in that document. Each of the nations could draw upon the agreed text to support their procurement programmes.'

The GCHQ input to the Canukus partnership ranged from listening in to the conversations of Soviet Army field commanders on exercise to plotting surface-to-air missile defences by pinpointing the location of their radar and intercepting the data sent from new missiles to their ground stations. GCHQ could monitor this traffic from land stations in the UK, Cyprus, Hong Kong or inside British embassies; from the specially-equipped Nimrod R1s of the Royal Air Force's 51 Squadron – effectively GCHQ's private air force – and from Royal Navy ships sailing as close as they dared to Soviet territorial waters, or indeed from submarines which often went inside them.

Experts from Cheltenham worked closely with colleagues in the Defence Intelligence Staff to build up a picture of Soviet forces and discover new weapons. Although principally an organisation for analysis, DIS also had its own network of information-gatherers in the defence attachés in embassies and in one of the most curious anomalies of the Cold War, the British Military Mission (BRIXMIS) in East Germany. BRIXMIS, with about forty staff, was a remnant of the four-power arrangements for the occupation of Germany drawn up in 1945. Its operatives were allowed to travel in East Germany, and were used to gather intelligence on the 380,000-strong Soviet garrison there – the field force that would have been the spearhead of any drive westwards. BRIXMIS's operations including rifling various Soviet Army rubbish tips; Air Marshal Michael Armitage, formerly CDI, remembers that 'it was amazing what could be found out. They were very untidy people.'

The Nato system of spreading English-speaking influence through information worked well as long as the sigint powers, critically the USA and UK, agreed. Most of the time the information concerned the minutiae of Soviet military dispositions and equipment and there were no problems, but arguments did sometimes occur when politically sensitive matters were under review. During 1983–5 the Pentagon used allegations that the Soviet Army was using chemical weapons in Afghanistan, and its Vietnamese allies a bacteriological agent code-named Yellow Rain in Cambodia, to vilify Moscow and help its own generals in arguing for a new generation of chemical weapons – binary nerve gas – for the US armed forces.

Repeated US attempts to include the Yellow Rain allegations in MC/161 were blocked by Britain. One official recalls, 'The Americans were banging on about this, saying there were tens of thousands of people dying in Cambodia because of it. We said, "Fine, produce some bloody bodies or samples!" And in the end it was all bullshit. It was an example of intelligence being driven by politics. We ended up agreeing in Nato that the allegations were not proven.' Undeterred by the fact that they could not get an endorsement through the classified forum of Nato's MC/161 document, the Americans went public with their claims in *Soviet Military Power*, which in 1984 stated that there was 'strong evidence of the actual use of chemical and toxin weapons by the Soviet Union and its client forces in Afghanistan, Laos and Kampuchea'. No independent scientific verification of these charges has ever emerged.

The cause of those in Whitehall who believed that the new Soviet leader should be trusted, and that the excesses of Caspar Weinberger's Pentagon analysts be ignored, was damaged in August 1986, after the General Secretary announced the withdrawal of six regiments of the 40th Army, the Soviet occupation force in Afghanistan. At the 27th Congress Gorbachev had publicly called the conflict a 'running sore', and the Foreign Office had received information that he had gone further in closed session, telling the delegates that the party had already made the decision to withdraw all Soviet troops from Afghanistan. One Soviet journalist told me in Kabul in 1988 that, shortly after taking power, Gorbachev had promised the Central Committee he would get the army out of Afghanistan within three years. Between those reported pledges of February 1986 and the completion of the withdrawal in February 1989, Gorbachev was in fact to abandon many of the preconditions for withdrawal, and the last Soviet soldier did leave within that three-year time scale. This central Asian war had become a *cause célèbre* for the Reagan administration, and by 1986 it was significantly increasing its covert military aid to the *mujahedeen* resistance fighters.

Following well-publicized departure parades in August 1986 for the six regiments of Soviet troops in Afghanistan, the Pentagon branded the whole withdrawal a hoax. Signal and photographic intelligence from satellites provided the proof. The USA then modified its line to say that some troops had been brought in specifically for the parades, others had withdrawn and then returned to Afghanistan, but that three anti-aircraft regiments had actually left. This mess – in part the result of a Soviet desire to generate propaganda at a difficult time in their own decision-making process, in part perhaps an early example of military foot-dragging in the face of Gorbachev's initiatives – damaged the Soviet leader's credibility in many Western capitals.

In truth, Soviet military policy in Afghanistan changed significantly in the summer and autumn of 1986, and some indicators of this were known to British and US intelligence. Frustrated by the effect of the long-running war on Soviet relations with other countries, the General Secretary had ordered the army to do everything possible to prevent casualties prior to withdrawal. Evidence of the new tactics – using Soviet artillery and air power but sending in the Afghan army to do the close-range fighting – was gathered by British diplomats near Kabul in September 1986 and sent to the Foreign Office. As a result of these new orders, subsequently-released figures would show that the number of Soviet troops killed in action fell from 2,343 in 1984, the peak year of their operations in Afghanistan, to 1,868 in 1985 and 1,333 in 1986.

Britain and the USA had in fact been supporting the *mujahedeen* almost since the beginning of the Soviet occupation in December 1979. SIS had been authorized by the Prime Minister to take active measures, known within the Service as Disruptive Action, within the first year of the campaign. Whereas the great majority of MI6's time – one Whitehall expert estimates 96 per cent – is spent simply gathering information, there are other occasions when it becomes involved in covert action.

SIS's assistance to the Afghan resistance was small-scale compared with that of the CIA, which from the outset began supplying large amounts of Soviet Bloc-manufactured weaponry, which it acquired from Egypt and later Israel, to the Afghan guerrillas. By mid-1986 the agencies were escalating their supplies to include modern shoulder-launched anti-aircraft missiles. The CIA, using the Department of Defence as its agent, purchased 300 Blowpipe missiles from Shorts of Belfast in the spring of 1986. These missiles were manufactured under the code-name Project 279. A further 300 missiles were bought later. One British intelligence expert remarks, 'We were helped by the Americans – they paid most of the bills.' By September 1986, when the first of the more modern US-made Stinger missiles appeared on the battlefield, British assistance in providing Blowpipes was no longer needed.

Early on in the war SIS had decided to focus its limited Disruptive Action effort on the units of a charismatic young commander named Ahmed Shah Massoud. Whereas most of the guerrilla commanders displayed few organizational skills, were corrupt and made blatantly dishonest claims about the scale of their 'victories', Massoud was a methodical organizer whose bases in the Panjsher valley, close to the major road connecting Kabul with the Soviet frontier, allowed him to mount effective ambushes on enemy supply columns. SIS's choice of him, so early in the campaign, was a shrewd one.

SIS sent an annual mission to Massoud to find out what he needed and, within the tight budgetary limits suffered by the British, to provide it. By early 1982, for example, several British-supplied tactical radios made by the firm Racal had arrived in the Panjsher. These played a crucial role in allowing Massoud to co-ordinate his forces. The annual missions, consisting of one or two SIS officers and a small number of 'freelance' military instructors, also concentrated their early efforts on giving organizational training to Massoud's junior commanders. One person with a knowledge of the operation notes that Massoud's forces 'had a communications system which was very nearly priceless and acquired the knowledge of how to use it and how to organize. Those were subtle things, but probably worth over a hundred planeloads of Armalites or Stingers.'

Both the CIA and SIS were constrained in what they could do by the Pakistani government, as almost all military aid to the *mujahedeen* flowed through that country. Pakistan's Inter-Services Intelligence (ISI) had its own agenda and sought to back the guerrilla groups with the toughest Islamic ideology. This did not produce problems with Massoud, who belonged to such a group, but in other cases involved large amounts of Western weapons going to anti-Western fundamentalist groups. A British expert remarks, 'The Pakistani intelligence community wanted to keep very strict control of things. There was tension with the Anglo-Saxons, so some things were done with the Pakistanis' knowledge, some without.'

In time, extraordinary claims were made about the effectiveness of

Stingers and the success of the Western campaign of covert action. Charles Cogan, a senior CIA Directorate of Operations officer, would later argue that the conflict had triggered the Soviet collapse: 'The hollow shell that was the Soviet system had first to be exposed in Afghanistan.' In fact, as the casualty figures show, the Kremlin was able to reduce the mortality rate of its soldiers at precisely the time that Western intelligence did its best to increase it.

For Margaret Thatcher, being able to 'do business' with Gorbachev did not mean stopping supplies to the guerrillas, who inhabited – to borrow her Private Secretary Charles Powell's term – a separate compartment in her political mind. The SIS campaign of Disruptive Action assisted the *mujahedeen* with missiles which were to be used to shoot down several passenger planes. When the supply of Blowpipes was revealed by a British newspaper, the ambassador in Moscow was summoned to the Soviet Foreign Ministry, where he denied knowledge of the scheme. The case shows the usefulness of intelligence services to a government pursuing apparently contradictory policies that it judges to be in its interest; in the summer of 1986, Afghanistan was a forum for Western as well as Soviet dishonesty.

During autumn 1986 the Foreign Office made one of its periodic diplomatic *démarches* into the field of chemical weapons. In talks in Geneva, the British were trying to play a leading role in the drive for a new chemical weapons convention. Officials and ministers decided that this especially abhorrent type of weaponry might provide a good litmus test for the honesty and openness of the new regime in Moscow – and in fact it was to play precisely that role during the coming years. Just as Britain tried to play a particular diplomatic role on the issue, so the intelligence community was tasked by the JIC to make Soviet chemical weapons a high priority.

Whitehall's centre of expertise in Soviet chemical weapons was the Defence Intelligence Staff. Neither the JIC Assessments Staff nor SIS had the experts to study the problem closely. Instead, a DIS cell under a Ministry of Defence civil servant made the key estimates. Judging a nation's chemical weapons capability is a difficult task: particular factories must first be identified, then their output measured and estimates of existing stocks made. Although the USA had photographic satellites with a reported ground resolution (the size of object they are able to distinguish) of ten centimetres, these were of limited use when judging chemical weapons, since they cannot tell you whether storage tanks at suspect plants are empty or full, or whether ammunition bunkers contain high-explosive shells or shells filled with nerve gas.

Nevertheless, in 1982 DIS made its estimate of Soviet chemical weapons one of its most important projects. The Prime Minister herself was briefed at the Defence Ministry on their findings. She was told that the Soviets had stockpiled 300,000 tons of the most lethal agents – nerve gases – across the Soviet Union and in eastern Europe. The DIS had based its estimate on the production capacity of the Soviet chemical plants identified through US satellite photography and certain GCHQ intercepts. Throughout Whitehall there was pride in their methodology, although the assumption that the factories had worked to their full capacity would prove a false one.

The 'made in Britain' figure of 300,000 tons became a diplomatic and intelligence shibboleth in Whitehall, and was used during summit meetings with General Secretary Gorbachev and Eduard Shevardnadze, his Foreign Minister. When they later denied that their country had anything like this quantity of nerve gas, those in the intelligence world who took a tough view of the new Soviet leader used these denials to cast doubt on his honesty on all other matters.

The US intelligence community had by the mid-1980s given up publishing estimates of the chemical weapons stockpile. Analysts in various agencies had produced figures ranging from 20,000 to 600,000 tons. The CIA felt the question was just too difficult. Although interested in what the British had to say, the USA did not endorse the 300,000 tons figure – it was left out of *Soviet Military Power*, for example. This was therefore a rare example of Britain going it alone on a substantial issue of intelligence. George Younger, Secretary of State for Defence, was to tell the House of Commons Defence Committee in 1988 that 'there are differences in the figures produced by various sections of the alliance. For instance, even in the United States there are different calculations made by different parts of the United States services. But generally speaking we compare notes with them and we stand by our calculation as being a reasonable estimate.'

There was just one problem with the DIS figure. It was completely wrong, an overestimate by a factor perhaps as great as nine. Years later, when the Russian Federation, as inheritor of the Soviet arsenal, signed the chemical weapons convention, it revealed stocks of 32,300 tonnes. Confirmation that the Soviet Union had produced only 30,000 to 35,000 tonnes of nerve gas came in a book by Lev Fedorov, a Moscow chemistry professor with many contacts inside the institutes that developed the weapons, who later became a dissident and was jailed by the authorities for publishing newspaper articles on the subject. The 32,000-tonne figure is in 1995 'the generally-accepted estimate', according to Derek Averre, a University of Birmingham expert. No evidence to support the assertion that chemical weapons were stockpiled on the territory of east European allies was found by those countries when they later broke free of the Communist system.

Many of the intelligence practitioners I interviewed for this book were unaware that the end of the Cold War had brought definitive figures for Soviet nerve-gas stocks, and instead repeated the accusations of official dishonesty which would become the central feature of British diplomacy on this subject during 1987–9. However, Lieu tenant-General Derek Boorman, Chief of Defence Intelligence from 1985 to 1988, is prepared to reassess the question, arguing that 'it was an incredibly difficult target. There was Soviet disinformation. There was geography; look at the size of the area we were covering. Good intelligence was available on manufacturing capability, but it was very difficult to estimate actual output, which was very tough in such a security-conscious state. All of us had to take a certain view based on capacity; that was the side to err on. In the circumstances it was prudent.'

Mikhail Gorbachev, already eighteen months into his leadership, had become frustrated at the lack of a breakthrough in arms control. He went to the Icelandic capital in October 1986 hoping to tempt President Reagan into joining him for a real breakthrough. During their talks Gorbachev made it clear that the SS-4 and SS-20 INF missiles could be the subject of a treaty separate from any agreement on Star Wars or strategic weapons, but he tried to exclude from any agreement the ninety or so SS-20s not within range of Europe – a caveat that would hold up negotiations for another year.

In their conversations, the two leaders did come close to agreement on two other matters on which they had previously been considered as irreconcilable. The US President, in an attempt to assure the Soviet leader that his intentions were not aggressive, offered to share Strategic Defence Initiative research with Moscow and agreed to keep US research 'in the laboratory' for the time being. Gorbachev suggested that the two countries move towards the abolition of long-range ballistic missiles, the most dangerous symbols of the Cold War arms race. The President was tempted by this offer, sharing with its proposer a fear of the missiles that could fly from one superpower to another in less than thirty minutes and so present decision-makers with a frighteningly short period in which to react. The two leaders agreed as a first step to work towards a 50 per cent cut in these weapons. Disagreement about the scope of Star Wars prevented a wider consensus.

When news of the Reykjavik conversations reached London, there was consternation in Downing Street. In her memoirs Margaret Thatcher wrote, 'My own reaction . . . was as if there had been an earthquake beneath my feet.' She saw that the proposals about SDI and moving towards the abolition of certain nuclear weapons could have a serious effect on Britain's plans to buy the US-made Trident submarine-launched ballistic missile. Only what she called 'Soviet duplicity' – Gorbachev's attempts to push his own agenda on SDI as part of the package – had stopped a deal. Billions of pounds had already been committed to Trident, and the Labour Party had pledged to scrap it if it came to power, arguing that Britain's nuclear forces were not truly independent and contributed nothing to international security.

Geoffrey Howe, then Foreign Secretary, remembers, 'We were, of course, conscious that an American abandonment of their missile deterrent could remove Trident from our armoury. Moreover, we were worried in a narrower sense that any agreements arrived at to share ballistic missile defence technology could endanger our deterrent's effectiveness.' Reykjavik exposed Britain's dependence on US nuclear weapons technology. The increasingly-frequent Soviet disarmament offers put Britain on the defensive; Howe publicly denounced one such Kremlin move as a 'gimmick', another as 'specious'. But what privately worried the foreign policy and defence establishments in London was that George Shultz, Reagan's Secretary of State, and experts at the White House seemed to see many of the Kremlin offers very differently.

The Prime Minister soon travelled to Washington to seek reassurances that nothing would be decided that would leave Britain without its future nuclear deterrent. Thatcher's inner circle regarded this as one of the first and most effective examples of her 'stiffening' the resolve of the US President, exercising an influence at a critical moment in Moscow's 'charm offensive'. In her campaign to ensure that nuclear disarmament did not proceed too quickly, Thatcher gained a powerful ally in the shape of General Bernard Rogers, the

Supreme Allied Commander in Europe at Nato headquarters in Belgium. General Rogers, a US officer, publicly denounced his commander-in-chief for proceeding to Reykjavik without consulting him about issues of such import. The SACEUR, as he was called in Nato, was like Thatcher a veteran of the political struggle earlier in the 1980s to deploy new US Pershing 2 and Cruise missiles in Europe in the face of mass protests by disarmament groups.

The Iceland summit had caused deep anxieties in London. There was a feeling that the Atlantic alliance might crack under the stress of the Kremlin's blandishments. Tom King, a Cabinet member at the time, believes that 'there was a feeling at Reykjavik that the Cold War was still very much on. That's why Margaret Thatcher was so concerned about what President Reagan might have been signing up to. The idea that he might have gone too far was an indication of people's lack of confidence that the world had really changed.'

At times such as the weeks following the Reykjavik summit, many in Washington watched with amazement the political influence Thatcher was able to exert over the President and the extent to which British intelligence was able to put its assessments across, often through personal visits by Percy Cradock and other key figures. Senior US officials comment on the degree to which these emissaries were able to make their conservative interpretation of Gorbachev felt, despite the small scale of Britain's intelligence effort. For his part George Shultz, the US foreign policy chief, was unabashed about what had happened at Reykjavik. He was convinced that deep cuts in strategic nuclear arms were within reach, and disregarded much of the assessment produced by US and British agencies.

Morton Abramowitz, Schultz's Assistant Secretary for Intelligence and Research (and head of the analytical agency known within the Washington intelligence community as INR), believes that history vindicated his Secretary of State rather than his colleagues in the espionage world: 'The leaders of the CIA were almost invariably wrong, and the British were in the same school. George Shultz was right. He was not an intelligence man, but he was meeting [Gorbachev and Shevardnadze]. The policy types were much better in their judgement than the intelligence types in Washington. As for British intelligence, you can never be to the right of them.'

Chapter 4

1986 Most Ridiculed Service

Although the intelligence community primarily fixed its view on the threat from the Soviet Bloc, there had always been other priorities too, and in October 1986 the Security Service and GCHQ proved themselves in what was to become a key area of operations: counter-terrorism. On 24 October a Jordanian named Nizar Hindawi was convicted of trying to smuggle a bomb on to an El Al plane at Heathrow airport the previous April. The aircraft was due to take off with 375 passengers on board, among them Ann Murphy, Hindawi's pregnant girlfriend whom he had duped into carrying the bomb. It was timed to explode when the Boeing 747 would have been at 39,000 feet over Austria.

Following the verdict, Geoffrey Howe announced the severing of diplomatic relations with Syria, because of what he said was 'conclusive evidence of Syrian official involvement' in Hindawi's 'monstrous and inhumane crime'. The Foreign Secretary said that the role of Syrian embassy and airline personnel in the case was clear. He alluded to 'independent evidence' that the Syrian ambassador himself had recommended Syrian Air Force Intelligence in Damascus to back Hindawi.

The case was a success for GCHQ, which had provided that 'independent evidence' in the form of an intercepted conversation between Loutouf Allah Haidar, the ambassador, and the authorities in Damascus. The Security Service was also involved; it had helped GCHQ to bug the embassy as part of stepping up operations against embassy officials from states regarded as terrorist sponsors. Whether the bomb was found by an observant El Al security man without further assistance, as was said in court, or whether MI5 had played a role in warning the airline of the likely plot is open to question. In court the security man, named only as Mr C, insisted that he had not been specifically tipped off about the bomb.

Some press speculation followed about how GCHQ might have intercepted the communications between Damascus and London. Experts suggest that this coup had not necessarily involved breaking the Syrian diplomatic cipher. Rather, the information may have come through the use of a bugging device known as an infinity transmitter. This can be planted on a phone line outside a building, so avoiding the need to infringe diplomatic immunity, and used to make a telephone still in its cradle go 'live' as a microphone. Had the ambassador had more than one telephone on his desk, then it could have been used to pick up the conversation he was having, even if the telephone he was using was scrambled.

In the days that followed Britain's breaking off diplomatic relations with Syria, the government attempted to convince its allies that they should follow this lead. In his memoirs Howe suggests that they would have done, had they enjoyed access to the same intelligence as the USA and UK. This admission is an interesting demonstration of the desire of these two countries to preserve sigint secrets, even when it would be to their diplomatic advantage to share them with what are, after all, close allies. Although European countries temporarily recalled their ambassadors and endorsed an arms embargo on Syria, they did not follow the UK–US lead in severing relations. The Syrian case provides an example of the role of intelligence in making foreign policy. Britain's Atlantic orientation, enshrined in the UKUSA sigint treaty, led London and Washington to take one view, while European partners adopted another. Britain's inability to share such secrets fed continental suspicions about a shallowness of Albion's commitment to the European project. At the same time, however, it was becoming more important for the UK to improve its security ties with those partners because of a resumption of Irish republican terrorism on the continent.

For Anthony Duff, the Director General of the Security Service, the Hindawi affair represented a strong case for a redefinition of MI5's roles. The DGSS had his own strategy for rebuilding the Service, which had the fledgling Counter Terrorist Branch at its centre. He diverted resources away from the more traditional 'ideological' areas of the Service's work despite the views held elsewhere in Whitehall and expressed by the Joint Intelligence Committee, that Gorbachev was a liar who shared traditional Kremlin aspirations. Despite the fact that he was above retirement age, Duff had been appointed by the Prime Minister, after a committee comprising Duff himself (then Chairman of the Joint Intelligence Committee), Brian Cubbon, Permanent Under Secretary at the Home Office, and Robert Armstrong, Cabinet Secretary, had met several times but had been unable to think of anyone to take over the Service. All agreed that it was wallowing, with dangerously low morale and a tarnished public image, and Armstrong eventually suggested to Duff in the autumn of 1984 that he take over the job.

Duff was an unusual figure in the intelligence world, more of a 'character' than his predecessor or successor at MI5. Gently spoken, with a patrician manner, he was highly successful at getting his way in the Whitehall system, leading observers to dub him both a 'bully' and a 'charmer'. One thing Duff had in abundance was nerve; during the Second World War he had commanded a submarine. Duff told colleagues that the war had been his university and that many of his close friendships were formed in those tough times. His *sang froid* was to come in useful in a Service which was frequently under fire and had become a political football. One intelligence figure who observed Duff's effect on the JIC and then MI5 remarks, 'His experience as a young man commanding a submarine which was little more than a tin can that could be destroyed at any moment had turned him into a real leader. He could talk to working-class people without fuss – his qualities were quite different from those of the average university-trained diplomat.'

The most damaging of the attacks on the Security Service during the early and mid-1980s were those arising from the public revelations of some of its own retired officers. These made many people believe that the organization was a crucible for conspiracies, staffed by peculiar right-wing extremists. The writer David Cornwell, later famous under his pen-name John Le Carré, served in MI5 during the 1960s. As he later described it in a piece of non-fiction, the atmosphere in the Curzon Street building hardly inspired confidence:

> For a while you wondered whether the fools were pretending to be fools, as some kind of deception; or whether there was a real efficient secret service somewhere else. Later, in my fiction, I invented one. But alas the reality was the mediocrity. Ex-colonial policemen mingling with failed academics, failed lawyers, failed missionaries and failed débutantes gave our canteen the amorphous quality of an Old School outing on the Orient Express. Everyone seemed to smell of failure.

The Tory MP Jonathan Aitken said in 1988, 'The tone of MI5 is one of sound mediocrity, often touched with an inferiority complex about its cousins at MI6.' In SIS, opinions about the quality of their colleagues at MI5 were often unflattering: one officer called them 'grey-shoed plodders'. MI6 thinks that it has the brightest graduates, and MI5 the academic also-rans. It is true that not all officers in MI5's General Intelligence (GI) group are graduates. This group, which mans most of the key officer postings, was about 300 strong in 1986. A 1993 public information pamphlet which states that 'approximately a quarter' of GI officers are Oxford and Cambridge graduates is, an SIS man claims scathingly, intended to impress other departments with how many personnel with these qualifications the Security Service has, rather than being a sign of Whitehall's customary sensitivity about the large number of Oxbridge graduates in its ranks.

The Service had taken a heavy blow after the uncovering of Michael Bettaney's attempted treachery in 1983. A Security Commission report had criticized the standards of management that had allowed Bettaney to develop a drink problem and suffer the personal collapse that led him to give secrets to the Soviet Union. The Prime Minister considered MI5's higher management discredited and therefore supported Duff as an outsider.

For MI5's managers, the biggest problem was simply that its mission of maintaining domestic security attracted far more public and parliamentary interest than the foreign operations of SIS or GCHQ. Nowhere was this question more vexed than in the issue of how the Service defined 'subversion', the countering of which was one of its principal missions. The work done by MI5's F Branch in the 1980s had its origins in the ruling class's fear of international Communism after the First World War. F Branch's aim was to infiltrate and disrupt extremist organisations, most of them on the far left, because such groups might be plotting to overthrow parliamentary democracy.

By the 1980s few people, even officers in the Service, believed that the factional remnants of the Communist Party of Great Britain or of Trotskyite groups such as the Socialist Workers' Party were able to mount any kind of effective insurrection. Public ridicule of such groups was such that they were considered a suitable subject for a highly popular situation comedy, BBC Television's *Citizen Smith*. F Branch, however, had displayed institutional inertia, rumbling on regardless of the post-war changes in society. Industrial agitation or rallies of the far left were labelled subversion rather than being regarded as a part of the democratic process. Dedicated counter-subversion officers pointed to the 1974 miners' strike, which had prompted a general election and change of government, as an example of subversion and used it to justify infiltrating the trade-union movement. For the tougher types at Curzon Street, the idea that subversion might 'undermine' democracy rather than overthrow it provided a fresh rubric for bugging and surveillance. F Branch's work caught up certain Labour MPs and trade-union leaders, which troubled some MI5 staff and poisoned the atmosphere with broad sections of the left, who regarded MI5 as an unaccountable, unscrupulous secret police.

Shortly before Duff arrived at the Service's Gower Street HQ, Cathy Massiter, a former F Branch officer, appeared on 20/20 Vision, a Channel 4 television programme, making public her disquiet about the way MI5 was defining subversion. She described how she had been asked by her superiors to conduct phone-tapping on members of the Campaign for Nuclear Disarmament, the National Council for Civil Liberties and the housing pressure-group Shelter. Her superiors had cited the 'Communist connections' of certain individuals involved with the organizations as the reason for taking an interest in them as a whole.

The CND phone-taps had, in her view, been carried out in support of government policy, the 1983 general election being the first in which Labour had campaigned for unilateral nuclear disarmament. Allegations that, because of their involvement with the NCCL, Patricia Hewitt, later the Labour leader's press secretary, and Harriet Harman, who later became a Labour MP, had been tapped were to involve the Service in protracted litigation. Massiter also described how phone-taps had been used to investigate the organizers of strikes and other industrial action.

The government had tried to prevent the showing of the 20/20 Vision programme, part of a battle Margaret Thatcher considered essential if the 'secret services' were to function. Officers of the Service knew that they could expect to be silenced, but several more chose to make public their concerns.

In May 1984 Miranda Ingram, a former K Branch officer who had worked with Michael Bettaney, published an article in which she complained, 'The concern of some officers is that there is a lack of flexible debate within the Service about the interpretation of "subversion" in the determining of policy. In the prevailing right-wing atmosphere, an officer who dissents from the official line does not feel encouraged to voice his concern. He feels that to do so would be futile, or unfortunately that it would be detrimental to his career.' Ingram wrote again when some of the Security Commission's recommendations on the Bettaney case became public. John Day, formerly Head of A4 Section, the Service's surveillance specialists, was later to write critically about early government proposals for tighter oversight of the Service.

While Massiter, Ingram and Day might all have been said to be broadly on the left of the argument about the Service, the greatest difficulties would come with Peter Wright when he attempted to publish his book *Spycatcher*. Wright was happy to reveal not only that the Service was cavalier about the law, relying on the maxim 'don't get caught' as it 'bugged and burgled' its way around London, but also that it was run in an inefficient manner, with senior officers retiring *en masse* to watch test matches. But Wright's allegations were centred on claims that the Service had not been thorough enough in investigating leads on Soviet penetrations.

Wright, in common with James Jesus Angleton, the CIA counter-intelligence chief, had placed great credence in the testimony of Anatoly Golytsin, a Russian defector who claimed that Western intelligence organizations were extensively penetrated and that much of the Kremlin's foreign policy consisted of lies aimed at lulling the West into a false sense of security. Wright's belief in some of these suggestions placed him on the far right, even within MI5, but his most damaging allegations concerned the possibility that Harold Wilson, the Labour Prime Minister, might have been a Soviet spy, and were therefore of great interest to the left. Wright wrote that he had discussed releasing information about MI5's investigation into Wilson and some of his friends shortly before the 1974 election and that 'up to thirty officers had given their approval to the scheme'.

Wright's allegations chimed with suggestions by Wilson himself, shortly after he left office in 1976, that he had been the victim of a Security Service plot. There was plenty of evidence that some of Wilson's friends and associates, particularly those who had emigrated to Britain from eastern Europe, had been investigated as part of a possible 'red cell' linked to the Prime Minister. Although Wilson later attempted to disown some of the allegations he had made, and although many of his friends dismissed them as part of the paranoia that had affected his last years in office, it was apparent that MI5 had investigated some of those around him. Wright's testimony inflamed the sensitive area of MI5 plots against the Labour government.

Many Labour MPs were already hostile to the Service because of its counter-subversion activities. The re-emergence of the 'Wilson Plot' allegations further damaged the possibility of MI5 being able to work harmoniously with any incoming Labour government. During a House of Commons debate in 1988, Roy Hattersley, the shadow Home Secretary and therefore the man who would have taken responsibility for the Service, said, 'In truth, since the war MI5 has been one of the worst and most ridiculed security services in the Western alliance.' His remarks shocked Home Office and Security Service officials, but were a good indicator of the scale of MI5's problem.

Duff therefore arrived at Gower Street in a time of crisis. His strategy for resurrecting MI5 had four principal planks: diverting resources away from counter-subversion into counter-terrorism; improving communication with staff; embracing the case for limited external oversight of the agency; and cultivating the media in order to improve the Service's image. These plans amounted to a revolution. In his interview for this book, Duff remarked, 'A little to my surprise, I found that, except for a handful of old sweats in middle management, they were very anxious to be made honest men of through legislation and independent oversight.'

Although the new DGSS enjoyed the confidence of the Prime Minister and key officials, it is apparent from talking to people who observed the changes that very little of what the DGSS did was specifically authorized by the government. Duff benefited from a constitutional freedom of the kind senior managers at SIS and GCHQ could only gaze upon with envy.

The information booklet published by the Service in 1993 noted simply that 'the Home Secretary is . . . kept informed about Service plans and priorities, as well as about matters of current concern, and by these means exercises Ministerial authority over the Service'. How simply being 'kept informed' of what MI5 was doing constituted authority in any positive sense was not explained. MI6 and GCHQ, by contrast, are 'tasked', or told what to do, by the Cabinet Office machinery. This lack of ministerial control over MI5 had its origins in the desire to keep it politically independent. The 1952 directive by the then Home Secretary David Maxwell Fyfe, which was the only real statutory basis for the Service when Duff took over, states, 'It is essential that the Security Service should be kept absolutely free from any political bias or influence and nothing should be done that might lend colour to the suggestion that it is concerned with the interests of a particular section of the community, or with any other matter than the defence of the realm as a whole.'

Duff therefore had considerable freedom to define what his organization was doing. One senior civil servant comments, 'The Security Service is very much a self-starting organization – which isn't to say they're not stimulated by ministers' comments. With their protection from day-to-day parliamentary and journalistic scrutiny, they could afford to be more introspective.' The key operational change made by Duff, switching resources from counter-subversion into counter-terrorism, suggested that he did not share the view of those running the intelligence machinery in the Cabinet Office that the Cold War was still very much on. Duff's decision involved reducing coverage of the Communist Party and organizations like the National Council for Civil Liberties which did not pose a noticeably lesser 'threat' in 1985 than they had in 1975. So it may be that Duff's aim was also institutional and political peace of mind.

The only real control exerted by the Home Secretary was over the granting of telephone intercept warrants, itself a procedure which was put on a statutory basis early in Duff's tenure. Although it was almost unheard-of for the Home Secretary to refuse such a request, someone who has been involved in the process says the warrants are 'in our rather English, pragmatic way, a powerful indication to a Director General of what the Home Office was thinking. It's a subtle process: for example, we might agree to an extension of one month instead of three, raise an eyebrow as it were, as a way of signalling the Home Secretary's supervision.' The warrant process involves the Home Secretary, the Permanent Under Secretary and a handful of civil servants. In effect, these seven or eight individuals are the only ones in the Department that has responsibility for MI5 who know what it is doing operationally. David Mellor, with his two innings as Minister of State, or second-ranking minister in the Home Office, confirms, 'I never had any direct dealings with it in five and a half years. It was entirely managed by the Home Secretary and a small group of his personal officials.'

The Security Service had acquired its initial counter-terrorist role in the early 1970s. The 1972–3 IRA campaign in Britain, which had included pub bombs exploded without warning, led to MI5 involving itself in the Northern Ireland troubles. Following the Palestinian attack at the 1972 Munich Olympics, counter-terrorist sections had been created within F Branch. F3 dealt with non-Irish terrorism, F5 with Irish. The work of both was circumscribed by various restrictions, mostly concerned with how the officers who worked for them fitted in their activities with those of the police.

When Duff became DGSS, probably no more than thirty officers worked in this field. They were led by Patrick Walker, the Service's first Director of Counter Terrorism, who was formerly Head of F5 and had considerable operational experience in Northern Ireland. Duff boosted Walker's resources and therefore increased his weight, and the priority of counter-terrorism, on MI5's Board of Management, which conducted key discussions about operational priorities and wider policy matters. Initially, Walker's empire was simply called F Branch (Counter Terrorism) with the counter-subversion branch retaining the same letter and its own director, but counter-terrorism soon got its own initial, becoming G Branch.

Duff and Walker's strategy exploited government disquiet over the shooting of policewoman Yvonne Fletcher in April 1984 by members of the Libyan People's Bureau (or embassy) and the bombing of an Air India Boeing 747 with 329 passengers on board after it had taken off from Heathrow airport in June 1985. The Libyan incident focused concern on the abuse of diplomatic privileges, mainly by Middle Eastern countries, to bring weapons into Britain, often to support terrorist groups. The Air India bombing reminded government that groups such as the Sikh extremists living in the UK might use this country and its airports as their battleground. The Hindawi case, which combined both elements, was therefore seen in Whitehall as confirmation of the soundness of Duff's approach. MI5 and GCHQ's role in pointing the finger at those responsible was seen as an effective use of resources.

G Branch was divided into several sections, covering Arab, Irish and Indian subcontinent (Kashmiris were added to the Sikhs) terrorism. With the counter-terrorism mission came agreement in Whitehall that MI5 should be responsible for protecting British interests against terrorism anywhere in the world – an important principle, given the historic rivalries with SIS.

In Northern Ireland about sixty MI5 personnel were responsible for running agents and bugging, and for supporting a senior officer, the Director and Co-ordinator of Intelligence (DCI), who acted as the Secretary of State for Northern Ireland's personal adviser. The vast majority of the human intelligence-gathering in Ulster was carried out by the Royal Ulster Constabulary Special Branch, with the Army's secret Field Research Unit running about 10 per cent of the agents. In this already-crowded operational arena, MI5's casework was meant to fall into two main categories: agents able to provide information on terrorist campaigns across the Irish Sea in Britain itself, and sources able to add political detail to what the RUC could gather from cells on the streets. At the time that G Branch was formed, the Provisional IRA was not mounting campaigns outside Ireland, so there was no urgent imperative for the expansion of MI5 activities in this area.

Fighting Indian subcontinent and Arab terrorism required the Service to find agents. Student populations were of particular interest, with MI5 recruiters able to exploit the fact that many of their targets were short of money and sometimes terrified of having to return to their native countries. Some of the successfully-recruited MI5 'assets' did leave Britain, and G Branch officers found themselves travelling to places like Beirut to run them. Counter-terrorism brought a little international glamour to a service often considered boringly parochial in Whitehall.

The switch towards counter-terrorism had little effect on A Branch, the part of the Service that conducted some of the most sensitive operations. Personnel from A4, one of the Branch's sections, provided the surveillance teams, known as Mobiles and Statics, which had traditionally kept Eastern Bloc diplomats under observation, but could increasingly be redirected to the new targets. Unlike some parts of MI5, A4 – often referred to as 'the Watchers' – retained a high reputation in Whitehall. One of the section's former officers notes, 'It was a curious mixture of people. We had a former RAF pilot who had flown Lysanders into France during the war and was confined to a wheelchair. He would sit in flats overlooking Warsaw Pact embassies. We had another couple of chaps who had been supermarket managers and joined us in their fifties – don't ask me why we recruited them. Then, of course, there were quite a lot of ex-Army NCOs.'

SIS officers being trained for agent-running found themselves pitting their wits against A4 watchers in exercises on British streets. One remarks, 'The truth is, it's almost impossible to spot them. They are very professional and they use an extraordinary variety of people: a black man driving a taxi, an old woman carrying her shopping, they can all be watchers.'

Other sections of A Branch were more controversial, and their activities went to the heart of the debate about the organization's operations and accountability. A1 was responsible for the many operations in which MI5 personnel secretly entered embassies or private property in order to plant bugging equipment or remove documents for copying. Such operations had traditionally been run on the 'don't get caught' principle, but Duff realized that they too would have to be regulated more stringently.

The Director General knew that some outside scrutiny of the Service would play an important part in rebuilding its image. The 1985 Interception of Communications Act applied to all government agencies, but the Commissioner appointed by the Act became the first outsider to have the right to delve into Security Service operational matters. However, the Service itself remained in a legal limbo, its rights and duties prescribed by often obscure Whitehall convention. Its staff, as Lord Denning had said in a report on the Profumo scandal more than twenty years before, had 'no special powers of search . . . they cannot enter premises without the consent of the householder, even though they may suspect a spy is there'.

Duff and Brian Cubbon came up with the idea of a Security Service Bill. For Cubbon, the chief Home Office civil servant, the proposal was closely tied to his plans for a new, more effective Official Secrets Act. The Permanent Secretary considered that the Security Service Bill would be a sweetener to MPs voting for a more focused and tighter secrets law. But Duff's plans first had to overcome the antipathy of the Prime Minister. He now reveals that Thatcher was 'much opposed', adding that 'her instinct was not to reveal anything at all to anybody, ever. She didn't use many arguments – she just said no.' Ultimately, however, she bowed to the advice of Duff, Cubbon and Robert Armstrong, and the legislation proposed by the Service against the wishes, for several months at least, of its political masters found its way into Parliament.

When it became law in 1989, the Security Service Act defined the purpose of MI5 – though leaving it with generous room for manoeuvre – enshrined its independence from the political interests of the government of the day, and appointed a Commissioner to look into any public complaints. Duff had wanted a tribunal of three commissioners to carry out this task, but had compromised with the wishes of Downing Street. The Act defined the organization's mission as the safeguarding of national security against threats, 'in particular its protection against threats from espionage, terrorism and sabotage, from the activities of agents of foreign powers and from actions intended to overthrow or undermine Parliamentary democracy by political, industrial or violent means'. It further added the role of safeguarding 'the economic well-being of the United Kingdom against threats posed by the actions or intentions of persons outside the British Islands'.

During the debate on the Bill, Roy Hattersley pointed out the paragraph (which became known within the Service as the In Particulars) that gave MI5 'the right to do whatever they choose . . . it is made up of word after word that has only subjective meaning'. The addition of 'undermine' to the phrase 'overthrow . . . Parliamentary democracy' was seen by Labour as an attempt to justify MI5's anti-union activities during the 1984 miners' strike. Other MPs were puzzled by the inclusion of economic threats; the Conservative Jonathan Aitken argued it was 'something very different from what MI5 has done in the past'. Douglas Hurd, Home Secretary at the time of the debate, said that the economic well-being clause was meant to cover such things as 'a threat from abroad in respect of a commodity upon which we are wholly dependent. One can think of oil as being such an example from the past.' In fact, people within the Service itself did not have a precise idea of what the 'economic well-being' clause amounted to, and there have been no operations of this kind since the Bill was drafted. One MI5 officer suggests that the clause was put in 'just in case'. If true, it is an example of the Service's tendency to seek maximum freedom in defining its role and so protecting its establishment.

The legislation had one big advantage: it gave civil libertarians and the left the feeling that MI5 had at last been placed on a legal footing and that a system for investigating complaints had been set up, while at the same time convincing even the toughest operational types within the Service that their freedom had been protected. What the Home Office had given with one hand it had taken with the other. The new Security Service Act would be difficult to put to the test unless someone like Harriet Harman could make a complaint with the force of a whistle-blower's evidence, as happened with Cathy Massiter and her allegations of bugging. The new Official Secrets Act however had taken away the 'public interest' defence for people like Massiter who went public, so making it less likely that authoritatively made charges would come to light in the first place. The Act had also given legality to MI5's phone-tapping or breaking and entering – although such acts had to be done under the Home Secretary's warrant – whereas the *status quo*, enshrined in the earlier statement by Lord Denning, had been that Security Service staff had no special powers in this regard.

Despite the misgivings of many MPs, including some Conservatives, the Bill became law. The one significant area that was to be augmented at a later date concerned the plans for oversight by the Commissioner, a judge given the power to inspect files and question staff. Jonathan Aitken MP said during the debate that 'the government do not even get close to proposing a scheme of genuine accountability'. In time, a growing band of Conservative MPs would come to share this view, and the pressure for greater accountability to Parliament grew.

Along with his organizational and legal changes, Duff tried to reinvent the Service's internal culture. He started a monthly bulletin for staff, hoping this would signal a change from the remote management of John Jones, his predecessor. He also encouraged staff to come to him direct with certain problems. Duff elevated David Ranson, the Director of F Branch implicated in Massiter's allegations, to the newly-created post of Deputy Director General (Administration). By creating a second deputy's post for Ranson and expanding Walker's G Branch, each attended by their own staffs, Duff had signalled what was to become another of the major changes in the post-Cold War intelligence scene: a proliferation of management posts.

The last element of the DGSS's plan involved the cultivation of the press. As a former diplomat, Duff had had plenty of contact with journalists, and the thought of speaking to them did not fill him with trepidation in the way it did many intelligence officers. He chose Bernard Sheldon, Legal Adviser to the Director General, to assist him in this. The Legal Adviser was sufficiently important in the Security Service hierarchy to have an office next door to the DG's on the third floor at Gower Street; he also sat on the Board of Management. Sheldon was in frequent contact with the police, Home Office and a wide circle of people, and was therefore, the DG assumed, a good person to deal with those most difficult of outsiders, the press. Duff and Sheldon focused their early efforts on the editors of quality newspapers, meeting them for lunch with the aim of convincing them that the Service was a modern, forward-looking organization which did not conspire against the Labour Party and was not stuffed with KGB agents.

These early contacts with the press took place without Margaret Thatcher's knowledge. What her response would have been, given the growing storm over *Spycatcher* and other secrets matters, can only be guessed at. As 1986 ended, another public battle involving the intelligence services and press freedom was about to break out. But Anthony Duff had already gone much of the way towards rebuilding the Security Service, along lines that ministers had played only the slightest of roles in defining.

Chapter 5

1986/7 ZIRCON

Throughout the latter part of 1986 and the first weeks of 1987, the investigative journalist Duncan Campbell was working on a BBC television series to be called *Secret Society*. Campbell had been a thorn in the side of the intelligence establishment for years. His articles, usually in the *New Statesman* magazine, uncovered matters ranging from which office blocks in London were used by the agencies to allegations of dirty tricks in Northern Ireland. An earlier attempt to convict Campbell and one of his sources under the Official Secrets Act had failed; this was one of several cases which had prompted the Home Office to draw up a new secrets law.

Campbell discovered that the government planned to build a new satellite which would enable GCHQ to eavesdrop on the Soviet Union. He believed the plan violated a 1982 government agreement to inform the House of Commons Public Accounts Committee of any military project costing more than a certain amount. During the course of his filming for the *Secret Society* programme, Campbell questioned former Ministry of Defence officials and Robert Sheldon MP, chairman of the Public Accounts Committee. Inevitably, word of his inquiries reached government, and the Prime Minister decided to act. Nigel Lawson, then Chancellor of the Exchequer, recounts in his memoirs that 'the government managed to lean on the BBC to ban the programme'. Faced with the prospect of an injunction, Campbell rushed his research into print in the *New Statesman* of 23 January 1987. The spy satellite, hitherto one of Whitehall's most cherished secrets, had become a major story, as had its code-name: ZIRCON.

The Falklands war of 1982 was regarded by most people in the defence and intelligence establishments as a textbook example of Britain's 'special relationship' with the USA in action. The Americans had made certain advanced weapons available to the British and had shared vital intelligence about the location of Argentine ground and naval forces.

In Cheltenham, though, there were people who knew that this assistance had sometimes required special pleading. The National Security Agency, GCHQ's US counterpart, had not achieved global coverage with its sigint satellites by 1982. The craft which was in a position to help Britain monitor Argentine communications was being used by the Reagan administration to eavesdrop on central America, principally El Salvador. One of the GCHQ officers who liaised with NSA recalls, 'We had to negotiate very hard to get it moved, and then only for limited periods.' During these spells of a few hours each, the satellite's listening dish was reorientated towards the south Atlantic in order to help Cheltenham. The NSA did not monitor the downlinked take during these periods, asking GCHQ to alert them if there was anything of US interest in the transmissions.

Although GCHQ was grateful for NSA's help, and learnt a good deal from the occasional use of its satellite, the senior officers in Cheltenham, notably the then Director, Brian Tovey, drew certain conclusions. As one former GCHQ officer says, 'We can ask the Americans to do things, but we cannot compel them. There may be targets they don't want to cover. The Falklands was a factor here. It brought going it alone back into fashion.' It was already apparent to GCHQ management that space represented the future of sigint and that gaining a British foothold in such technology might be possible, given the Prime Minister's largesse towards the agencies.

In 1968 the National Security Agency had launched the first of seven satellites code-named CANYON. This programme had alerted the US agencies to the extraordinary possibilities of communications intelligence-gathering by satellite. CANYON was able to pick off various types of voice and data traffic from space. It was followed by a type of satellite initially code-named RHYOLITE and later AQUACADE. RHYOLITE marked a breakthrough in the sigint world. It could pick up various types of transmission, but the most important take came from the microwave telecommunications links which by the 1970s had been installed across the Soviet Union. Microwave circuits had been considered highly secure by the Russians because they use a narrow beam of energy between a transmitter and receiver which have to be within line of sight. Trying to pick up the microwave transmission from even a few miles away is pointless. But the parts of the microwave beam which shoot past the receiver – 'spillage' in sigint jargon – continue in a straight line up into space. Microwave beams may also strike the ground in places, bouncing signals straight upwards. RHYOLITE was placed in a geosynchronous orbit – positioned 24,000 miles from earth with its speed exactly matching the turning of the globe – and so was able to 'hover' over the Soviet Union. It was equipped with a large parabolic dish so that the feeble fragments of microwave energy could be refocused on its receiver. Each microwave circuit could carry hundreds of conversations. The possibilities of RHYOLITE were, says one sigint insider, 'mind-blowing'.

Under the Anglo-Saxon sigint arrangements, GCHQ was a full party to the product of this satellite. Owen Lewis, then an Army officer working in sigint and now a communications security consultant in industry, remembers, 'When RHYOLITE came in, the take was so enormous that there was no way of handling it. Years of development and billions of dollars then went into developing systems capable of handling it.' NSA's response to the explosion of information coming from space included passing large amounts of it over to GCHQ for transcription and analysis. The USA developed two types of geostationary sigint payloads: one descending from RHYOLITE was used mainly to gather interesting UHF signals such as missile telemetry and various forms of communications; the other specifically targeted microwave traffic. Each type required three satellites continuously in geosynchronous orbit over the Equator to provide global coverage. The NSA found that the amount of information being picked up from microwave circuits was so large that it had to be immediately beamed down to an earth station within line of sight. For two of the three satellites, this required ground stations outside the USA.

From 1970 the NSA had built a new constellation of eavesdroppers initially code-named CHALET and later (after a US newspaper had published this code word) VORTEX. Two large ground stations were built to downlink the traffic from the two payloads that could not be run from the USA. At Menwith Hill in north Yorkshire, hundreds of NSA staff were involved in an expanded operation believed to be taking down the product of the CHALET over the Soviet Bloc. At Pine Gap in Australia they downlinked the product of another 'bird', probably the one covering China, south-east Asia and parts of the Pacific rim. Even by the mid-1990s, with a third generation of comint satellites in orbit in these slots, the NSA has still not found another way to relay this information; imaging craft, on the other hand, can send pictures back to the USA via a network of relay satellites. Menwith and Pine Gap had thus revitalized the UK–USA sigint alliance (to which Canada, Australia and New Zealand are also partners).

In January 1985 the space shuttle *Discovery* is believed to have deployed the first of a new, improved class of satellite code-named MAGNUM. This enormous satellite, thought to weigh 2.7 tonnes, was reportedly a descendant of the RHYOLITE series, designed to intercept Soviet missile test signals (telemetry) and data-links as well as microwaves. The cost ($300 million each even in 1985) and complexity of the project is such that few have been launched.

Despite Menwith's usefulness to the NSA, GCHQ officers felt that the quantity of material coming from these new satellites was tilting the sigint relationship so far in the USA's favour that there was a danger of the British contribution becoming insignificant. The Director and senior managers therefore frequently used the need to ensure continued access to US sigint as an argument in seeking funding for their own projects. In the 1960s it had been used to get money for GCHQ's listening post at Bude in Cornwall, placed to allow the interception of transatlantic telephone calls – which was of great interest to the NSA.

One civil servant who sat on the budgetary sessions of the Permanent Secretaries' committee on the Intelligence Services (PSIS) recalls, in connection with this GCHQ tactic, that 'the American card was played quite often. There was always this awkward question of how far can you pare away the commitment.' For the mandarins, it was often difficult to know how far the representations of a GCHQ Director in support of major new projects could be taken at face value. The one-time PSIS member reveals, 'One didn't feel very confident with technical matters, but that's always the case. It was like nuclear weapons, there were no neutral specialists. That is true of intelligence. The best we could do was prod and see how loud they squealed.'

In its daily tasking, GCHQ did the maximum to help the USA. As one officer remembers, 'The requirements from our friends across the water often had to be met first under the special relationship. They were quite clearly the Big Brother. If a suitably-worded request came in and the only way to meet it was to divert resources from a low-priority UK target to a "flash" US one, then it was pretty obvious what would happen. The special relationship was regarded with the highest possible esteem.'

Britain also tried to pass on any technological advances to the USA. During 1986–7 GCHQ installed in some of its signal interception systems a new software package which provided superior recognition of key words. It had been developed by a private company, PA Technology, at its centre near Cambridge, under a substantial GCHQ contract. The software marked a significant step forward in processing sigint, being based on a phonetic system of sound recognition superior to anything previously available. It is believed to have been offered to the NSA, which said it was impressed but had substantial projects of its own to develop similar packages.

By the mid-1980s the inequalities in the GCHQ–NSA relationship led some to believe that the USA was less than committed to it. Martin Morland, who left the Chief of Assessments post at the Joint Intelligence Committee in 1986, says, 'Everything is meant to be completely shared, but even then the Americans were gradually holding back a bit. It didn't happen on the central area of Soviet Bloc, but more where they had particular interests, like Cuba, or where commercial matters were concerned.'

One former GCHQ officer suggests that the ratio of US sigint intercepts of Soviet Bloc traffic to GCHQ ones was running at about five to one during the mid-1980s. The Director of the NSA between 1985 and 1989 was a tough-talking lieutenant-general, William Odom. Despite professing himself an Anglophile descended from seventeenth-century English founding fathers, Odom is brutally frank about GCHQ and the nature of sigint ties. He told me, 'It's a very uneven relationship, to put it mildly . . . the name of the British game is to show up with one card and expect to call all the shots.'

Lieutenant-General Odom suggests that the claims frequently heard in Whitehall (and often repeated by British interviewees during the writing of this book) that GCHQ remains a world-class player were by the 1980s self-delusion. The former NSA director notes, 'Technology has changed so much that what the British brought in World War Two, they do not bring any more. They had a great tradition for a kind of eccentric cryptanalysis. Well, today that and seventy-nine cents will only buy you a cup of coffee at Seven Eleven. Today, this business requires huge investment and Britain doesn't have that.'

ZIRCON had been conceived by Brian Tovey to keep the special relationship sweet and to take his organization into space, the next logical area of sigint development. Tovey, says a former GCHQ officer, 'was gung-ho, a real expansionist'. The Director's background, the sensitivity about the relationship with NSA, and a perception of the gains to be made from a sigint spacecraft all seem to have ensured that, from an early stage, Tovey's plan was for an eavesdropping satellite rather than one able to send back pictures.

The British satellite was conceived as a geosynchronous one that would sit over the Soviet Union. Tovey's vision of ZIRCON was to survive from 1983, when the Cabinet Office approved initial studies, to the autumn of 1986. A member of the Defence Intelligence Staff at the time says, 'It was held at an incredibly tight level. We knew that there was something called ZIRCON and we knew it would be incredibly expensive.' Just how expensive would be the subject of heated argument following the publication of Campbell's article, but given the costs of the US systems, it is unlikely that ZIRCON and its associated ground station would have cost Britain less than £500 million. Much of this enormous investment would have to be repeated after five years or so, the expected life of the satellite.

There was some debate within Whitehall as to how this expenditure could be justified, given that by this time the NSA had near-global coverage with its constellations of two different types of sigint satellite. ZIRCON's backers at GCHQ argued that it would allow the USA not to fill a certain slot, or give the British complete independence if they required it. However, the managers from Cheltenham conceded that three geosynchronous satellites would be needed for a complete stand-alone UK constellation – and nobody thought Whitehall would pay for that.

The publication of Duncan Campbell's article in January 1987 brought the hitherto 'black' project into the glare of publicity. Following publication, says Nigel Lawson in his book, 'Margaret instructed Michael Havers, the Attorney General, to issue an injunction against [Campbell] . . . in a somewhat unfortunate blaze of publicity, the police raided offices both of the BBC in Glasgow and of the *New Statesman* in London.' The sight of Special Branch detectives carrying off video-tapes and papers antagonized liberal opinion, and was evidence of how deeply entrenched the Prime Minister had become in her desire to protect the intelligence services from journalistic scrutiny, even if the political cost was high.

Nigel Lawson says in his memoirs, 'Well before all this blew up, I had succeeded in getting the ZIRCON project cancelled on grounds of cost.' He says the satellite 'did not in any sense leave the ground'.

In August of that year Michael Evans, defence correspondent of *The Times*, wrote a lead story in which he revealed that ZIRCON had been cancelled in February 1987, but that 'the Prime Minister and key Cabinet colleagues have decided to keep alive the idea of Britain having its own spy satellite by going ahead with a programme that will rely instead on American technology'. Evans's leak was authoritative and accurate, whereas the Lawson version was incorrect in saying that the British satellite did not leave the ground 'in any sense' – and probably also incorrect about the timing of the cancellation decision. What happened after the furore over the Campbell article died down has not been revealed before, but was discussed by key figures involved in the decision in their interviews for this book.

The Prime Minister's extreme sensitivity may have been connected with the fact that she was close to having to make a decision about ZIRCON at the time that Duncan Campbell's programme was being made. Despite Thatcher's generous attitude towards the intelligence services, she and the senior Cabinet colleagues who knew about the plan were coming to the conclusion that ZIRCON was simply too expensive. In 1987 GCHQ's entire annual budget was about £350 million. The cost to the UK of owning and maintaining a single ZIRCON satellite would have added about £100 million a year to GCHQ's budget in perpetuity. This was about twice the annual cost of the DIS, which had 800 staff at the time, and approached the budget of SIS.

A series of meetings between heads of agencies and senior officials in PSIS in late 1986 had been moving towards the view that Britain could not continue with the project in its original form. They sought an alternative arrangement that would allow GCHQ to enter the space sigint game. Lieutenant-General Derek Boorman, the Chief of Defence Intelligence, was party to those meetings and sums up their outcome: 'Getting that capability was essential. There was no divergence of opinion about it. We may have studied going it alone, but the UK simply isn't able to afford that geographic coverage on its own, so we subscribed to their system.' The 'subscription' that the spymasters had in mind was a cash payment to the NSA to cover part of the cost of one of their new sigint satellite constellations.

In February 1987 a small group of ministers, including Mrs Thatcher and Geoffrey Howe, met to discuss the issue. The intelligence committees had also put two other options to them: continuing with a 'made in Britain' satellite, or scrapping all UK involvement in the field. In the time-honoured Whitehall fashion, the ministers took the middle way and opted to buy into the US system. It was the right choice, says Geoffrey Howe: 'A decision to maintain access to that facility can be justified. Beggars can't be choosers. If you can't afford a wholly independent operation then you have to put in a share.'

At his headquarters at Fort Meade in Maryland, the Director of the NSA was relieved by Britain's decision to abandon the 'go it alone' national project. Lieutenant-General Odom says, 'I never thought they should even have tried ZIRCON. They thought about it for their industrial base, but it didn't make sense.' Not surprisingly, the general preferred the idea of a large GCHQ cheque being paid into his satellite programme rather than the money going to British industry.

The amount spent on ZIRCON up to that point was £70 million, according to the *Times* report of August. The size of Britain's contribution to the NSA was around £500 million. It was, says one senior figure in British intelligence, 'part of the way we kept up our subscription to the US country club'. Britain had paid a price equivalent to the cost of a single satellite, part of a three-craft American constellation. The complex arrangements were agreed in a super-secret memorandum of understanding between the US and UK governments which I believe was signed in the latter part of 1988. One of the satellites would, to borrow Ernest Bevin's phrase about the British nuclear bomb, have a Union Jack on the side, but Britain could also consider itself part-owner of all of them, sharing the take of the entire constellation. The UK would also have the right to 'task' any of the three satellites for up to one third of the time. On the other hand, the 'British' satellite would never actually be delivered to the UK and the highly-sensitive technology within it remained firmly within the NSA's security system. Furthermore, it is said that the NSA can override GCHQ even in the tasking of the 'British' craft.

Britain's decision to join this US scheme was a one-off financial transaction. Someone party to the deliberations says, 'There was a strong presumption that we'd never replace it.'

In 1994 the first satellite in the second generation MAGNUM

series was launched. The payload fairing on the rocket which carried it was around eighty feet long, indicating that the listening dish mounted on the craft may possibly have a diameter as large as 160 feet. Britain appears to have invested in the largest sigint satellite yet built. A second satellite in the series was launched in 1995. It is possible one of these was the British 'bird'.

The decision was a sensible one in several ways. It ensured that British money was going on the best possible technology; there was no duplication of what NSA was doing; and the UK was insulated from the possibility that the satellite might be blown up during launch or fail in orbit. The disadvantages were equally apparent: it transformed the UK from being a virtual client of the USA to being a literal one, reinforcing national dependence in intelligence; it left open the question of what happens when the 'subscription' runs out, particularly if, as some suggest, it was a once-only deal; and it opened up the possibility that a system Britain had partly paid for might be used by the NSA to spy on the UK's allies, further blurring the frontiers of the nation's sigint sovereignty.

These negative aspects made the February 1987 decision a watershed for British intelligence. There was, however, a choice that was not one of the three options presented to ministers: co-operation with France. There were reasons why such a decision would have been timely.

After the shock of Reykjavik, the Cabinet decided to start talks with France on another area central to the UK–US special relationship: nuclear weapons. In fact, the month after the ZIRCON decision, there were discussions about collaboration with the French in the development of an air-launched nuclear-armed missile that could have been used on Royal Air Force Tornado bombers. These talks did not pay off; the Ministry of Defence eventually stated its preference for a US missile, before having to cancel the project altogether owing to financial pressure.

France's intelligence services had also thought through the intelligence implications of the space age, and during the mid-1980s had come to very different conclusions. France had decided that its national commitment to space, exemplified by the Ariane rocket and the extensive complex from which it was launched at Korou in French Guiana, should be considerable. Spending heavily on military space projects did not frighten French ministers – in fact, it appealed to them. France committed itself to buying two photographic satellites code-named HELIOS. In 1986 funds were agreed for the development of a radar imaging craft called OSIRIS and later renamed HORUS. Research was also started into the only other significant area of space intelligence-gathering – the area that interested GCHQ – with the sigint project ZENON.

The price of developing three different kinds of space-based intelligence systems is obviously high. In 1995 the cost of the HELIOS project alone is estimated at about £950 million. France's annual spending on its military space programme grew from about £200 million in 1990 to around £390 million in 1994. Legislators in the National Assembly considered these plans too ambitious and tried to stop some of them. Paris tried to attract Spanish and Italian investment in HELIOS and to persuade Germany to contribute to HELIOS 2 – so helping to pay for a second generation of satellites – in return for allowing these allies to share in the tasking and product of the systems.

A British offer to take a large share – perhaps exploiting GCHQ's know-how to take the lead in ZENON – would probably have been welcomed by France, and would have had at least some benefits for British industry. To speculate along these lines misses the point, however; even in its 'go it alone' form, ZIRCON was at least partly conceived as a tribute to the NSA – a way of paying them back. Joining traditional rivals France in such a venture would have touched deep chords of national insecurity. Furthermore, taking even a one-third share in France's array of projects would, by the 1990s, have been costing Britain more than ZIRCON. One senior civil servant argues that the French programmes were not a real alternative: 'Investing anywhere else would have bought far less capability. The French don't even know how far behind they are.' By 1987 Britain had taken the decision, to borrow Geoffrey Howe's words, to play the role of beggar rather than chooser in the world of high-technology intelligence-gathering.

The saga of Britain's spy satellite, complete with court injunctions and police raids, coincided with episodes in two other difficult and long-running public dramas involving Thatcher and the intelligence services: banning trade unions at GCHQ and trying to prevent the publication of Peter Wright's book *Spycatcher*. In these three matters, the Prime Minister's determination to pursue her policies won her the admiration of many, but also the antipathy of others in the intelligence world who hated the fuss and public attention she had brought them.

In November 1986 the British government found itself in an Australian court, trying to stop Wright's publishers sidestepping a UK injunction against publication by bringing the book out on the other side of the world. The encounters between Malcolm Turnbull, acting for Wright's publishers, and Robert Armstrong, the Civil Service chief sent from Britain to defend the government line that the ex-MI5 man owed a lifelong duty of confidentiality, provided a daily drama in the British press. Armstrong, trying to deal with Turnbull's references to MI6 – which the Thatcher government did not want to admit existed – agreed to refer to it as 'the other place'. In one session, struggling under cross-examination, the Cabinet Secretary admitted, in a phrase which was to enter the language, that he had been 'economical with the truth'.

In March 1987 the Australian court rejected the UK government's request for an injunction. An appeal failed six months later and the matter then went to the House of Lords, where the government also lost. The Prime Minister had underestimated both the anti-English sentiment in Australia, which found its expression in the courts, and the practical impossibility of getting the *Spycatcher* genie back in its bottle once copies had begun to circulate.

In the Security Service itself, Wright was widely despised by the staff, who dedicated themselves to the principle of keeping secret what they knew, and who also regarded much of what he said as questionable or untrue. In a subsequent BBC television interview with *Panorama*'s John Ware, Wright's most disturbing allegation – that there had been a plot against Harold Wilson's government – fell apart on screen, with the ageing writer admitting that it had not involved thirty MI5 officers, as stated in his book, but had consisted of little more than idle chatter between Wright himself and a small number of his colleagues. What Security Service officers resented was the fact that the government attempt to ban publication had invested Wright's allegations with credibility. Anthony Duff, Director General of MI5 at the time the decision was made to proceed against Wright, told me, 'The whole thing was a disaster in terms of (a) making a lot of money for Peter Wright and (b) holding up the British state to ridicule. I went along with it. I should have tried to stop it.' Duff had deferred to his Legal Adviser, Bernard Sheldon, and other government law officers who had originally advocated prosecution.

Armstrong's grilling in the witness box had disturbed some civil servants. One Whitehall mandarin recalls, 'I felt very sorry for Robert. I'm absolutely certain he did it as a civil servant doing his duty, not being influenced by considerations of personal discomfort – which you might say is the understatement of the year.'

The banning of the trade unions at GCHQ was effectively accomplished by 1987. Thatcher had launched this initiative in January 1984; it married her instinctive dislike of union power with the desire on the part of some Cheltenham and Whitehall mandarins to remove such organisations from this field of intelligence work. Thatcher and her advisors believed banning unions was vital to the UK–US relationship, which they argued had been put under strain by industrial action at Cheltenham in 1979 and 1981. The union ban became a rallying issue for the left, later producing a Labour Party commitment to reverse the process once in power.

Subsequent verdicts on the affair from two figures who were closely involved and still believe in the principle of de-unionization, but who felt deep reservations about its 'handling' – in other words, the politics of what was done – are instructive. Michael Herman, a senior GCHQ officer until 1987, wrote after his retirement, 'The likely verdict on de-unionization will be that the consequences were not thought through – perhaps as was repeated with the Poll Tax . . . consultation with the Opposition seems to have been no part of the plan. It was not the Thatcher style.' Geoffrey Howe, who as Foreign Secretary had to carry the Parliamentary can for the de-unionization exercise, felt the GCHQ story said something deeper about the government's attitudes to secrecy, and shares Herman's view that the lack of consultation 'was our fundamental mistake. We made it because of our failure to appreciate the difficulties, the subtleties indeed, of moving . . . from darkness to light.'

Thatcher had spelt out her 'say nothing' approach in an interview in the summer of 1984, following calls for an inquiry into the Libyan People's Bureau affair. She referred to remarks made at the beginning of the Falklands crisis by 'someone who knew a bit about intelligence which was totally and utterly devastating in the amount which it gave away', and added, 'The moment you say too much, the sources dry up.' Her remarks were directed against Ted Rowlands, a Labour MP who had served as Foreign Office Minister of State from 1976–9. During the emergency debate on 3 April 1982 that followed the Argentine capture of the islands, he told the Commons that a possible invasion in 1977 had been deterred because of the quality of intelligence available, and said, 'I shall make disclosure. As well as trying to read the mind of the enemy, we have been reading its telegrams for many years.'

During the research for this book, more than one of the intelligence chiefs interviewed cited Rowlands's remarks as a textbook example of the sensitivity of signal intelligence methods and a reason for limiting the role of MPs in scrutinizing sigint activities. One suggested that Argentine intercepts had dried up within hours of the parliamentary disclosure. The Rowlands anecdote does, however, shed more light on the attitude of Thatcher and those mandarins to democratic oversight than it does on the real nature of the south Atlantic intelligence war. While writing this book, I put those allegations to someone with an intimate awareness of GCHQ's product during those months; they said, 'The Argentines were doing everything they could do within their knowledge and apparatus to protect themselves. Even if they were told a channel was unreliable they would not have been able to do anything differently.' In other words, the Labour MP's remarks had had no noticeable effect. They had, however, provided Number 10 with useful political ammunition.

The Prime Minister felt that matters of secret policy were the exclusive preserve of leaders and their intelligence agencies, and could not be understood by others, particularly the media. In her memoirs she notes her sympathy for Ronald and Nancy Reagan, who were 'hurt and bemused' by public comments on the Irangate affair, with much 'cruelty and contempt . . . pouring out from the liberal media'. Regarding Reagan as a friend, she could not help sympathizing with him when his honesty was being questioned by those outside the Administration.

The Irangate crisis had been growing since the autumn of 1986, as revelations emerged about the work of a secret group within the National Security Council (NSC) first in trading arms for US hostages in Beirut and later in using the profits from the sale of weapons to Iran to back the Contra rebels in Nicaragua. Congress had forbidden the use of US government funds to back the rebels, one of the President's right-wing *causes célèbres*. John Poindexter, the National Security Adviser, had resigned, as had Colonel Oliver North, the principal NSC aide organizing the project. The issues at stake in Irangate were serious enough, but it seems that the British Prime Minister still found it difficult to accept that a leader should come under media and legislative scrutiny for acts committed in their name.

During my research, I learned that SIS picked up information about Admiral Poindexter and Colonel North's activities before they became public. Washington had kept Britain in the dark about its covert hostage strategy, but MI6 learned about it through a Middle East agent. I asked one spymaster whether Whitehall told the Americans it knew what they were up to. He replied, 'All we could do was tuck it away in a box, we couldn't have discussed it with them. This was UK Eyes Alpha, after all!'

At one point during the long hostage saga, Britain received sufficient intelligence to plan a rescue mission. Interviewees suggest it was provided by the Americans. In *Immediate Action*, published in 1996, a former SAS sergeant writing under the pseudonym Andy McNab suggested that he had been part of such an operation. McNab claimed dozens of troops had been standing by in the Middle East; a small number of members of G Squadron were actually on the ground in Beirut as an advanced party when the operation was stood down. However close the SAS *may* have got, when the highly reliable information needed to launch such an operation was obtained there was not enough time. In fairness to SIS, which spent years trying to locate the British hostages, the captives were moved every few months (Brian Keenan suggests seventeen times in all) and held in areas where the kidnappers could ensure the discretion of local people.

Thatcher's desire to keep all intelligence matters shrouded in darkness was central to the union problems at GCHQ, the ZIRCON police raids and the *Spycatcher* court battle. Some senior figures, such as Anthony Duff at the Security Service, were already undermining this strategy by discreet briefings of newspaper editors. Others felt that the publicity attending all three cases had been truly damaging and that the Prime Minister lacked the sophistication to know what was in the best interests of her 'secret services'. One senior figure remarks, 'I did not have great respect for her mind – a 2.2 was about right.' These occasional tensions between the intelligence chiefs and the Prime Minister were eventually to become focused on the central issue of the day: Gorbachev and his sincerity.

Chapter 6

1987 Springtime for Sceptics

During the early weeks of 1987, as the ZIRCON affair rumbled away, Mikhail Gorbachev started the year as he had the previous one, with a series of domestic political initiatives and with measures aimed at speeding along the arms control process. At a Central Committee plenum at the end of January he paved the way for greater *glasnost* about the party's past mistakes. This was followed by a law allowing the setting-up of small businesses called co-operatives. This change was intended to bring the millions of Soviet citizens who earned money from private enterprise – for example, by giving haircuts or mending cars – from the black economy into the officially-recognized one. For many orthodox Marxists, this was a significant step away from traditional Soviet economic principles.

In his drive to mend fences with his own intelligentsia and gain the trust of the West, Gorbachev announced in February the release of 140 political prisoners. These were said by the Kremlin to be the last such people in custody: several noted dissidents, such as Natan Sharansky, had been freed the previous year, and in December 1986 Andrei Sakharov and his wife Yelena Bonner had been allowed to return to Moscow from internal exile in the Urals city of Gorky.

The Soviet leader's frustration that an Intermediate Nuclear Forces treaty had not yet been agreed prompted him to reiterate publicly in February that such an agreement need not be linked to any other commitments on Star Wars or strategic weapons. But it was Moscow's insistence on retaining ninety or so SS-20 missile launchers outside the European theatre that was the chief remaining stumbling block. Two months later Gorbachev announced the end of Soviet chemical weapons production, a move treated with some suspicion – rightly, as it would transpire – by the Joint Intelligence Committee in London.

The Prime Minister sponsored another of Whitehall's attempts to read the changes in Moscow, a conference at Chequers on 27 February 1987. In her memoirs she described it as a debate between 'enthusiasts' for Gorbachev and 'sceptics'. She wrote, 'The sceptics probably had the better of the argument.' The discussions were intended to help her prepare for her first Kremlin talks since the new leader came to power, and it was during this spring of 1987 that her own attitudes about Gorbachev seem to have matured.

Shortly after the Chequers conference, Oleg Gordievsky was taken to brief her, also at Chequers. Thatcher later wrote that she developed 'the highest regard for his judgement about events in the USSR'. Gordievsky says of the almost four hours he spent with her, 'I was very tense. I was trying to make a good impression on her. I was trying so hard to make each point that almost as soon as I had, I'd forgotten what I'd just said.' One senior Whitehall figure says the former agent had considerable influence: 'Gordievsky advised Mrs Thatcher to say certain things to the Russian people which they had not heard before. When she was there she made a broadcast and many of the things which she said were at his instigation.' Thatcher told the Soviet people why the West feared its conventional military strength and how relations might be improved.

In London, several influential figures in the intelligence community felt the mood of change, people who fell into the Prime Minister's category of Gorbachev 'enthusiasts'. Lieutenant-General Derek Boorman, the Chief of Defence Intelligence, recalls, 'There were those around the JIC table who thought instinctively that something was going on. I tended to be rather liberal and generous in the early days of Gorbachev; perhaps in retrospect I was too generous, but I saw it as pretty breathtaking stuff.' Anthony Duff, the Director General of MI5, was not quite in the same 'rather liberal' tendency as Boorman, but he too felt that the changes were substantial and significant.

Also, among the analysts who formed the second tier within the agencies there were those who began asking basic questions about the way they were examining the Soviet target. Michael Herman, a senior officer who retired from GCHQ that year, was to prove one of the most influential. Herman had been a Head of J Division, the Soviet Bloc element of GCHQ, and served his last few years as Head of L Division, in charge of liaison with other bodies including the JIC. He was tall, bespectacled, balding, ruddy-cheeked and singularly suited to the epithet that could be applied to so many senior managers in the intelligence services: 'donnish'. But in his case it was the right adjec‍tive, because on retirement his restless intellect soon drew him into the academic world.

Herman was to give several lectures which, with some reading between the lines, amounted to an apology for some of the analysis of Soviet Bloc questions by British intelligence. In May 1988 he told the US Army War College, 'It will be surprising if history does not point to more overestimates than underestimates . . . it is more satis‍fying, safer professionally, and easier to live with oneself and one's colleagues as a hawk than as a wimp.' He added, 'Western intelligence has claimed a special responsibility to lead thinking rather than to fol‍low it. It can hardly duck responsibility if its worst-case conclusions have been propagated and used.' In the same month he would tell cadets at the Royal Naval College, 'There is a risk of missing real opportunities of increased security if assessments perpetuate "worst case" stereotypes of the adversary.'

Herman had been putting forward similar arguments in his last months of service with GCHQ. In his interview for this book, he said, 'I went through a conversion of sorts in the 1980s because, hav‍ing run the Soviet side, I became concerned by the sort of picture we were painting of them. I became a bit of a Soviet revisionist; I thought we were exaggerating the Soviet threat.'

The JIC system and the personality of some of its key members ensured, however, that views like those of Duff, Lieutenant-General Boorman and Herman were rarely found in assessments. Martin Morland, formerly the Chief of Assessments, believes, 'It was very difficult for them to listen to a lone voice. The machine tried to reduce error.' The Central Intelligence Machinery booklet later published by the Cabinet Office says, 'It is a strength of the British system that Ministers do not receive conflicting or piecemeal intelligence assess‍ments on situations or issues of concern. Through the JIC they are provided with assessments agreed between departments which pro‍vide an objective background to the discussion of policy.'

Lieutenant-General Boorman remembers that Percy Cradock, Chairman of the JIC, usually argued for conservatism in assessments of Gorbachev and Soviet policy. He says, 'Percy Cradock took a harder line. He was tougher. When I used to say I had an instinct about something, he would look at me as if to say "good assessment isn't based on instinct".' One of the analysts who supported the JIC goes further, albeit anonymously: 'I don't think it was until about mid-1990 that he began having serious doubts about whether we'd got it right. He always took a very tough line. If the Assessments Staff had produced reports saying there was a major change of direction under way, they would have been in trouble with him.' In my interview with him, Cradock did not accept that there had been significant errors in JIC's reading of events in Moscow.

Cradock's supporters argue that he expected a rigorous standard of intelligence based on facts rather than speculation. The problem was that when it came to the central political issues of Anglo-Soviet relations, the intelligence agencies could provide very few facts. One analyst confirms, 'Nobody ever knew what was going on inside the Kremlin'; another adds, 'There was nothing really coming in from any intelligence source about what Gorbachev was up to, apart from the fact that he was a pragmatist.' It was for this reason that JIC's Soviet assessments at this time consisted of a conservative reading of publicly-available information. David Mellor, who in 1987 had gone to the Foreign Office as Minister of State, says, 'They used to bring the most sensitive reports in a sort of lead-lined box. It was on paper like fax paper, often smudged. I must say, though, that very rarely was the sense with which you opened the thing justified. It can't all be like Le Carré – in fact, it was humdrum. I can't say I learnt anything devastating.'

That spring, with Gorbachev's release of prisoners and arms-control initiatives fresh in everyone's mind – as well as the prospect of a general election in Britain – there was a seminal debate during one of JIC's Thursday sessions about the nature of the changes in Moscow. More than one of those present discussed the meeting with me. Cradock wanted to push through a paper from Harry Burke, the hawkish staffer who oversaw much of the Assessment Staff's Soviet work, which said that, whatever Gorbachev might say about abandoning the use of force in international relations and cutting arsenals to achieve 'defence sufficiency', the Soviet Union was still aiming for Communist domination of the world. Anthony Duff, the DGSS who also enjoyed the intellectual authority of having been the previous incumbent of Cradock's chair, disputed this thesis. It was, says one of those present, 'the clash of the giants'. Duff apparently argued that, although such an objective might occasionally be expressed by Soviet party bosses, it was no more than an old ideological mantra for a country increasingly crippled by economic problems. Cradock's line prevailed and a JIC view was duly minuted. Duff's last comment was, according to one person present, 'I wouldn't be so sure.' His dissenting view did not form part of the text circulated to government departments in that week's Red Book.

Although declining to comment on this specific meeting, Duff did confirm when I interviewed him that he had basic differences with Cradock and the general trend of analysis in this period. He says, 'To the time I retired from public service in December 1987, as far as I recall, JIC assessments were maintaining that nothing [in the Kremlin] had changed, and that it was extremely unlikely that it would change. I did not agree with this and said so.'

March 1987's edition of *Soviet Military Power*, the Pentagon's annual threat assessment, contained a view very similar to that which Cradock had steered through his committee. It said, 'The Party leadership remains committed to the long-term objective of establishing the USSR as the dominant world power.' It added, 'Gorbachev has tried to portray his approach to Soviet diplomacy as a new era in the USSR's foreign policy. This approach is more stylistic than substantive; it reflects the new leadership's more sophisticated use of propaganda and the foreign news media to influence international public opinions.' This notion of the Soviet leader as a charmer or deceiver who remained very much committed to the global victory of Communism was very similar to the arguments used by Cradock and Burke, who usually chaired the Soviet Bloc Current Intelligence Group of the JIC.

The JIC assessment was influential: it seems to have travelled with the Prime Minister on her visit to Moscow, which went ahead at the end of March 1987. She recalls in her memoirs that at her first meeting with the charismatic Soviet leader in the Kremlin, she told him, 'I knew of no evidence that the Soviet Union had given up . . . the goal of securing world domination for communism.'

This message was effectively a prepared statement by the Prime Minister, as were her denunciations of Soviet human rights policies and of the Soviet occupation of Afghanistan. It was the areas in which her visit departed from the prearranged script that were to prove the most interesting, however. Diplomats from both countries declared the four-day tour a new chapter in relations. Thatcher had been warmly greeted by the Soviet people during her walkabouts, and had cemented her personal relationship with Gorbachev. Some at the Foreign Office felt that her televised account of Soviet military strengths had been a great help to Gorbachev in his domestic struggle to cut these forces and divert resources into the civilian economy. She herself wrote in her memoirs that, by the end of the trip, 'I sensed that great changes were at hand, but I could never have guessed how quickly they would come ... there was no doubt in my mind that he was making the Soviet Union something better than a "prison house of nations" and we ought to support his efforts.'

The March visit marked a key moment in the development of the Prime Minister's, and therefore the national, attitude towards the changes in Moscow. She had formed a positive opinion of Gorbachev during their December 1984 meeting, but had remained deeply distrustful of him because of his Communist mind-set. The February 1987 Chequers conference had been dominated by the sceptics, who argued that Gorbachev would not transcend his Marxist indoctrination. Thatcher wrote in her memoirs, 'In retrospect, it is possible to see that this analysis was flawed by a confusion between the *intentions* of Mr Gorbachev, which at any particular time were limited both by his way of thinking and by the circumstances of the moment, and the *effects* of his reforms, which unleashed forces which could sweep away the Soviet system and the Soviet state' (original emphasis). This distinction between Gorbachev and the power of the forces he was unleashing need not have been discovered 'in retrospect'. It was the subject of much journalistic discussion at the time. The *Guardian*'s Martin Walker, for example, wrote in 1986, 'Social change has its own momentum and its own logic, quite apart from the decisions taken in the Kremlin.' It would hardly have been like Thatcher, however, to make policy on the basis of articles in the *Guardian*.

Cradock says that from an early stage he described Gorbachev's reforms to the Prime Minister as, 'cosmetic, i.e. not seeking fundamental change, but explosive [in terms of their possible effects]'. This formula allowed the JIC chairman the best of both worlds: it was consistent with his view of the Soviet leader as a deceiver, while admitting that tumultuous change might result from his policies. Most participants in the debate – including, it seems, the Prime Minister – regarded him as Whitehall's leading 'dry' in the interpretation of events in Moscow. What Cradock did do however was to differentiate early on between Gorbachev's foreign policy, which the mandarin regarded as unchanged, and his domestic policy, where he felt Thatcher could be more encouraging.

The essential flavour of the JIC's assessment of the continued aggressiveness of Soviet Communism and of similar remarks in *Soviet Military Power* was reproduced in an essay in that year's UK Statement on the Defence Estimates, which asked whether the 'friendly face' of Gorbachev meant a change in the USSR's long-term foreign policy objectives. It answered, 'It is difficult to ignore the lessons of past Russian and Soviet history, which has been living proof of the idea that the best form of defence is expansion.' The essay continued, 'As long as the basic tensions between East and West are undiminished, Nato will continue to rely on a strategy of nuclear deterrence based on an effective mix of systems.' Elsewhere the White Paper cautioned, 'Now is a time for steady nerves.'

Phrases about steady nerves and Nato's strategy of nuclear deterrence led some observers to label the 1987 Estimates an 'election White Paper', an unusually party-political version of the annual defence spending document. The Conservatives were, after all, about to go to the polls against an Opposition which argued that the new atmosphere in international relations made it the right time for Britain to abandon its own nuclear forces. Had Cradock intended the JIC minute to help the Conservatives in the coming General Election? All of those involved in the analysis of intelligence to whom I put this question insist not. Under the British code of civil service conduct, such suggestions of partiality are akin to accusations of dishonour.

On 11 June 1987 Thatcher's government was returned to power with a majority of 102. Labour's policy of unilateral nuclear disarmament was cited by many political pundits as one of the reasons for its defeat. Opinion polls suggested that most people shared the disquiet at Labour's proposals felt by so many key figures in the defence and intelligence establishments.

Much of the discussion in the Joint Intelligence Committee during this period extrapolated political meaning from Soviet military developments. Whatever the shortfall of data on political matters, the intelligence machine continued to provide large amounts of information on the armed forces and military-industrial complex of the USSR. The 'facts' essential to Burke's papers and Cradock's assessments were most often military in nature. With hindsight, it is possible to re-examine the way they were interpreted.

Soviet fleet deployments to areas such as the Indian Ocean, south Pacific and north Atlantic had grown steadily in the 1970s as part of a plan to create a blue-water navy. By 1987, however, the Soviet Navy was disappearing from the world's oceans as a result of fuel shortages and the Kremlin's desire to soothe Western nervousness. The 1988 Statement on the Defence Estimates conceded, 'Soviet naval deployments away from their home fleet areas have steadily reduced over the last two years', but perversely – given that the Soviet Navy already had a reputation for spending far less time training at sea than its Nato counterparts – went on to say, 'The result has been an improvement in combat efficiency and readiness.' In fact, a decline had begun which would culminate in a large proportion of the naval vessels acquired at such cost over the previous thirty years becoming, by the early 1990s, rusting hulks.

These naval developments were unusual in that hardly any indicators that could have been interpreted as a slowdown in Soviet military production or training in response to the new Kremlin foreign policy goals were included in Defence White Papers or *Soviet Military Power* during the period 1986–8. But there were many other unpublished indicators.

The adoption by the Soviet Army in Afghanistan of a casualty-saving defensive strategy late in 1986 was known to Western intelligence analysts. In 1987 this process continued with the redeployment of several outlying battalions to more secure locations; in effect, a prelude to withdrawal. This process was known to the West (a US diplomat in Kabul who I understood to be a CIA officer told me of it at the time) but neither it, nor the general trend in Soviet operations in Afghanistan, were confirmed by the British or US governments.

Certain areas of Soviet military production were also frozen or cut during 1986–7. But the language of Britain's Defence White Paper and the Pentagon's annual statements remained consistently that of the Cold War: the Soviet Union continued a 'ceaseless build-up' of its military power. Yet in 1990 *Soviet Military Power* revealed that 'output of conventional ground force equipment as well as helicopters and fighter aircraft has declined since Gorbachev took power in 1985'.

The more subjective aspects of Soviet military life, such as morale and efficiency, had always caused the analysts problems, being far harder to estimate than the cold fact of which Soviet divisions sat in Kabul or how many tanks the Nizhniy Tagil plant had produced. According to one analyst, JIC assessments apparently grasped the fact that morale was 'pretty bad' in the Soviet Army, but it was presumed that coercion would be applied in time of general war. On 28 May 1987 Matthias Rust, a budding German aviator, managed to land a light aircraft in Red Square, symbolically humiliating the Soviet military system. Gorbachev took the opportunity to sack his defence minister, but the incident did prompt many questions about the efficiency of the entire system.

During the spring and summer of 1987 military trends in the USSR were unclear to the experts at the JIC Assessments Staff and the Defence Intelligence Staff: some areas of activity were slowing down, whereas in others high rates were being maintained. It was a confused picture, but the experts analysing the information chose to perpetuate traditional views of the Soviet 'threat' rather than confess to their confusion or admit there were indications of the effects of Gorbachev's policies. The Kremlin was about to give the intelligence 'liberals' further cause to believe that the changes had developed from rhetoric into something concrete.

On 22 July 1987 Mikhail Gorbachev announced that he would agree to the elimination of all INF missile launchers held by the two superpowers, abandoning his earlier attempts to keep some SS-20s that were based close to the Chinese border. From then on, INF negotiations moved swiftly, a treaty being signed five months later. For both Reagan and Thatcher, the deal showed the value of tough bargaining with the Kremlin. It also demonstrated the real compromises the Soviet leader was ready to make: it was the first superpower agreement which actually reduced the number of nuclear weapons (earlier ones had simply attempted to limit them); the Soviet side had agreed to the principle of unequal reductions, and would therefore have to dispose of far more weapons; and stringent verification procedures were agreed, allowing US monitors to install cameras in missile factories hitherto among the most secret sites in the USSR.

As the treaty neared completion, the two sides conducted a 'data exchange'. The final episode in the ten-year battle of INF power politics and intelligence involved the two sides telling one another exactly what weapons they had of this type and where they were. The results shocked some Western analysts, but provide a vivid example of the limits of intelligence even in the age of the spy satellite.

The USA and its allies believed that the Soviet Union had 440 SS-20 missile launchers, but in fact they had 523. The error was not as bad as it might seem: since Gorbachev's freeze on INF deployments, 118 of the large launching vehicles had been held in storage, leaving 405 at missile bases.

With the older SS-4s, the Western experts had lagged behind as the systems were decommissioned, suggesting publicly that there were 112 launch pads for them whereas in fact there were only 79. Nato figures for the SS-12M system were the most impressive: the Pentagon estimated that there were about 104, Moscow revealed that 115 launchers were deployed.

It was over the deployments of a new missile and launcher system, designated SS-23 by Nato, that the most serious mistakes were made. The 1987 edition of *Soviet Military Power* had stated that there was a single brigade of SS-23s, normally twelve to sixteen launchers, in Byelorussia in the west of the USSR. It added, 'If the SS-23 follows the same sequence of deployment seen with the Scud B, the western Military Districts will receive it first, followed by the Group of Soviet Forces, Germany.'

The US said later that there could be about forty of the new launchers. The British assessment by DIS, revealed in briefings to journalists that spring, was that there were 'nearer twelve' and that the new weapon was being fielded more slowly than expected. The INF data exchange revealed that eighty-two were with operational units, eighteen of them at two bases in East Germany.

During 1987, few intelligence targets could have had a higher priority for US and UK agencies than these four types of INF missile and their associated military units. They were both a potential military threat and the subject of ongoing diplomatic negotiations; thus, any change in deployments was of great significance. In East Germany, Britain, the USA and France had the advantage of the military missions they were allowed under the old four-power agreements. These legalized spies spent their days travelling the roads, logging Soviet military movements and, when possible, peering into equipment hangars at Soviet bases. But they, the satellites and the sigint experts had completely missed the establishment of two bases for SS-23 nuclear missiles. It was not as if the objects in question were devices able to fit in a suitcase; the eighteen launchers positioned in the German Democratic Republic were the size of buses and were supported by dozens of ancillary vehicles.

The SS-23 story provides several lessons. Most simply, that a nation which tracks spy satellites can hide equipment at the times when the satellites pass overhead; and that having people on the ground, as the allies did in East Germany, will not necessarily help. The interpreters who studied the images beamed down by the two or three KH-11 CRYSTAL satellites that covered the Soviet Bloc at the time would eventually have found the new SS-23s, but it would have taken time – perhaps several years, just as the accurate estimate of SS-20 bases had. Within four years, many people would have forgotten these limitations, and huge resources would be committed to finding similar mobile missile launchers in the deserts of Iraq. Fortunately for Nato, the Kremlin had no intention of firing the SS-23s in Germany.

The INF data exchanges did set some intelligence specialists thinking about a wider question which loomed as several other series of arms-control talks progressed: how many nuclear weapons did the Soviet Union have? Even those with access to the highest security classifications in JIC and the Ministry of Defence had no precise idea.

The new policy of *glasnost* was beginning to reveal to the Soviet people the network of secret military-industrial cities, usually known only by their postcode, that had built the Soviet nuclear bombs. Arzamas-16 was the most important, analogous to the USA's Los Alamos or Britain's Aldermaston. The USA and Britain were aware of these places, and knew where most of them were and roughly what work was carried out there. But there were big questions about how the Soviet bombs were made, how many there were, even what most of them were called. An agent inside this secret industry would have been priceless, but there were none. Not since the early 1960s, when the SIS–CIA man Colonel Oleg Penkovsky was active, had the West received reports from high-level sources about how many ballistic missiles or nuclear warheads the USSR had.

Data given to Congress by the Defence Department and the Department of Energy showed a wide range of estimates. The DoD figures showed the Soviet Union might have up to 46,000 nuclear weapons by 1987; other US estimates put it at 36,000. The US nuclear stockpile at the time was about 23,000. A variation of 10,000 in warhead estimates was disappointingly vague given the vital importance of destroying such systems in the event of a third world war and would increasingly become of interest as the stability of the Soviet Union came into question.

The lesson for JIC and DIS experts from these attempts to pinpoint nuclear weapon storage points and estimate their overall numbers was that it was impossibly difficult. Whereas missile launchers could be found in time, many of the warheads being deployed by the 1980s were simply too small to be detected by satellites. There were disagreements among Nato analysts about whether the Soviet Army deployed nuclear artillery shells. Such rounds would after all be the same size as those filled with high explosive, and it was impossible to tell from overhead whether a bunker or storage box contained a shell of either type. Unlike in Britain, where nuclear warheads moved in special convoys of armoured lorries, complete with their own Royal Marine security detail, fire engine and police escort, the DIS could not work out how the thousands of Soviet nuclear warheads that would have required servicing each year were being transported. Trying to spot such an operation became one of the most important tasks of Britain's military mission in East Germany BRIXMIS, over a period of twenty years. Yet as Air Chief Marshal Michael Armitage, who headed the DIS from 1982–5, confirms, 'We never once detected the movement of a Soviet nuclear warhead in East Germany.'

With the INF treaty, the traditional task of monitoring Soviet military forces in case of a surprise attack was, for British intelligence, supplemented by the need to provide information for verifying arms-control agreements. The numbers of warheads or missiles was to become important less because of the possibility that they might be heading for Portsmouth or Whitehall, more because the West needed to know that they were being taken out of commission. This was also a difficult task, but would be made a little easier by the verification terms of the new agreements, which allowed on-the-spot visits to various Soviet facilities.

Many in the military and intelligence establishments did not regard the coming of the INF treaty as good news. Some detected a plot by the Kremlin to use the treaty as the first step in removing all US nuclear weapons from Europe, so 'decoupling' the two halves of the Atlantic alliance. That summer, Gorbachev had indeed been attempting to link the INF forces with the short-range nuclear weapons – the so-called 'battlefield weapons' such as artillery shells, air-dropped bombs and certain remaining missiles – although he didn't pursue it, accepting instead that there would be separate talks on the issue.

General Bernard Rogers, the Supreme Allied Commander in Europe, retired at the end of June 1987 and gave several interviews lambasting the Soviet leader and casting doubt on his sincerity. Rogers told the BBC's *Newsnight* programme, 'Gorbachev and his henchmen didn't vote in the British election. What I'm saying is they are moving towards the achievement of that objective, which is intimidation, coercion, blackmail and eventually neutralization in western

Europe.' The general, who had fought hard to get Nato's INF weapons deployed in the early 1980s, could not bear to lose them. He described the Pershing 2 missile, which was to be scrapped under the treaty, as 'one of the most valuable tools' and argued that 'for me, a bad deal is worse than no deal at all'. Although the INF treaty would actually shape up to be a very good deal, scrapping far more Soviet warheads than Nato ones, General Rogers did not regard it as such, and had begun preliminary work in Nato headquarters on what would be called 'compensatory' or 'buttressing' measures: the deployment of new nuclear weapons by Nato, effectively to replace those lost under the treaty.

Margaret Thatcher did not share the general's view of Gorbachev, but she did agree that keeping nuclear weapons in Europe was essential to the future of the Atlantic alliance and to peace generally. She and those in the foreign policy and security establishment who had long argued that the Soviet Union needed to accept the principle of 'lopsided' arms control – agreements which imposed deeper cuts on the Soviet side – had got what they wanted. The whole logic of Nato's 'Twin Track' decision in the early 1980s to deploy Pershing 2 and Cruise was that the West would be ready to get rid of such weapons if the diplomatic talks produced results. Now that this had happened, the Prime Minister had, in the words of her later memoirs, 'mixed feelings'. It was precisely the transformation of Moscow's appeals for arms cuts from rhetoric to substance, something the intelligence sceptics had suggested in the early Gorbachev days would never happen, which triggered her reservations. She worried about decoupling and about the USA's longer-term commitment to the Trident deal. During her July visit to Washington, knowing that the INF Treaty was looking inevitable, she made an early appeal to the President in support of General Rogers's package of new nuclear weapons deployments.

The 1988 Statement on the Defence Estimates welcomed the INF treaty, particularly its tough verification regime and the fact that Moscow was dismantling more weapons, saying, 'In both respects the agreement is a major advance.' But the treaty simply intensified the differences in Whitehall between those who believed Gorbachev and those who didn't. One British general told me at the time that the Soviet leader had sacrificed his SS-20s, as the price of removing Nato's Cruise and Pershing missiles, in order to 'clear the way for nuclear war in Europe'. Similar views existed in the Pentagon; the April 1988 edition of *Soviet Military Power* described the US President's diplomatic triumph of four months earlier as being 'designed to a large extent to support Soviet efforts to decouple western Europe from its alliance with the United States'.

The improvement in East–West relations continued, despite Pentagon scepticism. In February 1988 it became clear that a deal had been finalized for the withdrawal of the Soviet Army from Afghanistan. The Geneva Accords would be signed on 14 April. Moscow promised to have its soldiers out by 15 February 1989, with half of them out by 15 August 1988.

Thatcher hoped the summit of Nato leaders held in Brussels at the beginning of March 1988 would reaffirm the alliance commitment to keeping its short-range nuclear forces. The Federal Republic of Germany, however, was already having its doubts about the kind of 'compensatory' nuclear modernization that General Rogers's successor, General John Galvin, was formulating. Whereas the INF missiles had also been deployed to Britain, Belgium and Italy (from where they could have hit Warsaw Pact targets), short-range nuclear weapons were by their nature more likely to be stationed in Germany – and in any conflict, used there. Thatcher's relations with Chancellor Helmut Kohl were to become increasingly strained over the issue. Geoffrey Howe later wrote in his memoirs, 'Margaret persisted in attaching huge importance to the continuance of land-based nuclear weaponry.'

The INF treaty and the Afghanistan withdrawal agreement provided exactly what the hard-line voices in the JIC had wanted – something more concrete than Kremlin rhetoric. Given the Prime Minister's public welcome for these moves, the tone of assessments had to change subtly. But key figures like Percy Cradock did not alter their basic view of the Soviet leader because of it. They still regarded him as a committed Communist cutting weapons for tactical reasons, in order to try to reinvigorate the economy.

In the Ministry of Defence an influential band of officers and civil servants maintained that the agreement did not justify freezing defence spending or Nato's nuclear deployments. Tom King, the Cabinet minister who would later change all that, was asked whether this band of Cold Warriors had been too slow to revise their views before his arrival, and replied, 'When you have somebody who for forty-five years had been focused on that area, they obviously weren't going to say "Please may I be redundant?"'

Chapter 7

1988 A Brilliant Intelligence Operation

Whitehall's uncertainty about the significance of the INF Treaty was shared by the intelligence agencies, with some managers favouring the early redeployment of at least some resources away from Soviet Bloc targets. During 1988 they were to learn some of the pitfalls of the new operational priorities. At the beginning of that year the Secret Intelligence Service and the Government Communications Headquarters were still very much guided by the conservative interpretation of events within the central intelligence machinery, under the Joint Intelligence Committee chairman Percy Cradock. By the end of 1988, SIS would be under a dynamic new Chief and taking its first tentative steps towards shifting its priorities.

The Security Service, on the other hand, had acquired considerable momentum along the path set by Anthony Duff. He recalls, 'By the end of 1987 counter-espionage was still the prime activity, but counter-terrorism was running it close and we were running down counter-subversion very fast.' The DGSS had retired in December 1987, aged sixty-seven, to be succeeded by Patrick Walker, the former F Branch officer, first Director of Counter Terrorism and Deputy Director General (Operations). As such, Walker was inevitably an apostle of the new faith.

Walker's appointment as DGSS followed a blueprint drawn up by Anthony Duff. When Duff arrived in 1985, Walker had not been considered as a front-runner for the succession. John Deverell, Director of G Branch, had been the leading candidate. He had run the F5 Section, countering Irish terrorism, at the beginning of the 1980s, before getting his first branch directorship in 1982. After two years he moved on to be Director of K Branch, the counter-espionage element of the Service, and with Walker's elevation (in succession to Cecil Shipp) to Deputy DG (Operations) in 1986, Deverell moved over to become

Director of G Branch, the expanding counter-terrorist empire created under Duff.

The other candidate who had caught the eye of the Cabinet Secretary and Home Office Permanent Under Secretary was Stella Rimington. She was a long-time F Branch officer, having been Head of F2 Section, watching the trade unions for signs that they might, by Gower Street's definition, be 'undermining' parliamentary democracy. Having reached branch director rank by his early forties, Deverell apparently had the advantage at this stage; Stella Rimington did not get her branch directorship until she was several years older, succeeding Deverell first as Director of K Branch and, in the latter part of 1988, as Director of G Branch.

Duff decided, however, that Deverell was not the best person to lead the Service into the 1990s. Gower Street insiders suggest that the DG's assessment was based on the broad issue of management ability rather than on any particular failure. One of them recalls that, the day after Deverell received this disappointing news, he went from Curzon Street, where G Branch was based, to Gower Street to tell Duff that he would serve whoever was chosen in his place with complete loyalty.

Rimington was later to tell pupils at the annual prize-giving of her old school, Nottingham Girls, that women were treated as second-class citizens in MI5 when she joined it, and that 'it is no good me pretending that for a woman it is easy getting to the top'. However, her appeal to Whitehall as a possible successor to Walker, even in 1988, was at least partly due to the fact that she could become the first woman to head a UK intelligence agency.

Appointing Walker and securing Rimington's eventual succession was all part of Duff's vision of the Service as one that would be involved in what had previously been police business, one in which the traditional distinction between intelligence and evidence would dissolve. Before retiring in 1987, Duff recruited David Bickford, a Foreign Office lawyer, to be Legal Adviser to DGSS. I asked Bickford whether he and Duff agreed from the outset that the Service should be transformed into a British version of the US Federal Bureau of Investigations. He replied, 'You don't go in without having an idea of where the organization should go, at least on the legal side, to achieve greatest effectiveness.'

As an outsider, Bickford pursued MI5's new agenda with little respect for usual Whitehall conventions, and as part of this he stepped up press contacts. In 1988 the Editor and two reporters from the *Independent* were invited for lunch at Gower Street. As they sat in the Director General's dining room on the third floor, Walker told them about his vision of the Service as a more open one so that members of the public who felt they had a crime to report would find MI5's number in the telephone book, 'just like the FBI'. In time, the ambitions of the Service's management would lead them to push towards tackling organized crime, the core of that American agency's work, but in 1988 the focus of change was counter-terrorism.

From February 1987 the G Branch workload had expanded in a new direction. A 300 lb bomb set off by the IRA at the British Army headquarters at Rheindalen in Germany had been the first attack by Irish terrorists on the garrison there since 1980. The Provisionals had also begun to build up the support network for a new campaign in Britain, which was to begin on 1 August with a bomb at a barracks in north London – the first attack of its kind for four years.

After the Rheindalen bomb there was a lull in IRA activity in Germany for several months. The IRA knew from secret documents it had obtained from inside British intelligence that MI5, MI6 and the British Services Security Organisation (a civilian agency involved in protecting overseas bases) had failed in their attempts to recruit informers from among the Irish community in Europe.

Operation SCREAM, the documents revealed, had been started by SIS in 1980 after the previous wave of IRA attacks in Europe, with the aim of 'offensive penetration' of Irish expatriate communities. The British Services Security Organisation and MI5, which maintained a liaison office in Cologne, had been unaware of SCREAM when it started. Operation WARD had been launched a year later; it was an attempt to put the matter on a proper footing by placing sixteen Irish sources under a control group of Army Intelligence, British Services Security Organisation and Irish Joint Section (a combined MI5–MI6 section) officers. Unlike previous Army and MI6 recruitment efforts, WARD at least observed Western intelligence protocol by informing the German authorities of the plan and undertaking to share any worthwhile intelligence. Deverell had been involved in the operation as the Head of MI5's F5 Section. The results, however, had been disappointing: secret papers written in 1984 said of the WARD agents, 'Only two can be said to be active in the sense of reporting anything at all.' The British Services Security Organisation officer writing one of the reports concluded, 'Operation WARD has not so far produced any worth-while intelligence.'

When it resumed its European campaign, the IRA now knew two vital things: that its operatives should steer clear of Irish expats, as they could be agents, and that the British and German authorities they were up against consisted of myriad different organisations between whom there was mistrust as well as poor communication.

The Provisional IRA was positioning weapons and Active Service Units – generally two to six strong – in preparation for further attacks. While this was happening, an informer gave the security forces a tip-off that would trigger a major overseas operation by MI5's G Branch. The identity of the source remains unknown, and it is unclear whether the informer was handled by MI5 agent-runners in Ireland or by the Royal Ulster Constabulary Special Branch. However, once it became known that two prominent IRA figures were flying to Málaga, close to Gibraltar, the operation became MI5's.

The first intelligence of the presence of IRA personnel in southern Spain had reached MI5 as early as November the previous year. IRA reconnaissance and support teams had identified a British military target in Gibraltar, as well as placing explosives and probably firearms nearby. There is little reason to doubt the subsequent official version of what the Provisionals aimed to do: bomb a British military cere-mony on the Rock.

On 8 November 1987 an IRA bomb killed eleven people at a Remembrance Day service at Enniskillen in Northern Ireland. The attack triggered widespread revulsion throughout the island, and many people were deeply moved when Gordon Wilson, a survivor of the blast, described how his daughter had died in his arms. The ter-rorists had placed the device with a simple timer – which meant that once it was planted, there was no way to stop its indiscriminate effects. Phoning a warning so that people might be evacuated did not appear to have been part of their plan.

Both the IRA and the security forces drew lessons from the Enniskillen incident. Republican spokesmen labelled the Remem-brance Day blast a 'disaster' for their movement. Unnamed IRA sources claimed in the press that the unit which had carried out the operation had not been authorized to do so and had been 'stood down' afterwards. So-called 'no-warning' bombs in public places had not been part of IRA strategy since the early 1970s. The IRA drew its conclusions about how to carry out future attacks on targets where the risk of bystanders being killed was high: it would either employ command detonation (using radio signals or wires) or give a warning. Intelligence analysts noted that a car prepared for use as a bomb discovered in Brussels on 21 January 1988 had been intended for detonation by radio control.

For months MI5 and the RUC Special Branch struggled to learn more from their sources about the IRA's plans to attack the British Army in Gibraltar. It seems that late in February 1988 or during the first days of March they received hard intelligence of the forthcoming operation. The head of the section in MI5's G Branch dealing with the Provisional IRA (referred to at the subsequent inquest as 'Mr O') thereupon met officers of the Military Operations department and of the London-based Special Forces HQ, and it was decided to mount a major operation, code-named FLAVIUS, to disrupt the expected IRA attack.

An SAS team, drawn largely from A Squadron of the 22nd Special Air Service Regiment based at Hereford, was prepared for the operation. The soldiers chosen were long-time veterans of the regiment. A Squadron was chosen because it happened to be on standby as the Special Projects Team, the SAS duty counter-terrorist force available for action at short notice. Their commander, a major called 'Soldier F' at the later inquest, attended a briefing at the Ministry of Defence in London prior to leaving for Gibraltar. As well as about a dozen SAS troops, the Security Service committed a mobile surveillance group from its A4 Section. Several MI5 officers travelled to the Rock with them.

The IRA terrorists who were to carry out the attack assembled in Málaga on 4 March 1988: Sean Savage, Danny McCann, Mairead Farrell and probably two others (a woman and a man). Savage had hired a white Renault 5 car. A red Ford Fiesta was prepared for the operations with 64 lb of Semtex explosive. The IRA team were under intermittent Spanish police surveillance during this time. Although the Spanish were able to relay a general warning to the British about the presence of the Provisionals, they were unaware of the Ford Fiesta, did not detect the arrival of the explosives in their country, and never found the IRA cache presumed to contain one or more Kalashnikov assault rifles, a magazine for which was later found in the red Fiesta.

At midnight on 5 March, the SAS men, the 'watchers' from MI5's A4 Section and selected members of the Gibraltar police gathered for a briefing. The sources of the intelligence contained in that briefing remain highly sensitive, and those who were present did not allude to them at the inquest. Some of the information had clearly been relayed by the Spanish authorities. Other information had come from the source within the republican movement. One could speculate, for example, about why the soldiers were told at the briefing that the IRA team would definitely be armed, since the Spanish never found the weapons. Mr O, who had remained in London, said at the inquest, 'All that is known is fragments and we have to put forward an assessment of the likely course of events.' From these fragments, if the inquest account is to be believed, the MI5 and Army briefers made an assessment which led to the SAS soldiers and watchers being told that certain suppositions were certainties. Some proved correct: most obviously, that the IRA team would enter Gibraltar the following day. Others did not: the IRA team was not armed, they did not have the bomb with them, and the bomb itself was not primed for detonation by remote control as the soldiers were told. Perhaps most importantly, the soldiers took away the impression that they were all that stood between the terrorists and a major atrocity.

On 6 March Savage entered Gibraltar in the Renault 5. The government said later he was not spotted as he crossed the Spanish border, despite the presence there of a police officer who was looking out for them. McCann and Farrell were spotted not far from the frontier at 2.30 p.m. They were followed for about half an hour, when they met up with Savage. As this was happening, there was a debate within the operations room about what to do. Soldier F, the major, conferred with Soldier E, an SAS captain who was the troop's tactical commander, and the police. Another Army officer, Soldier G, a bomb expert, was there with them. The police apparently felt unsure about the identity of the three and whether they had a bomb with them.

At 3.25 p.m. the three were positively identified by the soldiers and A4 members watching them. At this point Soldier G left the operations room and inspected the Renault which Savage had parked. He took the presence of an old aerial on the new car to mean, in the later words of Soldier E, that 'we are definitely dealing with a car bomb'. This dispelled whatever doubts may have remained in the mind of the Gibraltar police chief, who was listening to events unfold over the radio in his operations room, and at 3.40 p.m. he signed over control of the operation to the SAS major, Soldier F.

Soldiers A and B approached McCann and Farrell from behind as they walked along the street. McCann apparently turned around, and the smile left his face as he made eye contact with Soldier A. The soldier decided the IRA man was making an aggressive movement and began shooting at him. At the inquest Soldier A was asked what the purpose of that movement might have been; he said, 'I didn't know then and I don't know now.' Uppermost in the SAS man's mind, however, was the possibility that McCann might try to detonate the bomb by remote control; Soldier A stated at the inquest, 'We were told it was 100 per cent certain to be a button job.'

In a rapid sequence of actions, Farrell was then shot eleven times, and Sean Savage, who was not with the other two terrorists, was approached by two SAS soldiers who shot him sixteen times. Savage had apparently spun round on hearing the sound of gunshots. At the later inquest, pathologists confirmed that some of the rounds which hit Savage could have been fired by someone standing over him after he had fallen to the ground.

For about twenty minutes there was uncertainty in the police operations room, then Soldier F told the local police chief that the three were dead and signed a paper relinquishing control of the operation.

Subsequent examination of the Renault 5 parked by Savage showed it did not contain a bomb but had been placed as a blocking car, to keep the parking space for another vehicle that would be brought over in time for the expected attack two days later. It took the Spanish police two more days to find the red Fiesta that had been prepared as the bomb; they discovered it had a timing device rather than a remote control device – although the purpose of a wire leading from the bomb to the dashboard was unclear.

In the weeks that followed the incident, the Prime Minister and the media engaged in another of their battles, with the Independent Broadcasting Authority refusing a government request to stop the Thames Television documentary *Death on the Rock*, which cast doubt on the official version of the shootings. The government pondered for months over whether it should allow the security personnel who had taken part to appear at an inquest, but eventually agreed. The legal examination of the IRA trio's deaths took place in September; it did not censure the soldiers' actions, although two of the eleven jurors did dissent from the verdict.

The killing of the Gibraltar Three, whether justified or not, set in train a spiral of violence. When the three were being buried in Belfast's Milltown cemetery, Michael Stone, a loyalist terrorist, attacked the ceremony with a pistol and hand grenades, killing three people. The funeral of two of those victims became in turn the scene of a grisly confrontation, when two soldiers in plain clothes driving an unmarked car blundered into the cortège. They were dragged from the car, beaten and killed. Margaret Thatcher says this event disturbed her more than any other in Northern Ireland during her term of office. Nobody who saw the film of this event, she concluded in her memoirs, could say 'that reason or goodwill can ever be a substitute for force when dealing with Irish republican terrorism'.

The Gibraltar operation divided public opinion. Although many supported the use of force against the IRA and did not care that the three had been unarmed when they were shot, others saw the incident as confirmation that the SAS was a force of state executioners who had been ordered to take no prisoners. People at the cutting edge of counter-terrorism during this period have told me that deep recriminations followed between the Army and the Security Service.

From the outset the MI5 watchers had expressed doubts about the SAS men, whose 'civilian' disguise – virtually identical outfits of jeans, training shoes and bomber jackets – became the subject of scathing jokes. Operatives from A4 felt that the SAS men were too obvious, which was why McCann apparently realized that he and his companions were about to be arrested or attacked. When giving evidence to the inquest, the SAS soldiers effectively placed the blame on their Security Service briefers for allegedly insisting that their hypotheses about the bomb being set off by remote control and the IRA terrorists being armed were '100 per cent certainty'.

There was, it seems, no order to kill the IRA team. They were shot because the intelligence information available prior to the operation meant different things to people from the very different worlds of MI5 and the SAS.

Most of the SAS soldiers involved in Operation FLAVIUS had served in Northern Ireland, where the regiment had built up its own style of operating. The twenty-man resident SAS Troop in Ulster had killed eighteen IRA members between 1983 and mid-1987. The other twelve thousand or so Army troops had shot dead two. These statistics resulted from the strategy of using the SAS in situations where the best possible intelligence of a forthcoming attack was available, thus allowing the soldiers to be placed in a position where they could obtain a 'clean kill' of IRA terrorists – one in which their actions would be deemed reasonable by the legal system. In Northern Ireland there were no explicit orders to kill Provisionals, but a different wording was used in orders for arrest operations from that used when soldiers had discretion about how to react if they spotted armed terrorists.

For five years, from December 1978 to the end of 1983, the SAS killed no one in Northern Ireland because its orders clearly labelled missions as 'hard arrests' or surveillance. After that, according to SAS men who served there, the orders had changed, and soldiers who lay in wait for IRA terrorists were told that they were manning 'aggressive Observation Posts' or involved in an 'Observation Post/Reactive' or 'OP/React'. The congratulations and medals that followed incidents where they had shot dead terrorists left members of the SAS in no doubt that such a response was appropriate when their orders specified an OP/React mission. The Army regarded these tactics as legitimate in its battle against the Provisionals. One general in Northern Ireland had, according to one of those present, said to officers manning one of the centres that co-ordinated special operations of this sort, 'A crate of champagne to the first man who puts a body in my in-tray.'

Although Army intelligence and Special Forces commanders in Northern Ireland came to view the killing of IRA members in preplanned ambushes as a success, they were aware that the courts might take a different view if it could be shown that the same foreknowledge which had allowed them to place SAS troops in the path of an IRA cell might also have been used to avert a confrontation and make arrests. Over the years following the commitment of SAS troops to Northern Ireland, lawyers of the Army Legal Service had acquired an understanding of the kind of statements that would make the soldiers' actions appear reasonable in the eyes of a court. This involved convincing judges (in the case of any Northern Ireland criminal proceedings, as juries do not preside in such courts) or juries (in inquests) that the force used had been necessary. Various cases had established the precedent that a soldier simply had to believe that his life, or the life of some colleague or bystander, was in danger to be justified in opening fire without warning – even if anyone killed by this action was subsequently found to have been unarmed or even simply a bystander.

The language used by the soldiers at the Gibraltar inquest therefore owed as much to the well-proven approach of their Army Legal Service lawyers as it did to being a genuine account of the events. Soldier A said that McCann moved his right arm 'aggressively across the front of his body', Soldier C that Savage 'spun round very fast'. These statements were almost identical with those of SAS men defending similar actions in Ireland during the previous years.

William Hanna, an unarmed bystander shot dead by the SAS in Belfast in 1978, 'suddenly moved in a twisting motion', according to an inquest statement by one of the soldiers. Patrick Duffy, an unarmed IRA man shot in Londonderry in 1978, had also 'spun round' and raised his hand, according to the SAS man who killed him. William Price, an IRA man who was not carrying a gun, made 'a sudden movement of his hands', according to the SAS soldier who killed him in July 1984 in County Tyrone.

Why, after what the republican leadership itself described as the 'disaster' of Enniskillen, the terrorists should have wanted to set off a remote-control bomb when the streets around what the soldiers believed to be the primed car were packed with civilians was never explained. Savage, Farrell and McCann all seemed to be making sudden movements or reaching for weapons which they were not carrying.

Subsequent press reports suggested that the Spanish police had been keeping continuous surveillance on the IRA team, and had cast doubt on the British version that the three had not been detected until they were inside the colony. If the Spanish were right, why hadn't the SAS simply apprehended the IRA members as they crossed the airfield near the border checkpoint? Tony Geraghty, in his book on the SAS, suggests that the Spanish were sending their reports to London; they did not want to relay them direct to Gibraltar because of the long-running dispute over the sovereignty of the Rock. The fact that Mr O, the MI5 officer, remained in London during the operation might be seen as confirmation that an operations centre was being run there, possibly channelling the Spanish information. But how long would it have taken him or another person to communicate the fact that the IRA members were about to cross the border? The failure to apprehend the three Provisionals earlier seems to have owed much to a desire to observe them for as long as possible in order to detect any other members of the IRA team who were in the colony with them. It was clear that Savage, McCann and Farrell were not the only people involved; the *Sunday Times* later published the name of a female IRA operative who, it said, had escaped death that day in Gibraltar. Although the woman denied the charge, there was other evidence to suggest that more than three people were involved in the IRA attack.

At the inquest, the emphasis on the mistaken assumptions arising from the soldiers' briefing placed a good portion of the blame on the Security Service. It is highly probable that the briefers did *not* tell the SAS men that it was '100 per cent certain' this would be a remote-control bomb, but that this line was emphasized by Army lawyers during the extensive coaching of the men before the inquest. Instead, the assessments made by MI5 briefers at the fateful meeting of 5 March probably matched those of Mr O, their Head of Section in G Branch, at the later inquest: they used careful phrases, in which they were frank about the limits of their knowledge of the IRA plan. What united MI5 and SAS operatives was the desire to avoid an Enniskillen-type blood bath. This was stressed, rather than the need to make arrests. The result, given the track record of the SAS during the preceding years in Ulster and the particular individuals involved, was 'hardly surprising', says one SAS officer.

There were recriminations afterwards. One non-Army figure close to the operation told me forcefully that FLAVIUS was a 'brilliant intelligence operation', but conceded that MI5 would think twice before using the SAS to arrest terrorists again. An SAS officer serving at Hereford at the time confirms, 'Things went very quiet on the counter-terrorist front after Gibraltar – there were very few requests for help.' Later MI5 operations mounted against IRA operatives in Britain – some of whom were armed and, in one case, were carrying a bomb – involved, according to the evidence given in trials, a combination of armed police and MI5 surveillance operatives rather than members of the SAS.

Further ambushes did take place in Northern Ireland itself. The SAS Troop killed three Provos at Drumnakilly in August 1988, a gunman from a republican splinter group in Armagh in April 1990, two Provisional IRA men at Loughgall in October 1990, an Irish National Liberation Army gunman in Strabane in November 1990, three Provisionals in Coagh in June 1991 and four in Coalisland in February 1992. Fourteen republican gunmen ambushed and killed in less than four years. Both the Security Service and senior police officers, however, seem to have been convinced by Gibraltar that such methods were unacceptable outside Northern Ireland. George Churchill Coleman, the police anti-terrorist chief in London at the time, revealed to me that while 'the military option was appropriate to the known circumstances [in Gibraltar] . . . I do not personally think the British public would stand for too many of them. It is just not our way of doing things in a democratic society.'

A few months after the Gibraltar incident, G Branch officers received another hard lesson in international counter-terrorist operations when police investigations led detectives to a flat in Hull where they discovered 90 lb of high explosive, several Kalashnikov assault rifles, hand grenades and other bomb-making materials.

The killing of Ali al-Adhami, a Palestinian political cartoonist, in London the previous summer had prompted a murder investigation by the Metropolitan Police. Their inquiries soon focused on Abed al-Salah Moustapha, a member of Force 17, Yasser Arafat's personal security group. Moustapha had come to Britain in 1983 using an alias. He had run a garage in Essex as a cover while at the same time playing an intelligence role at the PLO's London office. Moustapha's presence indicated a failure of vetting on the part of MI5 and the immigration authorities, since there was an international warrant out for his arrest. Inquiries into the PLO man's social circle soon focused on Hassan Ismael Sowan, a Palestinian student who had honoured Moustapha by making him best man at his wedding.

After police raided Sowan's flat in Hull and discovered the arms cache, a story of international espionage unfolded. Sowan had sold himself to Israeli intelligence. As a young man growing up in the occupied West Bank, Sowan had accepted Israeli offers of financial help with his engineering studies. He became an informer first for \, the Israeli equivalent of MI5, and then for the foreign intelligence service Mossad. Sowan's task as an agent had been to report on the operations of Arafat's Force 17 in Europe. When detectives investigating the al-Adhami killing and the Hull arms find questioned officials at the Israeli embassy, they were surprised when the officials admitted that Sowan was an agent. My own researches suggest the Israelis said that they had failed to relay certain information to the British because their Palestinian agent was not co-operating fully with them.

Sowan was put on trial and received an eleven-year jail sentence for possessing the weapons. Ariel Regev, the Mossad station chief in London, and one of his station officers were asked to leave the country. A PLO official believed to have helped Moustapha kill al-Adhami was also ordered out. British authorities leaked a letter written by Margaret Thatcher to the Israeli Prime Minister warning that his intelligence services would find themselves losing British co-operation if they continued to act in Britain without liaising with British officials.

A deep chill in the Anglo-Israeli intelligence relationship persisted for years, long after press reports suggested that fences had been mended. The affair demonstrated that the secrecy involved in intelligence agency casework often makes them poor partners in the fight against international terrorism.

In contradiction to British officials who frequently stress their willingness to co-operate, Yigal Carmon, Director of Counter-Terrorism in the Israeli Prime Minister's office from 1988–92, says that there have been few meaningful exchanges in recent years. According to Carmon, 'Britain co-operates to a very limited extent with other nations on counter-terrorism. Other Western nations were absolutely more open with Israel, more co-operative, which is as it should be.' Carmon believes that MI5 and MI6 are excessively secretive, although he says their caution is understandable given the possibility that nations with whom there had been good relations, like Argentina or Iraq, can suddenly become enemies.

Israeli experts say that many opportunities have been lost because of poor Anglo-Israeli co-operation. They believe the British did not inform them that Abu Nidal, one of the most notorious Palestinian terrorists, was in London during the mid-1980s, and they also say that there was little effective co-operation in watching certain key figures from Hamas (the Islamic Resistance Movement) who took refuge in London in the early 1990s. The exchange of military and foreign intelligence between the two countries did begin to pick up during the Gulf crisis, however, and in 1994 there were agreements aimed at improving counter-terrorist co-operation.

Complaints about the way British intelligence officers hoarded information also came from the German authorities hunting the IRA at the time. One senior detective involved in the hunt told me that he found the Security Service liaison officers very difficult to deal with and preferred to maintain ties with experts from the Metropolitan Police. The Israeli and German criticisms show that the organizational shift in MI5 moved faster than the cultural transformation. So many members of the organization were saturated in Cold War counter-espionage techniques that they could not easily change their approach to sharing information.

*

On 3 July 1988 the US guided-missile cruiser *Vincennes* shot down an Iranian airliner in the Persian Gulf with the loss of everyone on board. This incident was the dramatic, unintended consequence of a growing hostility between the Western nations patrolling the Gulf waters under US leadership and the Iranians. Iranian leaders vowed revenge, and a National Security Agency sigint intercept, later declassified in the USA, showed that Ayatollah Montazeri, a hard-liner known for his support of the Hizbollah movement in Lebanon, discussed paying several million dollars for a retaliatory action against a US airliner.

The destruction of a PanAm Boeing 747 that December, with the loss of 259 people on board and eleven on the ground when the falling debris struck the Scottish town of Lockerbie, was widely regarded as being that retaliation. The Lockerbie case was to become a conundrum that potentially involved the three Middle East nations most heavily involved in backing terrorist groups.

Jim Swire, father of one of the victims and subsequently spokesman for the Lockerbie families, later said, 'In Britain we have a healthy scepticism about the integrity of our intelligence services.' Among other things, he was concerned that warnings of a possible attack may not have been heeded. It seems unlikely, however, that either SIS or the CIA would have allowed the flight to go ahead if there had been any specific warning – if for no other reason than that several US intelligence officers were travelling on board and perished.

Evidence indicated that the bomb which destroyed the aircraft had been built into a Toshiba radio-cassette player identical to several that had been seized earlier in Germany. The design of the bomb and the identity of the people caught in the German operation pointed to a Palestinian group, the PFLP General Command, headed by Ahmed Jibril. He had been responsible for several previous aircraft bombings. Jibril's apparent involvement suggested that the Syrian authorities might be implicated, since he was based in Damascus and depended on them for support.

The police's inquiries led them to Malta, where clothes found in the suitcase containing the bomb had been bought. They subsequently issued warrants for the arrest of two men, believed to be intelligence operatives working for Libyan Airlines in Malta, who had bought the clothes and checked the suitcase through on to a flight to Frankfurt and from there to London.

The Lockerbie trail therefore led to Iran, Syria and Libya. Iran and

Libya both seemed to have the motive of revenge: Iran for their destroyed airliner, Libya for the US bombing two years earlier. Matters were further complicated by the suggestion that the operation might have been a collaborative effort between one or more of these parties and Jibril's group. Another theory, enthusiastically endorsed by lawyers acting for PanAm, suggested that the tragedy might have been the result of a US drugs intelligence mission that had gone wrong.

Britain and the USA were eventually to focus on Libya as the culprit. This assessment was based on the work of the Scottish police and the Federal Bureau of Investigation rather than on intelligence; many in the secret world have believed in Iranian involvement from the outset. GCHQ could not produce a sigint 'smoking gun' linking the attack to any of the suspected nations – although, of course, the NSA's intercept did undermine the notion that Libya was entirely responsible. The success achieved with the Hindawi case of the previous summer was not possible, evidence of the limits of intelligence in the counter-terrorist arena.

By mid-1988 two issues were moving up the foreign policy agenda that were to affect the future roles of GCHQ and the Secret Intelligence Service: drugs, and the proliferation of weapons of mass destruction.

In 1988 SIS set up its Counter Narcotics Section. This was prompted by a growing awareness within government of the seriousness of drug trafficking and by a desire to help the US authorities in what was for them becoming an increasingly difficult area. Although intercepting drugs was the task of the Customs and Excise, SIS was able to profit from the fact that Whitehall officials did not regard that organisation as having an effective intelligence network. The principal concern at the time was heroin originating from Pakistan, Afghanistan and Iran. In time, there would be growing anxiety about the activities of the Colombian cocaine traffickers.

At about the same time, attention began to focus on weapons proliferation, although it would take more than a year for this to have organizational consequences for SIS. John Gordon, the Head of the Nuclear Energy Department at the Foreign Office, wrote a paper setting out the dangers of countries using Britain to gain access to technology that might be useful in nuclear weapons programmes, and suggesting what might be done about it. Initially, he drew attention to six states: India, Pakistan, Israel, South Africa, Brazil and Argentina.

By mid-1988 there were only two SIS officers working on proliferation. They helped collate information; but even at that stage, Gordon says, 'SIS's assessment of who was breaking the nuclear trade regime and which countries were building a nuclear capacity was absolutely crucial'. In time, this would grow into a major operational commitment for the Service, but this had not yet been agreed by the Cabinet Office.

In November 1988 Colin McColl took over as the Chief of SIS. Whereas his predecessor Christopher Curwen had been a traditional, quietly-spoken 'safe pair of hands', McColl had more flair and a temperament better suited to selling the Service in Whitehall during the coming years. Balding, with an infectious grin, McColl eschewed the normal Whitehall dress code, looking more like the marketing manager of a large company in his sharp suits and Italian designer ties. He was also fond of wearing an Australian bush hat. McColl's expansive character first showed itself at Oxford, where he was known for his parties, and then in his diplomatic postings, where he indulged his passion for amateur dramatics. The overall effect is summed up by one of his senior intelligence colleagues, who calls McColl 'the last of the old actor-managers'.

Whitehall procedures prevented McColl from redefining his organization with the same speed as MI5. As McColl would later explain, 'The agencies don't pluck priorities out of their hat. They are tasked.' This statement needs a little qualification; an energetic Chief can campaign among the key Cabinet Office officials for a change in direction. John Gordon feels counter-proliferation began moving up Whitehall's agenda at this time because 'certain departments of the Foreign Office, MoD and MI6 were all looking for new tasks ... it was inevitable that they should expand into the non-proliferation field'. It is fair to say, however, that when McColl took over the Service that November, neither the key figures at Downing Street nor the new Chief himself wanted any major change in SIS priorities.

Although McColl was known for his broad grounding in Third World matters, his rise had been typical of the 'Sovbloc master race' as they were known within MI6. He had been posted to Warsaw in the 1960s and to the UK Mission in Geneva in the 1970s. Both were key hunting-grounds in SIS's attempts to recruit sources within the Soviet Bloc diplomatic community.

Barrie Gane replaced McColl as the Director of Requirements and Production, the number two job in SIS (there was no Deputy Chief, although there had been one earlier in MI6 history), and therefore as the new Chief's heir apparent. Gane's three predecessors as Director of Requirements and Production had all gone on to the top job. Gerry Warner remained as Director of Counter Intelligence and Security, the third-ranking post in the organization. Both Gane and Warner were tied to McColl by close professional bonds.

MI6 occupied several 'diplomatic' posts in the British embassy in Warsaw. In 1966, McColl replaced Warner in one of them. Gane and McColl thus served in Warsaw at the same time, where they both played a part in a Cold War drama legendary within SIS. Adam Kaczmarczyk, a twenty-eight-year-old communications clerk in the Polish Ministry of Defence, had been recruited by MI6 in 1967. At meetings in the flats of British embassy staff, Kaczmarczyk had provided intelligence on the organization of the Polish army, its communications systems and the Soviet forces stationed there. Polish counter-intelligence officers somehow became aware of his actions, and he was followed to a meeting with his SIS handlers. Shortly after the meeting, Kaczmarczyk was arrested and three British embassy personnel detained in possession of incriminating papers. Gane was given twenty-four hours to leave the country – which he did, bringing his Warsaw posting to an end after less than a year. McColl, who had presumably escaped the Polish surveillance operation, managed to stay on until 1968. Kaczmarczyk was tried *in camera* and executed.

McColl, Warner and Gane were all therefore part of a tough Cold War school of espionage. They did not have any significant disagreement with Percy Cradock and his interpretation of events in Moscow, and they still regarded recruiting Soviet agents as their top priority.

Chapter 8

1988/9 The Wall Comes Tumbling Down

On 8 December 1988 Mikhail Gorbachev went to the United Nations General Assembly with another of his carefully-crafted arms-control proposals. His desire to cut military spending and move the West towards a treaty reducing armies in Europe led him to take an action that produced a dramatic worsening of relations with his own military.

Gorbachev spelled out his plan unilaterally to cut the Soviet armed forces by half a million troops. Many of the provisions of this plan seemed designed to convince Western leaders such as Margaret Thatcher, who had expressed scepticism over Moscow's shift to a defensive military posture. The Nato summit had issued a communiqué that March setting 'as a high priority, the elimination of the capability for launching surprise attack'. Gorbachev talked of moving five thousand Soviet tanks out of eastern Europe and cutting a further five thousand in the western Soviet Union. The cuts to armoured forces and artillery amounted to about a quarter of Moscow's front line facing Nato. He announced that special airborne and bridging units, which Nato considered essential for the Warsaw Pact's offensive war plans, would also go. These measures angered the army. On the day Gorbachev had left Moscow for his trip to the United Nations, Marshal Sergei Akhromeyev, his chief military adviser, resigned.

In September, Marshal Akhromeyev had said in a lecture in Stockholm that there could be no agreement with Nato on cuts in conventional forces 'without reciprocity'. In a private meeting with journalists he admitted that the Soviet General Staff had been guilty of mistakes in its previous build-up – for example, in deploying the SS-20 missile – but that he had advised the Soviet leader not to make any unilateral cuts in the armed forces. His resignation on 7 December was because his advice had been ignored. In Stockholm, Marshal Akhromeyev also referred to the lesson of the earlier unilateral cuts made by General Secretary Nikita Khrushchev in the early 1960s, arguing they had been mistaken. In articles in the Soviet press, several other generals warmed to the idea that previous cuts had brought nothing but misery – part of a growing campaign by the military against Gorbachev's strategy.

Ever since Gorbachev had come to power, it had been an article of faith in the assessments of the Joint Intelligence Committee that he would not get rid of the Soviet Union's superiority in conventional weapons. As the year ended and 1989 began, British ministers reacted with curious diffidence to Gorbachev's UN speech. They repeatedly stressed that the reductions did not go far enough to remove the need for a treaty cutting conventional weapons in Europe. It was true that even after the cuts the Warsaw Pact retained a superiority in tanks and artillery, but Gorbachev had never billed the proposed reductions as an alternative to the treaty, simply as a way of moving things along.

The Cabinet was becoming increasingly concerned about the pressure growing from within the Treasury for defence cuts, something the Prime Minister had set herself against. On 20 January 1989 came the inauguration of the incoming Administration of US President George Bush. The change of President caused profound anxiety for the Prime Minister. Bush's assessment was that the changes in the Soviet Union merited an overall freeze in defence spending, announced soon after he took power. By mid-1989 his Administration was ready to announce a $64 billion programme of defence cuts spread over five years.

It became clear that President Bush would not be the same soft touch for the Prime Minister as his predecessor. She noted in her memoirs, 'I found myself dealing with an Administration which saw Germany as its main European partner in leadership.' Geoffrey Howe, Foreign Secretary at the time, says, 'The consciousness among American administrators that Margaret had such a pull with Reagan was always in their mind. When President Bush came in, he and the people around him were anxious to have a "UDI" from the special relationship.' Under President Bush, the change in the substance of the UK–US relationship was accompanied by one of style too; the Prime Minister noted somewhat undiplomatically, 'I had learned that I had to defer to him in conversation and not to stint the praise.'

Thatcher felt less need to tailor her language for others lower down the US hierarchy, even if it embarrassed her own officials. On a visit to London, William Webster, then the Director of the CIA, paid a courtesy call. Percy Cradock was also there. According to Lieutenant-General William Odom, then Director of the US National Security Agency, 'Webster was sitting there with this tirade coming from Mrs Thatcher. Percy Cradock was so embarrassed he was almost in a foetal position. She looked across at him and said, "Percy, am I boring you?"'

Whatever the Prime Minister's manner, the UK–US intelligence relationship remained largely immune from the general Foreign Office or Downing Street gloom about the Bush Administration's pro-German policy. Some in Washington came to regard it as the only really 'special' area of co-operation remaining between the USA and Britain. Morton Abramowitz, head of the Intelligence and Research branch of the US State Department until 1988, notes, 'Britain made an extraordinarily astute investment buying into the US intelligence system, particularly in sigint. They were able to parlay themselves all sorts of durable ties which spilled into other areas, creating a pro-British lobby in the American system. So the UK, with its intelligence links, had a wider impact on the whole relationship.'

During the winter of 1988–9 several JIC assessments attempted to justify continuing high levels of defence spending in Britain. Tom King, who took over as Defence Secretary in 1989, says, 'It seemed an anomalous situation at the time in Nato, as our adversary appeared to be retreating but it was too early to start dismantling . . . we certainly could have cut earlier with hindsight, that's true. But we would have been taking a risk. We have to remember certain things had changed irreversibly and certain things hadn't.' The intelligence establishment provided much of the meat for the inner Whitehall discussion about what had and had not changed.

The picture of Soviet military activity early in 1989 was one of retreat on almost all fronts. The last of 100,300 troops were withdrawn from Afghanistan on 14 February. Moscow had committed itself to pulling out a four-division garrison from Mongolia. On 9 January the Kremlin's Cuban allies had started withdrawing their expeditionary force from Angola. Gorbachev was putting into effect a substantial programme of cuts in the production of military equipment that he had pushed through the previous year.

Underneath the Soviet structure, the tremors of nationalism – the force that would rip apart first the Warsaw Pact and then the Soviet Union itself – were becoming more powerful. Within the Soviet borders these were making themselves felt in the three Baltic republics and in the Caucasus.

In November 1988 the Supreme Soviet of Estonia had declared itself 'sovereign'. The Soviet constitution accorded supreme legal authority to these bodies, but the Communist system had in fact been designed so that they would never use that authority against Moscow's interests; Supreme Soviet members were also usually Party members and they were meant to put their loyalty to 'Soviet internationalism' before their identity as Estonians. The Estonian vote marked the beginning of the collapse of this system. The Kremlin knew that this action contained profound dangers because the Soviet Union's founding fathers had made another constitutional promise they never intended to keep: the right of the fifteen republics to secede from the USSR.

The Caucasus was the other cockpit of nationalism. In November 1988 thirty thousand people had demonstrated against Soviet influence in Georgia. Two neighbouring republics, Armenia and Azerbaijan, were growing increasingly hostile over the status of the Nagorno-Karabakh enclave. Most of the people there were Armenian, but the area was under overall Azeri rule. Because of growing intercommunal violence, Gorbachev imposed direct rule on Nagorno-Karabakh on 12 January 1989. Soviet paratroopers were soon in action against Armenian nationalist guerrillas.

Gorbachev's policy of freeing political prisoners had put dozens of people previously jailed for nationalist agitation back into the community. As popular frustration grew over the continued economic decline and Party corruption, these nationalists emerged as credible figures untainted by association with Communism. Moves towards multi-candidate elections begun by the Kremlin provided them with a ticket into local Supreme Soviets.

British intelligence found that this enormous change taxed it to the full. For years there had been evidence in Soviet military journals of the problems of nationalism in the ranks of the armed forces. This included the use of bribes to avoid conscription, an activity prevalent in the Caucasian and some Central Asian republics. This trend began to grow during the Gorbachev years, with the eventual result that a substantial slice of the Soviet Army's manpower melted away as thousands of youths evaded conscription.

The phone-calls of local officials and ordinary citizens carried over microwave links and so sucked up by American sigint satellites must have contained daily signs of the growing nationalist sentiment. But the centres for analysing the Soviet Bloc – J Division at GCHQ, DI3 at the Defence Intelligence Staff and so on – did not contain personnel with the specific task of examining nationalism. The lack of organizational readiness for the problem resulted in part from the desire of intelligence and foreign-policy bureaucracies to keep life simple by dealing with Moscow rather than a host of smaller national groups.

One of the principal Soviet analysts in the British intelligence system remembers that almost no consideration was given to nationalism during late 1988 and early 1989: 'I don't recall that it was ever regarded as a significant factor, something which would affect the policy of the Soviet Union.' He adds, 'I consoled myself by the fact that the Americans were doing the same thing.' This intelligence 'group-think' is described by another senior analyst, one of the more thoughtful members of the JIC Assessments Staff, who believes, 'An analytical culture develops among people looking at the same problem. It's always one of the hardest tasks to keep on challenging the assumptions of that culture. All the great misjudgements of history have been made by experts.'

Ministers and officials felt the absence of good analyses of the growing nationalist sentiment. Margaret Thatcher wrote of her visit to the Ukraine, the most powerful Soviet republic outside Russia, during 1990, 'I found that I had not been properly briefed ... everywhere I went I found blue and yellow bunting and flags (the colours of pre-Soviet Ukraine) and signs demanding Ukrainian independence.'

During early 1989 the prime focus was not on the growing evidence of nationalist unrest within the Soviet Union itself, but on the unrest within the wider family of nations under Moscow's traditional domination: the east European states of the Warsaw Pact. The Soviet Army had intervened in East Germany in 1953, in Hungary in 1956 and in Czechoslovakia in 1968 to prevent political developments which were not to Moscow's liking; would Gorbachev do the same, or would he honour his principles of non-violence in international affairs?

The Pentagon's Defence Intelligence Agency believed that force would be used. Its published annual statement *Soviet Military Power* said in April 1988, 'The General Secretary is, however, unlikely to alter traditional relationships that retain the non-Soviet Warsaw Pact nations firmly under Soviet dominance.' One year on, with Hungary and Poland moving towards multi-party elections, the JIC found itself struggling with the same conundrum. One Soviet analyst recalls, 'We found it extremely difficult to answer that question. We didn't know what he would do. I think we felt that if the situation developed to the point where the social fabric began to disintegrate, he would order the tanks in.'

Gorbachev did draw a line around the borders of the USSR, and there were to be several attempts to use tanks to prevent the secession of Soviet republics; an early sign of this uncompromising attitude was the killing by Soviet troops of twenty demonstrators in the Georgian capital Tbilisi on 9 April 1989. But the JIC had arrived at the wrong conclusions about Gorbachev's view on eastern Europe. Although the Soviet leader attempted through political pressure to persuade the more recalcitrant east European party dictators to reform their regimes, he remained committed to his principles of non-intervention. The 1968 invasion of Czechoslovakia had spawned the Brezhnev Doctrine, circumscribing the independence of east European states; Gorbachev's press spokesman Gennady Gerasimov would soon be joking about the 'Sinatra Doctrine' – the right of those same countries to 'do it their way'.

Early in 1989 Mrs Thatcher predicted that she would not see the end of Communism in her lifetime. Lieutenant-General Derek Boorman, formerly the Chief of Defence Intelligence, says, 'I don't think any of us substantially got 1985–8 right. None of us – intelligence people, journalists, commentators – got the timing right. We were all completely overwhelmed by the pace of it.'

During the preparations for the Thatcher–Gorbachev summit in April 1989, two of the long-term preoccupations of the intelligence community loomed large on the agenda: Soviet policy on chemical weapons and their espionage activity in Britain.

The Kremlin was trying to move forward its political campaign for a chemical weapons treaty. In January, Eduard Shevardnadze, the Soviet Foreign Minister, had announced that the destruction of the chemical weapon stockpile would begin in 1989. British experts, including the DIS man responsible for the oft-publicized British estimate that the Soviet Union had 300,000 tons of nerve gas, were allowed to visit the chemical warfare centre at Shikhany. The Soviet officers declined to show the visitors a facility which they said would be used to destroy the chemical agents, but which the British suspected was still producing them. The chemical weapons displayed on previous visits had not included the most modern ones, Nato experts believed. One of the most sceptical intelligence analysts says that the 1989 visit 'was an exercise in obfuscation. It seemed to confirm what we expected: that Russian statements on chemical weapons were disinformation.' From early on Lieutenant General Anatoly Kuntsevich, Deputy Commander of Chemical Troops and the organizer of the Shikhany visit, attracted the suspicions of DIS and MI6 experts. They believed the general was one of the men with most to hide; he had formerly been director of the complex in southern Russia and was believed to be responsible for the development of new agents.

Assessments made early in 1989 formed the basis of a British diplomatic counter-offensive on chemical arms. The 1989 Statement on the Defence Estimates, published that May, accused the Soviet side of 'secrecy and evasiveness'. It said, 'We strongly suspect that, contrary to Soviet claims, production of CW agents in the Soviet Union is still continuing . . . we estimate the size of the Soviet stockpile . . . to be several times higher than the 50,000 tonnes claimed.'

This was to be the main item on the agenda during the April summit. The Prime Minister later wrote, 'I raised directly with Mr Gorbachev the evidence which we had that the Soviets had not been telling us the truth about the quantity and types of chemical weapons which they held. He stoutly maintained that they had.' Geoffrey Howe also took Eduard Shevardnadze to task; he says, 'We all took the view that we were being led up the garden path. I raised the issue many times, but there's a limit to how far you can go before it becomes apparent that you are calling the leader of one of the world's superpowers a liar.'

It is now clear, however, that Soviet answers about the quantity of their nerve gases were true, and that the British intelligence community's evaluation of the question was faulty. The Soviet Union had no more than 35,000 tonnes of nerve gas, as their subsequent treaty declaration and accounts from dissident chemical weapons scientists in Moscow would confirm.

However, evidence from those same unofficial and open sources would show that the British had been right to question the sincerity of the publicly-stated Soviet desire to get rid of chemical weapons. However, as some intelligence analysts admit, the debate was obscured by Britain's faulty estimates of Soviet stocks, a mistake which allowed the other side to maintain that they were telling the truth. The issue of the continued development of such weapons was to prompt a further and increasingly important question: were Gorbachev and Shevardnadze lying, or had they been deceived by the military?

Vil Mirzayanov, a department head in the State Scientific Research Institute for Organic Chemistry and Technology in Moscow, was later imprisoned for publicly alleging Soviet military duplicity. He wrote that the period 1987–9 saw the development of two new nerve gases. In 1989 Soviet scientists tested A-230, a weapon based on the V type of gas, but considerably more toxic than previously-manufactured variants. They were also developing A-232, a binary version of the nerve gas which allows the lethal compound to be stored as two harmless chemicals. In December 1995 I was able to discuss the issue of this continued research with Mikhail Gorbachev himself in an interview for the BBC's *Newsnight*. The former General Secretary told me the scientists may have been 'completing some of the programmes that had already started . . . perhaps there were loose ends to tie up'. It is true that while A-230 was produced in development qualities, neither it nor any of the other agents described by Mirzayanov were turned out in large quantities or fielded in Soviet munitions. In this sense, Gorbachev and the generals apparently felt their actions were compatible with the unilateral declarations that they had halted production. Continued Soviet research on biological weapons, lethal viruses and bacteria was less easy to reconcile with a convention signed by Moscow in 1972 banning all work on such weapons. The areas of Soviet chemical and biological weapons research became matters of prime importance for MI6 and the CIA.

The other Cold War issue at the time of the April summit was espionage activity in Britain. Geoffrey Howe's memoirs relate that Soviet intelligence officers under diplomatic cover were observed meeting a British spy while preparations for the summit were under way. The Prime Minister decided not to expel anyone before the meeting so as not to spoil the diplomatic atmosphere.

Within the Security Service, David Bannerman, the Director of Counter Espionage, K Branch, discussed what action might be taken with Patrick Walker, the Director General. Bannerman – who, through the death of a brother, had unexpectedly inherited the baronetcy of Elsick, a Scottish title dating back to 1682 – was a tough officer with a long track record in counter-espionage who considered that the Cold War was still very much on. After the summit, Howe writes in his memoirs, 'Within two weeks Margaret was told by the

Director General of MI5 that the level of KGB and GRU activity remained high and the case for further expulsions as strong as ever.'

How high the level of Soviet espionage activity really was is open to question, because it was at about the time of the May expulsions that Walker and his Board of Management at Gower Street began to carry out a new shift in resources. Counter Subversion, F Branch, had by this time already been run down to a cadre of thirty to forty officers and its resources switched to counter-terrorism. MI5's senior managers had then started taking away resources from K Branch, traditionally the most important part of the Service. K Branch officers, like those in F Branch before them, found themselves thrown into counter-terrorist work; the cuts represented a Board of Management view that the Soviet espionage threat was declining substantially, at around the same time as the Service was urging ministers to expel more KGB and GRU officers.

By spring 1989 Stella Rimington had taken over the fast-growing G Branch, and it was probably at some time in 1989 that senior civil servants confirmed the moves begun under Anthony Duff to make her the next Director General. Her rival John Deverell – and predecessor as Director of Counter Terrorism – had been posted to Northern Ireland as the Director and Co-ordinator of Intelligence. Given these shifts in resources, it is probable that Bannerman saw himself as fighting a rearguard action at K Branch, and he may have received the DGSS's backing for the expulsions as a kind of consolation prize.

The Prime Minister decided not to announce that eleven Soviet diplomats and three journalists had been thrown out, and instead wrote a letter to Gorbachev explaining that her actions were not intended to damage the friendly relations between the two countries. The Soviet leader did not take it well, and a retaliatory expulsion of British diplomats and journalists from Moscow duly followed.

On this occasion, Moscow had the last word. Thatcher did not order further expulsions, and the May 1989 action was to prove the last large-scale *persona non grata* of Soviet diplomats from London. Had intelligence hard-liners in Britain played too great a role in setting this particular agenda? Geoffrey Howe told me, 'MI5 was in no sense dominant in our deliberations. Margaret Thatcher was actually the doveish one. Margaret didn't want expulsions to rock the boat, which is why she went to such great lengths, writing to Gorbachev and so on, to cushion the blow. But whenever we tried to handle it softly, it was thrown back at us by them.' The time for such diplomatic *machismo* was over, however. To have continued large-scale expulsions at a time when SIS was trying to exploit the growing feeling of collapse in the Soviet Union to build up its own agent network might have struck even the toughest Whitehall mandarin as hypocritical.

Throughout the spring and summer, chemical weapons and espionage had proved irritants in Anglo-Soviet relations. The former Foreign Secretary relates in his memoirs that Shevardnadze said to him, apparently jokingly, 'Ah! Here's Sir Geoffrey, who's been making life difficult for us by going on again about chemical weapons and the KGB.' How far had the British initiatives on these matters simply wasted time at summits that might instead have been used to discuss the implications of the rise of nationalism or accelerate arms control? Howe says, 'I don't think, quite frankly, that they inhibited the process of détente in the aggregate at all. That process was acquiring a momentum of its own.' Someone who was senior in the Foreign Office at that time is less sure; he concedes that such issues 'used up an awful lot of time, but that was inevitable once we got started'.

At the end of May 1989 Gorbachev made a long-expected visit to China. Soviet officials had stressed since he came to power that the General Secretary intended to broaden the scope of foreign policy from its traditional preoccupation with the USA and Nato. Repairing relations with China was an important priority. The two giants of the Communist world had been rivals since the 1960s, and at times border clashes had even threatened to develop into war. The resulting military build-up in the Soviet Far East was, in the view of Gorbachev and his advisers, a thorough waste of resources. The General Secretary wanted 'normalization' in order to cut these forces and stimulate trade.

However, his visit to Peking, designed to mark this change, was overshadowed by China's student democracy movement. Since early May tens of thousands of young Chinese had flocked to Tiananmen, the huge square in central Peking, to take part in a series of protests appealing for party reform. A statue called the Goddess of Democracy was built, and became the focus of much attention from Western journalists covering the demonstrations. For China's ageing party leaders, the protests were an unacceptable challenge; they brought units of the People's Liberation Army into the capital in preparation for a showdown with the 'counter-revolutionaries'.

The students attempted to fraternize with the soldiers, hoping to persuade them to refuse orders to disperse the protest. But on 4 June 1989 the People's Liberation Army was ordered into Tiananmen, where it set about gunning down hundreds of the young demonstrators. As these events unfolded, reports from correspondents in Peking and from Chinese dissident groups suggested that some army units had refused orders, and that others might even be fighting on the students' side.

GCHQ experts had been following these events with close attention. Although the Chinese, in common with other Communist countries, had a system of secure land lines and codes for their high-level communications network, the deployment of army units into the capital caused a great deal of traffic over insecure tactical radios that was easily intercepted by a combination of GCHQ's station in Hong Kong and US sigint satellites. The product, which included conversations between divisional commanders entering Peking, was analysed at GCHQ, in the Defence Intelligence Staff, and in the Far Eastern Current Intelligence Group in the Cabinet Office.

Assessments based on this sigint provided one of the intelligence community's success stories of that tumultuous year. The Red Book told ministers, and the DIS took the unusual step of putting on a briefing for journalists: there were no major splits in the Chinese People's Liberation Army, the leadership's orders were being obeyed by units throughout the country, and the student democracy movement had been crushed. Prompt and accurate assessment allowed the government to deal with the Chinese authorities accordingly.

Throughout the summer of 1989, nationalism gathered pace in eastern Europe and certain Soviet republics. Vacláv Havel's release from a Czech prison in mid-May set in train the later 'velvet revolution' there. One million people joined anti-Soviet demonstrations in the Baltic republics on 23 August, and two weeks later a government coalition led by activists of the previously-banned Solidarity trade union took power in Poland. The most dramatic changes in eastern Europe began in Hungary, where the government had decided, despite pressure from Moscow, to dismantle the barbed-wire fences and other restrictions on its frontier with Austria. Thousands of people soon took the opportunity to travel from the German Democratic Republic through Hungary to the West – an exodus that progressively destabilized the government in East Berlin.

As the Prime Minister returned from an economic conference in

Tokyo that September, she stopped in Moscow for talks with the Russian leader. As had happened with the INF Treaty, Thatcher was finding that the pace of change in Europe was forcing her to confront the logic of some of the West's earlier standpoints; she confesses in her memoirs, 'Although Nato had traditionally made statements supporting Germany's aspiration to be reunited, in practice we were rather apprehensive.' She considered Europe's largest nation to have oscillated historically between aggression and self-doubt, and argued that Germany was 'by its very nature a destabilising rather than a stabilising force in Europe'. She received little comfort from the General Secretary, who had apparently concluded that there was little Moscow could do to stop events, given its own equally insincere history of statements in support of German reunification; the Communist Party in the GDR was even officially called the Socialist Unity Party.

Thatcher's Cabinet colleagues were almost unanimous – after they had left office – in criticizing her for persisting at this time with two strongly-held views: slowing the pace of German reunification, and stressing the need for Nato to deploy new nuclear weapons – an issue that also brought tension with Bonn. David Mellor says, 'One of the surest signs that she'd lost her grip on foreign policy was to try and stop the reunification of Germany. Her self-delusion that she could have any influence over it – which she saw in terms of helping Gorbachev – sowed seeds of bitterness in Anglo-German relationships which remain to this day.' Her usually loyal Private Secretary Charles Powell feels that the pace of change had become too great: 'With hindsight, she was obviously wrong. Having got it right, against all the policy advice, in the early and mid-1980s, it was very difficult for her to convert her whole view in the late 1980s.'

After her Moscow meetings the Prime Minister said that she expected a Conventional Forces in Europe treaty, cutting armies from the Urals to the Atlantic, before the end of 1990. As diplomats struggled to complete the treaty, the basis upon which it was to be negotiated – between two military blocs – was fast becoming a footnote of history. The triumph of non-Communist nationalist forces in eastern Europe led to polite invitations to the Soviet Army to leave the four countries in which it was based and the subsequent collapse of the Warsaw Pact military organization.

With nuclear weapons as with Germany, the Prime Minister now had to deploy considerable political effort to evade the consequences of one more change she had previously sought: the end of the Soviet

Union's superiority in conventional weapons in Europe. That October, at a meeting of defence ministers in Portugal, British diplomats pressed their Nato colleagues to endorse the drive for additional, 'compensatory' nuclear weapons begun in 1987 by General Bernard Rogers, the Supreme Allied Commander in Europe.

Throughout Nato's forty-year history, the existence of superior Warsaw Pact ground forces had been given as the reason for stationing US nuclear weapons in Europe. Now, even though the Iron Curtain was falling, hundreds of thousands of people were flooding into the West, and there was the prospect of a Conventional Forces in Europe treaty, British diplomats took satisfaction that the Nato Nuclear Planning Group meeting of ministers in Portugal ended with a communiqué saying 'the removal of the imbalance of conventional forces would provide scope for further reductions in the sub-strategic nuclear forces of Nato, though it would not obviate the need for such forces'.

On 10 November 1989 East German border guards began breaking down the Berlin Wall. The Warsaw Pact was in collapse. The effects on Britain, its foreign policy and defence posture, were direct and quantifiable. Regiments of Sukhoi Su-24 bombers based in Poland would have to move back to Russia, out of range of the UK. Tank divisions previously stationed within an artillery round's fall of the forward garrisons of the British Army of the Rhine were being loaded on to flat cars and moved east. Huge quantities of equipment would be destroyed; other tanks and field-guns would be seized by the embryo armies of the republics struggling to free themselves from the Soviet Union. The logic that high levels of defence spending by Britain were necessary because of the 'Soviet threat' had collapsed.

Could the intelligence establishment have done more, or was it inevitable that a Prime Minister who had 'lost her grip in foreign policy', but was in no danger of losing her hold on government, would have insisted on continuing with high defence spending and policies that soured relations with the most powerful state in Europe? Certainly, at key moments during 1989 the agenda of the intelligence services, notably where chemical weapons or spy expulsions were concerned, had become hers. However, those agencies had, in the view of many of their own members, been structurally and philosophically unable to see growing nationalism for the decisive force that it was, despite the warning signs as early as autumn 1988.

No one in Whitehall doubted the ability of JIC Chairman Percy Cradock to produce clear assessments from the intelligence machine, but he had never been particularly charitable towards the Russian leader; in fact, few of his colleagues exhibited a deeper scepticism about the Kremlin's reforms. Thatcher disagreed with him about Gorbachev, and in fact saw her German policy, at least in part, as helping the Soviet leader. However great or small the JIC's influence on the Prime Minister, its minutes, by emphasizing uncertainty and traditional Russian aggressiveness, were more likely to have fed her concerns about nuclear weapons and Germany than to have diminished them. But despite the reservations of intelligence sceptics such as Cradock, she stuck to her approach of supporting Gorbachev personally. In fact, it would become more entrenched as the future of the Soviet Union itself came into question.

Part Two

Chapter 9

1990 Supergun

The collapse of Communism in eastern Europe heightened White-hall's interest in the possible proliferation of weapons of mass destruction. There were concerns about certain Middle Eastern states running programmes to make nuclear, chemical or biological bombs. At the beginning of 1990 worsening inter-ethnic violence in Azerbaijan led to a Soviet Army intervention during which armoured forces took the city of Baku, killing ninety-eight people. At this time, the US intelligence community announced that Moscow had evacuated a large nuclear weapons storage site in Azerbaijan, presumably because of fears that it might be overrun by militant nationalists. There was growing concern that nuclear weapons might go astray in the increasingly chaotic Soviet Union. The key committees running intelligence service budgets and tasking directed British agencies to increase their commitment to counter-proliferation. This came just before the politically-sensitive matter of arms sales to Iraq became public.

The Secret Intelligence Service, the Security Service and the Defence Intelligence Staff had all devoted small-scale efforts to counter-proliferation before, but during 1989 and early 1990 this changed and attempts were made to improve interdepartmental co-ordination. DIS remained the main centre for specialized expertise; its Scientific and Technical Directorate had long enjoyed the advantage of being able to take some of the best boffins from the Ministry's own research establishments on attachment and use their highly-specialized skills.

At MI6, Counter Proliferation followed Counter Narcotics in acquiring its own section within the Requirements and Production empire. Instead of the two officers who had previously dealt with the subject, several were now involved. SIS recognized the need for improved technical expertise, traditionally the province of DIS. The

Service therefore recruited several new experts, poaching some from the Ministry of Defence – including the DIS civil servant who had been in charge of the Soviet chemical weapons estimate. SIS had problems finding the right officers to manage this new area; the high-flyers of its Intelligence Branch stream were more often versed in the classics than in the science of uranium centrifuge enrichment or anthrax preparation. It was the same at King Charles Street: John Gordon, who had headed the Nuclear Energy Department in the Foreign Office, says that none of his officer-grade staff had a science degree. An MI6 officer jokes, 'Most people in the Foreign Office would be better at talking to Julius Caesar than discussing matters of technology.'

The Security Service also became involved, adding a Counter Pro-liferation Section to K Branch. One officer commented, 'We needed convincing that there was a job to be done.' This might seem surpris-ing in retrospect, but it appears that the new section was formed with counter-espionage specialists, and K Branch felt it was already losing enough of them to other areas.

A proliferation Current Intelligence Group in the JIC staff was used to collate intelligence reports. However, this group's remit was limited to collating information about the traffic in weapons of mass destruc-tion or the technology that could be used to make them. The growing lobby of MI5, MI6 and DIS staff concerned with counter-proliferation therefore used the Restricted Enforcement Unit (REU), a secret Whitehall committee set up in 1987 principally to prevent the illegal export of conventional weapons. The REU was chaired by the Depart-ment of Trade and Industry, the body that granted export licences to British industry, and was made up of experts from the Foreign Office, MI6, Customs and Excise and other government departments.

The REU differed from the proliferation CIG in the Cabinet Office in that it was empowered to take timely action to prevent ille-gal exports. Peter Pigden, Deputy Chief Investigating Officer of Cus-toms and Excise, sat on the REU: 'There was a free and frank exchange of views. It wasn't just government departments listening to the intel-ligence services, it was a committee where everybody had a voice.'

Although this expansion and reorganization was encouraging for Whitehall's initially small band of proliferation experts, they knew the system had major faults – a fact that would soon become publicly apparent. Historically, Whitehall had put very few resources into the field. The work on nuclear weapons by John Gordon's Foreign

Office department had centred on India, Pakistan, Brazil, Argentina, Israel and South Africa. Even in these cases, the intelligence available to HMG often represented little more than warmed-over international gossip.

Information released by the South African government after it opted to move the country towards majority rule showed that it had a successful nuclear weapons programme. It had actually built six nuclear devices: the end-point of a complex technological process that all aspiring nuclear powers seek to master. South Africa was a major SIS target: the agency ran one of its biggest operations there, staffed in the late 1980s by five officers. But it probably comes as no surprise, given the failure of Western intelligence to make an accurate estimate of the Soviet nuclear stockpile, to find that Britain did not know whether South Africa had the bomb. John Gordon confirms, 'We were suspicious of them, but we were under-informed.'

The Israeli nuclear weapons programme had produced scores of nuclear devices by 1990, possibly as many as two hundred. Israel had become a nuclear power on a par with the UK. Here again, Whitehall decision-makers had few hard facts, although for different reasons. John Gordon says, 'The Americans were giving us masses of information on the nuclear side – except about Israel, where they gave us nothing.'

Gordon, who was considered one of Whitehall's principal experts on proliferation, had gone on a sabbatical to Imperial College and was to leave the Foreign Office later in 1990. He had identified the export licensing office in the Department of Trade and Industry as the Achilles' heel of British attempts to restrict the sale of sensitive technology. He says, 'The export licensing regime was under very serious pressure from the volume of applications and from understaffing. It was an area where a scandal was waiting to happen. The DTI licensing department was run by some very overworked, junior people without any real technical knowledge.' Early in 1990 that scandal became public.

Throughout his war against Iran, Saddam Hussein had used Iraq's oil wealth to acquire weapons in prodigious quantity. His spending on foreign military hardware during the 1980s was, according to some estimates, £50 billion. Iraq's main suppliers were the Soviet Union and France. Moscow had provided thousands of tanks, hundreds of fighters and Scud ballistic missiles. The French had sold the Iraqis some of their most potent weapons, including the Mirage F-1 fighter-bomber and the Exocet anti-shipping missile. Some newcomers to the arms exporting business had also been cashing in: Brazil had sold the Iraqis powerful multiple rocket launchers, Chile a family of munitions and bombs.

The international arms trade with the Gulf belligerents had taken place at two levels: providing advanced, highly-visible systems such as the French Mirages, and the low-key supply of support materials, including munitions. Although Britain would not provide the former, it did supply both sides with the latter. According to guidelines drawn up in 1985 by Geoffrey Howe, then Foreign Secretary, Britain claimed it would not provide equipment that would 'significantly enhance the capability of either side to prolong or exacerbate the conflict'. The guidelines also stated that the government would not allow the export of 'lethal equipment to either side'. These words, notably the phrase 'significantly enhance', were open to a variety of interpretations. The government had also left some loopholes – for example, by saying that it would honour existing contracts. Under this heading, Britain provided Ayatollah Khomeini's regime with spare parts and ammunition for the fleet of Chieftain tanks bought when the Shah of Iran was in power.

During 1987–8 Britain had followed the US lead in inclining towards Iraq. US warships became involved in several battles with the Iranian gunboats that harassed oil tankers in Gulf waters. As part of this shift, Britain had in September 1987 closed down the Iranian government arms procurement office in London. At the same time, British companies hoping to sell to Iraq looked for a more liberal interpretation of the export guidelines.

In October 1987 TDG, an Iraqi concern headed by Safa al-Habobi, who was also a senior official in the Iraqi Ministry of Industry and Military Production, bought a British machine-tools firm, Matrix Churchill. The firm had already sold Iraq machinery for manufacturing artillery shells. Whitehall officials could have justified these sales – to themselves at least – as counterbalancing the Chieftain support trade with Iran; officially, they maintained the fiction that the machinery was to be used in the civil sector. But the new Anglo-Iraqi company was soon to play a part in Baghdad's ambitious plans to create a substantial indigenous arms industry and acquire weapons of mass destruction.

During the summer of 1988 MI6 received reports that the Iraqis were interested in building an enormous cannon and that a British firm called Walter Sommers might be making parts for it. The components of the gun barrel were so large, however, that there was scepticism about the project's feasibility among the few intelligence officers who heard about it.

Although the espionage agencies could provide little concrete information about Israel or South Africa, because British firms were not directly involved, they had acquired an impressive variety of sources able to tell them about Iraq's procurement drive to build the gun, nuclear weapons and long-range missiles. One senior MI6 officer told me, 'You might almost say that we were getting too much intelligence,' alluding to the problems this was later to cause ministers.

The Security Service already knew about Matrix Churchill's business with Iraq because it had recruited its export sales manager, Mark Gutteridge, as an informer. MI5's interest in the firm had been aroused because of the possibility that it might do business with the Soviet Bloc. MI6 decided in mid-1988 to reactivate Paul Henderson, a former source from the 1970s who had become Matrix Churchill's managing director. An agent runner using the pseudonym 'John Balson' began seeing Henderson between his regular business trips to Iraq. It soon became apparent to SIS that Iraq's objectives in its commercial marriage with British business went much further than providing equipment to make field artillery shells. In August 1988, as documents released in the later court case were to reveal, Henderson told Balson about Project 1728, an Iraqi factory where Scud missiles were to be modified, using British-made tools to extend their range.

From early 1989 another agent became active: John Grecian, managing director of Ordtec, started supplying Special Branch with information. Grecian's firm sold conventional artillery fuses to the Iraqis, but had become drawn into the supergun project. Grecian's intelligence was fed through to MI5.

The flow of information about Iraq's ambitions to acquire weapons that might destabilize the region (principally by putting Israel within range of an attack) had to compete in ministers' in-trays with assessments from other government departments that struck a rather different note. The Iran–Iraq war had ended in August 1988. An internal Foreign Office report after the ceasefire identified Iraq as the big prize in Middle East business. Mark Higson, the civil servant who ran the Iraq desk in the Middle East Department, says, 'We knew Saddam was a murderer. On the other hand, we knew the French and

Germans were going to jump in. Britain plc had to deal with him, even if he was a nasty man.' During 1988 Alan Clark, Minister of State at the DTI, and Lord Trefgarne, Minister of State for Defence Procurement, lobbied hard for a relaxation of the restrictions on exports to Iraq.

For some officials, the intelligence emerging about Iraq was sufficiently important for them to drop their objection to exports. Rob Young, Head of the Middle East Department at the Foreign Office, was in favour of approving Matrix Churchill's licence applications because he feared losing what he described in a memo as 'our intelligence access to Habobi's network'. Therefore when Alan Clark wrote to William Waldegrave, Minister of State at the Foreign Office, in November 1988 seeking a relaxation of export guidelines, Waldegrave agreed. Five months later, the guidelines were relaxed.

On 14 February 1989 the Iranian leader Ayatollah Khomeini issued his *fatwa* against the British author Salman Rushdie: an incitement to Muslims to kill Rushdie because of the allegedly blasphemous content of his book *The Satanic Verses*. Foreign Office appeals for the *fatwa* to be rescinded led to Iran breaking off diplomatic relations with the UK on 7 March; they had only been re-established three months earlier. These events reinforced Alan Clark's argument that Iran was Britain's real enemy in the region, not Iraq.

At about the same time as the *fatwa*, however, one of Clark's civil servants minuted him to the effect that some of the technology destined for Iraq had unconventional uses. Tony Steadman, head of the DTI Export Licensing Department, wrote to Clark: 'The applications are sensitive because of the possible use of such machines for the development of nuclear weapons.' Advocates of the sales used the time-honoured argument that a screwdriver or a nail could also be used for the same purpose. Allowing such exports would risk infringing not just the government's own guidelines about sales to the Gulf, but also the international treaty aimed at preventing the spread of nuclear weapons. By deciding to allow the export of certain machine-tools the government had already, in John Gordon's view, 'broken its obligations under Article 1 of the Non Proliferation Treaty, which says nuclear weapons states mustn't help those trying to acquire them "in any way". We had applied nuclear export controls to the six suspect states pretty religiously, but hadn't in the case of Iraq, where the Middle East Department seems to have applied the conventional arms export criteria.'

Saddam Hussein's use of chemical weapons against his own Kurdish population gave some ministers cold feet about trade ties. British Aerospace's plans for a major contract with Iraq – the sale of fifty Hawk training jets – were therefore vetoed by the Cabinet in July 1989. Although Iraq was now at peace with its neighbour, the Hawk deal was too visible for the tastes of most ministers; the supply of machine tools and know-how continued, however.

On 5 September 1989, Grecian told his Special Branch contact that he had heard of an Iraqi plan, code-named Operation BABYLON, to build a gun with a 600-mile range. This vital tip-off took some months to find its way, via MI5, to the SIS counter-proliferation section.

In October, at around the same time as MI6 finally received Grecian's tip-off, its own agent Henderson supplied his handlers with details of Iraqi plans for a 'long-range projectile'; in fact, a rocket-powered shell for the 'supergun' being designed by ballistics expert Gerald Bull and his Space Research Corporation. The key MI6 officer – subsequently entitled 'Mr Q' in the report that Lord Justice Scott conducted into the affair – had been energetic in pursuing leads on the Iraqi plans, but had difficulty in believing that a cannon with a calibre of around one metre could be built to fire a shell 600 miles. It appears that Henderson's intelligence was fed through by MI6 to a Restricted Enforcement Unit subgroup meeting on 10 November 1989. Peter Pigden, who attended for Customs and Excise, recalls the tone of the discussion: 'There was talk of a large gun, but I don't think anybody realized the scale of the thing. Some people there just couldn't believe something that size was feasible.'

While argument continued within intelligence circles about the feasibility of the BABYLON project and the desirability of trade with Baghdad, the government fended off Parliamentary questions. At around the time of the REU meeting – which had heard evidence that UK firms were helping to build the supergun – Margaret Thatcher told the House of Commons that British defence sales to Iran and Iraq would continue to be guided by the 1985 Howe criteria of even-handedness and the supply of only non-lethal material. But a secret DIS report also produced in the autumn of 1989 said almost the opposite: that the British exports were 'a very significant enhancement of the ability of Iraq to manufacture its own arms and thus to resume the war with Iran'.

In March 1990 Saddam Hussein's execution of the *Observer* journalist Farzad Bazoft intensified the inter-departmental angst over sales to Iraq. This became still more profound with the impounding of a shipment of krytrons – so-called 'nuclear triggers' – at Heathrow airport on 28 March. US intelligence had alerted the British to the shipment. Krytrons are used to give off a charge of energy to an accuracy of a fraction of a second. They can therefore be used to trigger the high explosive that surrounds the fissile core of a nuclear weapon. Another application of krytrons is for igniting the stages of a missile, which might also have interested the Iraqi military. The Heathrow operation was seen in Whitehall as a coup for the REU, although those convicted have insisted that they were shipping the devices for non-military use.

As the debate continued in Whitehall, another agency – one more ruthlessly committed to preventing the Iraqis from acquiring a supergun – took its own initiative. Gerald Bull was the world authority on long-range cannons; he had worked for the USA for years on a project to use them to launch spacecraft. When funds dried up for that project, he worked on extended-range artillery, producing a 155 mm cannon with a range one-third greater than any other on the battlefield. The Iraqis bought this gun during their war with Iran, and later bought Bull's expertise for the supergun. On 16 March Bull was assassinated outside his flat in Brussels. Mossad, the Israeli intelligence service which throughout the 1980s had waged its own campaign to sabotage the Iraqi quest for weapons of mass destruction, was believed by many to have been responsible.

At around the same time as the Heathrow krytron seizure, the SIS officer 'Mr Q' received a tip-off from yet another informant. David James, finance controller of Walter Sommers, told MI6 that he believed tubes under construction at his firm and at another called Sheffield Forgemasters were being made to Iraqi specifications for use as artillery. James later told Mr Q that a small-scale version of the supergun had already been shipped to the Middle East. These new reports were put before the Restricted Enforcement Unit on 30 March.

Although the espionage agencies had plenty of sources of their own, it appears to have been a tip-off from a foreign agency (possibly German) during the first week of April that alerted Whitehall to the fact that the main sections of the BABYLON gun were about to be shipped from Teesport. Mr Q and Peter Pigden took urgent action. Their investigation led them to Teesside. Pigden recalls, 'We only had a couple of days to see what we'd got. We did some initial checking . . . we asked whether an export licence had been granted and the answer was no.' On 10 April Customs and Excise impounded the sections of the gun barrel. Once the tubes had been seized, parallel investigations were carried out into Sheffield Forge-masters, which had built the sections, Matrix Churchill and Ordtec.

According to someone who was party to the deliberations by the Restricted Enforcement Unit, 'everybody agreed that [the gun] should be picked up'. The REU and Customs had acted in the belief that the supergun exports were illegal. But almost as soon as Customs had seized the tubes, certain people in government began to argue that because of changes in the export controls – changes denied by the Prime Minister in the Commons six months earlier – there was noth-ing unlawful about the proposed exports

Alan Clark had altered the guidelines for the DTI's Export Licens-ing Department. The change meant that Matrix Churchill only had to get clearance if it knew the goods were for military use. It also emerged later that Clark had encouraged firms to be extremely flexible in their interpretation of 'civil use'. A civil servant close to the operation says that the Restricted Enforcement Unit and Customs and Excise were unaware of this change when they decided to go ahead with the Teesside raid, believing that any unlicensed export by the Anglo-Iraqi firm was illegal. This represented a remarkable failure of communica-tion between the private office of the DTI Minister of State and the DTI representative on the Restricted Enforcement Unit.

In a further instance of poor co-ordination between government departments, the DIS refused to provide Customs and Excise with expert advice during the investigation that followed the Teesport seizure. This left the Customs team angry and bewildered, as it had been a DIS expert's assessment of intelligence early in 1990 that had played a key role in the decision by the Restricted Enforcement Unit and Customs to seize the tubes.

Not only had the debate within Whitehall about changing the export rules left everybody thoroughly confused, but problems were to arise when Customs pursued its Matrix Churchill investigation, coming closer and closer to Henderson, SIS's main source of intelli-gence. An MI6 officer says it was 'a miscommunication between Whitehall departments of monumental proportions . . . the magni-tude of what went wrong was quite awful'.

As Customs investigators probed Matrix Churchill, any hopes MI6 might have had that the investigation would leave Henderson untouched were dashed. The civil servant close to these events says the lawyers consulted by Customs and Excise as they planned their prosecution were unaware of Henderson's SIS role.

The DTI also had hopes that the prosecution might peter out: a memo from Michael Coolican (an official who later headed the Restricted Enforcement Unit) to Nicholas Ridley, the Secretary of State for Trade and Industry, on 14 June pointed out that the 'action proposed by Customs will add to the problems posed by the gun. For the DTI the timing is extraordinarily embarrassing.' By September 1990 a government solicitor had decided that Sheffield Forgemasters had not acted illegally and the supergun case was dropped. The investigators pushed ahead, though, with their case against Matrix Churchill, and in late June they raided Paul Henderson's office. MI6's prime source had become Customs and Excise's prime suspect.

Nobody found this reversal of fortune harder to believe than Henderson himself; he co-operated fully with the Customs investigators, thinking he was quite safe. He would later say that he had been motivated by patriotism: 'The fact that the intelligence services kept returning meant that what I was giving them was useful and that it was helping my country.'

By October 1990, following the invasion of Kuwait, preparations were under way for British military action against Iraq – and Henderson was in jail. SIS and MI5 distanced themselves from their sources. Gutteridge was told by an MI5 officer not to mention their connection if he was interviewed by Customs. Customs had also become aware of Henderson's work for MI6, but the intelligence services were ready to drop him. A memo later made public remarked unsympathetically that the Matrix Churchill managing director had been told by his handlers that 'any illegal activity . . . was entirely his own responsibility, and we could not, nor would we, help him in any way'. Ministers were later to prepare Public Interest Immunity Certificates for the court case, in an attempt to prevent the role of the intelligence services – and with it, the possibility that ministers had known about the firm's actions all along – becoming public.

Events in Kuwait compounded the government's embarrassment, producing a flurry of Parliamentary questions, an investigation by the Trade and Industry Select Committee, and finally the Scott inquiry. The allegation by Hal Miller, Conservative MP for the constituency containing Walter Sommers' works, that he had told the intelligence services about the supergun project in 1988 was particularly damaging.

Amid the furore, Percy Cradock asked Colin McColl, Chief of SIS, for an explanation.

McColl's written reply of 28 November was subsequently obtained by the Scott inquiry. In it, the SIS Chief muddied the waters by suggesting that the confused reports in 1988 had alluded either to a normal-sized artillery piece of 155 mm or to larger tubes that were 'not recognised as artillery'. In his report published in February 1996, Scott wrote scathingly about the way McColl had handled the matter. He said that the SIS internal briefing notes McColl had relied upon in writing his 28 November letter to Cradock 'lent no support to the view that there had been any confusion'. Scott's investigation found that MI6 knew the key details of the project by October 1989, but had not told the Foreign Secretary about it. Scott concluded that McColl's letter to Cradock had been 'apt to mislead': the Chief of SIS had tried to cover up his organization's failure to pass on vital intelligence.

When the Matrix Churchill trial went ahead in 1992, the judge, Brian Smedley, threw out the ministerial Public Interest Immunity Certificates. Alan Clark dropped the fiction he and other government ministers had previously sustained, that they had not known the machine tools had military applications, and the court case collapsed, at a cost of £3 million to the taxpayer. In court Clark paraphrased the words of Edmund Burke, and of Robert Armstrong in the *Spycatcher* hearings, by saying of the government line: 'It's our old friend being economical . . . with the *actualité*.'

At the subsequent Scott inquiry, several government figures were to claim ignorance about aspects of the intelligence on Matrix Churchill's activities. Iraq's arms procurement network and Britain's place in it had been the subject of several intelligence reports circulated to ministers; DIS had produced one in 1989, for example. Assertions by Waldegrave that, while at the Foreign Office, he had not known the purpose of the machine tools caused raised eyebrows among mandarins, one of whom adds, 'I'm very sceptical about these "If only I'd known" statements.'

Was there a possibility, however, that ministers like Waldegrave had simply been overwhelmed by the number of reports crossing their desks? That warnings about Iraq which seemed so ominous in the light of the later invasion of Kuwait had at the time appeared no different from warnings about several other countries that were developing their defence industries? Most of those to whom I put these questions were sceptical, but one former member of the JIC

Assessments Staff did concede these possibilities and the need to share the blame, adding, 'As far as I'm concerned, it's an intelligence failure if you don't sell your intelligence properly to the ministers who ought to be reading it.'

The birth of counter-proliferation as a post-Cold War intelligence priority was hardly an easy one. As with counter-terrorism, a variety of agencies jostled uneasily with enforcement authorities and politicians. Government hypocrisy in supplying machine tools to Iraq while publicly claiming there had been no change in policy had its parallels in many other trade relationships, according to civil servants. Until Iraq bought into Matrix Churchill in October 1987, exports had in any case been minimal compared to those by France or a host of other countries. The really painful lesson of the affair lay in the bureaucratic incompetence with which officials unsure of their respective roles had fumbled top-grade intelligence, and in the readiness of MI6, MI5 and government ministers to throw their informers to the courts.

Already during the summer of 1990, attempts were being made to improve counter-proliferation procedures in Whitehall, to strengthen export licensing and to commit greater resources to information-gathering. The deeper questions about how government and the agencies could stand by the people who provided such vital information would not even begin to be asked until the Matrix Churchill trial, and with it the attempt to cover up Whitehall's knowledge, collapsed in November 1992. Mark Gutteridge, the long-term MI5 source, commented, 'British intelligence has relied on businessmen as sources of information. Who on earth would want to talk to them now?'

The key period of the supergun saga, from mid-1989 to the summer of 1990, coincided with another drama for British intelligence concerning weapons of mass destruction. In this particular case, these concerns dovetailed with long-running disputes about the nature of reform in the Soviet Union and the honesty of its principal architect.

Chapter 10

1990 Black Death
on the Nevsky Prospekt

On 8 June 1990 Margaret Thatcher was driven across Moscow for a meeting with Mikhail Gorbachev at the Kremlin. Among the items on the agenda was one placed there by British intelligence – an issue which they regarded as a basic matter of trust in the Russian leader.

During the autumn of 1989 the Secret Intelligence Service had welcomed a defector whose information was to prove critical both for the uncovering of some of Moscow's darkest Cold War secrets and for the fortunes of MI6 in Whitehall. It would also lead to the long-simmering disagreement between the Prime Minister and her principal intelligence adviser over the sincerity of Gorbachev developing into a rift.

Vladimir Pasechnik, Director of the Research Institute for Especially Pure Biological Preparations in Leningrad, defected to Britain because of his deep concern about the uses to which his research was being put. In 1993 I became the first journalist to interview him. Pasechnik explained his decision to defect as resulting from 'feelings like misunderstanding, anxiety and then disgust – disgust towards this programme and to himself and to the people who have been involved in the programme'. This programme involved creating bacteria and viruses for use in biological weapons.

Although Pasechnik had been the institute's director since 1975, he says he was never made aware of the fact that his research violated the 1972 Biological Weapons Convention signed by the USSR. The treaty specifically banned all development of offensive weapons, although it accepted that minute quantities of biological warfare agents might be used in laboratories to help in developing antidotes and other defensive precautions.

SIS had long known about the Soviet programme. Arkady Shevchenko, the Soviet UN diplomat who had defected in New York several years earlier, had told Western intelligence about his role in preparing the Warsaw Pact papers for the 1972 convention and the cynicism of the military leadership towards it. The USA had publicly accused the Soviet Union of pursuing such research after an anthrax outbreak in Sverdlovsk, a city in the Urals, in 1979 killed scores of people. Moscow had blamed the infection on bad meat. What neither MI6 nor the CIA had realized before Pasechnik's defection was that they had been looking in the wrong places for this research. Western intelligence had assumed it was going on in army laboratories – the Sverdlovsk outbreak came from a closed area of the city ominously known as Military Compound 19. In fact, an entire network for developing biological weapons had grown up under the cover of the Ministry of Health. Pasechnik's institute was one of the four principal ones of the organisation, which was named Biopreperat. Douglas Hogg, later Minister of State at the Foreign Office, confirms that Pasechnik's intelligence 'reinforced a whole range of suspicions and information that we already had, but the information he gave us was very significant'.

By the early 1980s Biopreperat had 25,000 staff. Some of them were involved in emerging areas of civil biotechnology – an activity that was both a cover and, increasingly, a source of revenue for the organization. Its Leningrad laboratory worked on 'weaponizing' agents, trying to find the right concentrations of powder for filling bombs and the best way for the bombs to disperse those agents. A special chamber for studying how they would be scattered was built there. The actual manufacture of the agents went on elsewhere, however; a Biopreperat facility at Obolensk – a secret place, not far from Moscow, known in the late 1980s by its postcode only – worked on the bacteria themselves. It sent vaccine strains (that is, harmless if they escaped the lab) to Leningrad, where techniques for the mass-production of such agents in time of war and 'weaponization' were investigated.

The biological warfare arsenal also contained another whole family of diseases: viral infections. An institute at Koltsevo in Siberia, thousands of miles to the east, studied military uses of certain viruses. At Vozrozdeniye Island in the Aral Sea, a *poligon* or test range was constructed to try out the lethality and dispersal of the preparations on tethered animals.

Pasechnik's early work had involved tularaemia, a debilitating but not usually lethal bacterial infection. According to Pasechnik, this work went on from 1983 to 1985. Late in 1984 Pasechnik attended a meeting of the Biopreparat scientific council in Moscow which endorsed a work plan for 1985–90. It included a new programme to develop plague – the Black Death of medieval times – for use in weapons.

Part of the research involved breeding plague bacteria in vats containing antibiotics so as to create strains that were immune. The aim, of course, was to prevent the potential targets of such weapons from immunizing or treating their population. Biopreparat executives understood both the virtues and the limitations of such weapons. A bomb containing plague was not suitable for use on the battlefield, because the disease would take some time to incubate; chemical or nuclear weapons could produce the immediate results that might result in a breakthrough. On the other hand, biological agents were the only weapons of mass destruction that could be denied. An outbreak of plague which killed 100,000 people could be blamed by its perpetrators on nature.

Pasechnik says there were discussions 'about the possibility of using biological preparations in various military actions, including subversive activity . . . because it can be produced very easily and applied in such a way that it could be very difficult to discover . . . terrorists might introduce it in a city and then deny it.' It was the 'feeling of horror' engendered by such research which led him to defect.

Although the objectives of Biopreparat's work were startling, Pasechnik also brought evidence that they had not yet overcome certain scientific hurdles and that the entire organization functioned with the inefficiency typical of bloated secret bureaucracies in the Soviet system. The cultivation of plague bacteria that could resist antibiotics presented many difficulties, notably that with each exposure to a different type of possible antidote, the resulting bacteria became more feeble. Pasechnik says, 'The loss of biological activity during all technological processes was quite high, extremely high, I would say . . . this problem is quite complicated, in fact, and as far as I know it wasn't solved efficiently.'

As the work went on year after year, says Pasechnik, considerable cynicism grew up among the staff, particularly those from a military background who had previous experience of expensive but unproductive military research in the Soviet system. At the same time, scientists at the institute were well treated by Soviet standards. The result was mixed feelings typical of the Soviet 'era of stagnation'. 'People used to say, "We're involved in a highly-paid job, there's no reason to change it,"' says Pasechnik, 'but at the same time there were sad feelings about the uselessness of this programme and its vicious characteristics.'

The fact that the Biopreperat labs were not meeting the scientific targets set for them by the Moscow hierarchy – in that they hadn't succeeded in making an effective plague bomb –was of only limited interest to SIS. Their managers saw in Pasechnik's testimony *prima facie* evidence of a breach of international law, as the 1972 treaty banned any work on the offensive uses of biological agents. The Cabinet Office was kept informed as debriefing progressed.

The evidence SIS got from Pasechnik was complemented by the researches of a group of analysts in London into how the Biopreperat programme had been hidden in the Ministry of Health. They charted the evolution of this covert programme from its creation in 1973 by General Vsevolod Ogarkov. Key figures in the supposedly civilian hierarchy turned out to be 'retired' generals. The combined dossier was used to brief the Prime Minister prior to her departure for Moscow in June. Percy Cradock, Chairman of the Joint Intelligence Committee, convinced her that she should raise the biological weapons question in the Kremlin.

Thatcher wrote in her memoirs that she used the 8 June meeting 'to raise with him the evidence which we had gleaned that the Soviet Union was doing research into biological weapons – something which he emphatically denied but nonetheless promised to investigate'. Those in British intelligence who had never trusted Gorbachev deduced that he was lying. He had given a similar response to President George Bush when they met a few days before the British leader's visit.

That summer, there was an exchange between Cradock and the Prime Minister over whether Gorbachev knew about this continued biological and chemical weapons development. According to one person who saw a note of their conversation, she told him that she believed Gorbachev was being deceived by his generals. Cradock replied that this was about as likely as her being deceived by hers. Ever since the December 1984 meeting, the Prime Minister had decided to place her trust in Gorbachev. Although they had had many lively disagreements during the intervening years – notably about how best to ensure the future security of Europe – she remained a strong believer in his integrity and felt that he was the right man to reform the crumbling Soviet empire.

For the JIC Chairman, Thatcher's emphasis on her personal relationship with Gorbachev had gone too far, obscuring wider issues and other key personalities. In his interview for this book, Cradock praised the Prime Minister's early rapport with Gorbachev, saying, 'It allowed us to encourage change in the right direction.' But he added, 'The relationship got out of hand and developed an intense, almost emotional quality which warped judgement. It became difficult to persuade her that Gorbachev was aware of some of the darker aspects of the Soviet system. More seriously, there was a failure to recognize that, for all his remarkable qualities, he was a transitional figure.'

Charles Powell, her Private Secretary, witnessed these disagreements. He notes that the Prime Minister 'was horrified and found it very hard to accept' that the Kremlin was party to the continuing nerve-gas and biological weapons development, and confirms, 'She was convinced that Gorbachev had been misled by the military establishment. Percy disagreed about that, but I wouldn't be so sceptical as Percy.'

Thatcher does not comment directly on this argument in her memoirs, but does say that 'doubts were increasingly raised about the wisdom of supporting Mr Gorbachev'. She says she decided to maintain her policy because of personal loyalty to him, and because 'it did not seem to me that at the time anyone was better able than Mr Gorbachev to push ahead with reform'. Who was right, Thatcher or Cradock?

Pasechnik says that the Biopreparat network was run by a special section of the Communist Party of the Soviet Union Central Committee and by a department of the VPK, the Military Industrial Commission. Gorbachev stood at the apex of both these structures.

Vil Mirzayanov, the scientist who exposed the continuing nerve-gas development in later newspaper articles, points to the award of the Lenin Prize to senior officers by the General Secretary in person in April 1991 as evidence of Gorbachev's complicity in the other area of suspected covert weapons development. Lieutenant-General Anatoly Kuntsevich, a senior Chemical Troops officer who was later put in charge of destroying chemical weapons, and Viktor Petrunin, Director of the institute in which the new A-230 nerve gas was developed, both received the honour.

After Gorbachev's fall, the Russian government admitted that there had been an offensive biological warfare programme, in contravention of the 1972 treaty, and banned it. Officials at the Soviet (later the Russian) Foreign Ministry, who had themselves been kept in the dark about the continued development of such weapons, said that the Soviet government had not answered British and US questions honestly. Asked why Gorbachev had not been frank, Gregory Berdennikov, the Russian Deputy Foreign Minister who dealt with arms control, replied, 'I can only speculate. Maybe it was the fact that it was in violation of an agreement [the 1972 treaty].'

British intelligence analysts would argue that Gorbachev had encouraged the scientists to keep on working as a response to President Reagan's Strategic Defence Initiative. During their early summit meetings, the Soviet leader had indeed threatened unspecified action if the US continued with Star Wars research. Had the chemical and biological research been held as a military reserve or some sort of diplomatic bargaining chip?

In my 1995 interview with Gorbachev, I asked him whether he felt he had been deceived by his generals on the issue of chemical weapons. He said that while such men had been 'in no great hurry to introduce conversion [to civilian production], rather they preferred to preserve their military industrial complex', they had ultimately followed his lead in agreeing to a whole variety of arms control agreements. It seems likely that the Soviet leader was aware that certain research was still being conducted (and in this sense he was not telling Thatcher everything that he knew), but he did accept that there was foot-dragging among certain elements of the military. He was probably reassured during the 1987–9 period that the Soviet Union could still hold some stocks of nerve gas quite legitimately as some of the Geneva negotiations did envisage the US and USSR each retaining up to 5,000 tonnes. On the issue of biological agents, even people in the institutes working on the preparations appear to have succumbed to the delusion that the absence of 'weaponized' plague or anthrax (agent stored in shells or bombs) meant their programme accorded with the 1972 Convention. So while the Prime Minister did place too much trust in Gorbachev's assurances, the frequent suggestions by intelligence analysts in Whitehall that he was telling lies over such matters were an over-simplification.

In time, Biopreperat would argue that its work, including the testing of agent dispersal from bombs and the slaughter of hundreds of animals at Vozrozdeniye Island, had been purely defensive. Coming after so many years of denials that the organization was involved in military activity at all, this lacked credibility. When I eventually managed to visit Pasechnik's former workplace for the BBC, one scientist there told me the director 'would put Black Death on the Nevsky Prospekt if Moscow told him to'.

Pasechnik had been a defector rather than an agent in place. The Biopreperat episode and others encouraged the intelligence mandarins to retain Moscow as their number one target for the recruitment of human sources. SIS saw in the increasingly corrupt and chaotic environment of the Soviet Union fertile ground for recruitment. Although it is clear that the CIA traitor Aldrich Ames was doing his best to betray any Western attempts to recruit new agents, SIS was only sharing information with its main partner to a limited extent, precisely because of the risk of compromise. There would be signs that MI6 succeeded in recruiting several new Russian agents during the period 1990-1.

Colin McColl, Chief of SIS, and his number two Barrie Gane, Director of Requirements and Production, saw in the ferment of the former Soviet Bloc a chance to realize the dreams of their professional lives and gain a decisive advantage over their old foe, the KGB. According to an intelligence community insider, the new Chief had, shortly after taking office, begun a review of SIS activities that had continued throughout 1989. The east European revolutions caused much last-minute debate among McColl and his directors. The result was a blueprint for an improved, post-Cold War Service. On the administrative side, this involved the move to a new headquarters and the installation of the latest information technology. Operationally, it meant rapid adjustment to the new realities.

SIS stations in the formerly Communist countries of eastern Europe were transformed, beginning in Poland and Czechoslovakia. The resources devoted to these bases were reduced, and the remaining SIS officer was in each case 'declared' to the newly-installed democratic authorities. Their role was transformed into one of liaising with and assisting the intelligence services of eastern Europe. At the same time, the growing freedom of movement into and out of the Soviet Union allowed greater opportunities for deep-cover SIS officers to travel and find new agents. The Soviet economic crisis, which meant that everything had its price – in Western currency – would soon, according to MI6 officers, produce more 'walk-ins' than the Service wanted.

The worsening shortages back home led increasing numbers of KGB officers stationed abroad to concentrate on money-making rather than spying. Vladimir Kryuchkov, the First Chief Directorate head elevated to the Chairmanship of the KGB, was by inclination a Cold Warrior, but found himself under orders from Gorbachev to co-operate with Western agencies and gather political intelligence with the aim of boosting the Kremlin's foreign policy drives. Yuri Shvets, the KGB Washington station officer who later wrote a book, recalls that even in the late 1980s an analyst in Moscow told him, 'Kryuchkov is at a loss regarding the kind of information he needs ... we are painfully looking for a new concept that could serve as a guide when preparing analytical reports.' KGB and foreign service officers in the field were looking after their own interests, their bosses uncertain of what organizational strategy to follow.

In mid-1990 a new officer took over from Gerry Warner as the new Director of Counter Intelligence and Security at Century House. His job was to take advantage of the faltering morale of the KGB to recruit as many of its key members as possible. He had served in some of the traditional hunting-grounds for agents in foreign espionage and diplomatic services: Geneva and New York, both centres of international organizations. SIS's method – to use station officers in embassies anywhere in the world to talent-spot the discontented KGB or GRU operatives, and then to have visiting deep-cover officers from London run the new case – did not change. However, the circumstances had become more favourable, and McColl wanted to use the officers freed up from eastern Europe to help with this new drive.

In Moscow, the leadership found itself increasingly besieged by radical reformers who wanted faster change and conservatives who believed the achievements of seventy years were being betrayed.

On 7 February 1990 the Central Committee of the Communist Party of the Soviet Union abandoned one of its basic principles – one-party rule – thus clearing the way for genuine elections. Supreme Soviets, the self-styled 'parliaments' of the republics, were now making increasingly explicit references to independence. The Central Committee's historic declaration, an attempt to head off the political stresses within the Union, simply seemed to encourage the radical reformers. A month later, the Lithuanian Supreme Soviet declared itself independent. Three weeks after that, the Estonian assembly followed suit by announcing that it would seek secession from the Union. Western Kremlin-watchers were puzzled by the nationalist agenda: political statements like those from the Baltic republics sounded explosive, but equally seemed unrealistic, given the interdependence of the different elements of the Soviet Union in everything from energy to air traffic control.

As the nationalists in the Soviet republics felt their way towards the independence which they could see achieved in Poland or Hungary, a similar process was going on, little-reported, in the Socialist Federation of Yugoslavia. There, the unhappy marriage of Serbs, Croats, Muslims, Slovenes and Macedonians through constitutional arrangements drawn up after the Second World War was being put to the test. Slovenia, bordering on Austria and Italy, echoed the role of the Baltic republics by spearheading the nationalist agenda. Croatia followed close behind. The Slovenes and Croats were both motivated by economic factors – the feeling that they, as the most advanced republics, were propping up the other members of the Federation – as well as by purely political nationalism. There were multi-party elections in Slovenia in April, and in Croatia in May. These installed nationalist leaderships that would soon be at work pulling apart the Federation.

There were a number of parallels between Yugoslavia and the USSR, the most important of them for western Europe being the attitude of their armed forces. Decades of propaganda had billed the Yugoslav People's Army and the Soviet Army as 'schools of internationalism' or of 'the brotherhood of nations'. The general staffs of both armies considered themselves the guardians of internationalist values, and viewed the increasingly bold actions of the nationalists with alarm. In time, the most deeply-ingrained sentiments of most Yugoslav and Soviet generals would emerge – the desire specifically to serve their Serbian and Russian heritage respectively – but before that could happen they first had to try (and fail) to protect the internationalist order by force.

In the Soviet Army, soldiers withdrawn from eastern Europe were living in tents. Officers felt the worsening shortages of basic goods along with everyone else. Down south in Nagorno-Karabakh, troops were dying fighting the nationalists. Evidence of disquiet in the Soviet General Staff was being picked up by British intelligence.

At the Cabinet Office, Gloria Craig, a Ministry of Defence civil servant, had taken over the running of the Soviet Bloc Current

Intelligence Group from Harry Burke. Gordon Barrass, the SIS analyst who had debriefed Gordievsky, was one of the two Deputy Chiefs of Assessments who ran the groups of experts analysing intelligence. Both were temperamentally less inclined to be tough on Gorbachev than Burke had been, and saw dangers in the growing unrest. Craig put a number of papers up to the JIC on the possible consequences of military discontent. Margaret Thatcher says in her memoirs, 'Throughout the summer of 1990 there were disturbing reports of possible rebellious activity within the Soviet military. Their authenticity was never certain, but they carried some credibility.' The uncertainty arose from the continuing absence of high-level human sources or sigint, but the papers indicated the JIC's growing belief that a military coup was possible.

The spread of armed conflict, particularly in the Caucasus, led certain nationalists, initially in the Baltic republics, to begin supporting draft-dodgers. Estonian or Latvian youths did not want to go to Armenia to suppress the nationalist movement there. This development was viewed with the utmost concern by the Soviet General Staff. In London, Tom King, then Defence Secretary, noted, 'The failure of conscription was one of the things that really indicated that the thing was coming apart. In a way, conscription had been the cement for the whole system.'

Under the Soviet Constitution, which dated from Stalin's time, the Russian Federation, at the core of the Soviet Union, lacked many of the institutions and trappings of the other republics. An Azerbaijan KGB or a Ukrainian Foreign Ministry existed, for example, even though traditionally they were firmly in the grip of local party élites linked to the CPSU and pledged to the continued existence of the Union. As the traditional system of Party control broke down in the outlying republics, certain organizations were therefore at the disposal of the new leaders. Russian nationalists took note.

On 29 May 1990 members of the Supreme Soviet of the Russian Federation voted to appoint Boris Nikolayevich Yeltsin as their chairman. This legislature was one of the very few specifically Russian institutions. Yeltsin was a traditional Communist boss who had successfully reinvented himself as a reformer while working as the head of the Moscow party organization. His outspoken style had led Gorbachev to sack him from the Politburo, creating bitterness between them. Increasingly, members of the Supreme Soviet saw Yeltsin as leader of the opposition to Gorbachev. From a base in the

1970s block on the Moscow River dubbed the 'White House' by locals, Yeltsin began the slow process of creating a power base for himself.

The growing assertiveness of this Supreme Soviet appealed to ordinary Russians, who entertained a variety of prejudices about the inhabitants of the outlying republics. Many believed that Russia would be better off if it could go it alone and stop subsidizing the other republics. Long-time Communists in the Supreme Soviet reflected on these arguments, as they also reflected on those from the other extremes: members still loyal to Marxist ideology who believed that Gorbachev was throwing away decades of 'socialist gains', and the small number of radical nationalists who saw Russia's relationship with the Georgians or Kazakhs in traditional imperialistic terms – and also wanted to protect the sizeable Russian minorities in many of the outlying republics. Russians dubbed this latter tendency the Red–Brown Alliance – red for old Communists, brown for fascist nationalists. Red–Brown ideas began taking root among army officers.

On 2 July 1990 the 28th Congress of the Communist Party of the Soviet Union opened in Moscow; it was to be its last. The 27th Congress in 1986 had provided Gorbachev with an early platform for mapping out his vision of reform; in 1990, however, the Congress was for him more a battle for political survival. The party faithful were nervous about the Central Committee's decision to renounce its monopoly of power. Gorbachev had taken the title of President and was hoping that assuming greater personal power would help to hold the crumbling Union together. The Congress showed how embattled he had now become, fighting off criticism from all sides. Many began to look to new leaders.

In London, few on the JIC could predict what the emergence of Yeltsin's Supreme Soviet as a new Russian power base would bring. A memo which described as 'exaggerated' the suggestion that Yeltsin might become more powerful than Gorbachev was later quoted by the Prime Minister as a 'less than perspicacious' reading of events. Someone who served in the Cabinet Office suggests that the report Thatcher obliquely refers to in her memoirs was prepared by Gloria Craig and Percy Cradock. The fact that she mentioned it in her book is unusual, not only because it was a quotation from an intelligence assessment (although she does not say so explicitly) but also because she used it to make an implied criticism of these officials. It does indicate how difficult it was during this period for the JIC to predict events with authority, and how politicians were aware of these limitations.

The fact that the Prime Minister was being accused by her principal intelligence adviser of 'warped judgement' was not perhaps so extraordinary in view of how beleaguered she had become by that summer. Arguments about policy over Europe and financial integration had seen the departure of Nigel Lawson and Geoffrey Howe, two of her key Cabinet ministers, from the posts of Chancellor and Foreign Secretary the previous year. There was growing dissent within her party over the poll tax, her attempt to reform local authority finance. The belief that she had 'lost touch' became a familiar refrain among those who sought a challenge for the Party leadership that autumn.

However, Cradock was an official, not a Conservative grandee. His disagreements with the Prime Minister can therefore be regarded as quite different from the Cabinet rough-and-tumble. He had never really believed in Gorbachev, but ever since her visit to Moscow in 1987 Thatcher had been an enthusiast of his internal programme of *perestroika* if not for aspects of his foreign policy. The disagreement was therefore symptomatic of a divergence of opinion about the central question of foreign policy – and of the marginalization of intelligence over that issue. The absence of good agents or sigint blunted the JIC's impact on policy and meant that on many matters it was only able to 'analyse open source' or, to put it another way, to read the newspapers or watch television like everyone else. The verdict of Charles Powell, the Private Secretary so often by the Prime Minister's side during those tumultuous years, is damning: 'I don't think intelligence as such played a big role in our view of Gorbachev.'

At the Nato summit held in July 1990 at Turnberry in Scotland, the alliance's leaders gathered to reshape the organization now that its adversary had ceased to be part of an effective alliance. The meeting brought further disagreements between Thatcher, the Germans and the USA about nuclear weapons. The leaders agreed on a communiqué which talked about adopting 'a new Nato strategy making nuclear forces truly weapons of last resort'. They also accepted that Soviet withdrawals in eastern Europe and the prospect of a Conventional Forces in Europe treaty made deep defence cuts possible. Their communiqué declared the Cold War officially over; this would soon have direct financial consequences for Britain's armed forces.

However, unlike the Prime Minister, virtually everyone in the Cabinet and the leaders of the Nato member states, Cradock did not consider that the Cold War had ended. He told me that, for him, the decisive moment did not come until after the failure of the 1991 Moscow coup. Cradock's views were representative of those of many intelligence chiefs in Whitehall. They pointed to the possibility of a reversal of fortunes in Moscow, the reimposition of a rigorous Communist dictatorship. They were deeply worried about instability and what might become of the Kremlin's weapons of mass destruction. The continued existence of the Communist Party in power in Moscow was for many in intelligence a vital indication that change had not been, in the words of the 1989 Defence White Paper, 'fundamental and irreversible'. The fact that the spymasters still believed in the Cold War was reflected at this time in the absence of any review of their activities to match the one that was under way in the Ministry of Defence.

The MoD's rethink, entitled Options For Change, was formally announced in the House of Commons on 25 July 1990, after extensive leaking of the various proposals. Tom King, the Defence Secretary, revealed that the principal cuts would be in forces stationed in Germany: the British Army of the Rhine would be reduced by half, and RAF Germany would be cut from four air bases to two. He described the aim of the exercise as 'smaller forces, better equipped, properly trained and housed, and well motivated'. The overall reduction in manpower was planned to be around 18 per cent. King commended his blueprint for change as 'an orderly and planned transition to the new world that is now unfolding'.

Many within the armed forces criticized the plans as 'Treasury-driven'; the planners started with the sum by which they wished to reduce expenditure, and then had worked out which forces or equipment programmes would need to be cut to comply. But the way in which the military would have preferred to see the rethink carried out – deciding on the UK's defence needs and then working out the kind of forces needed to meet them – would have been so full of subjective judgements that ministers and officials would find it impossible to agree on. The country had, in any case, for years been spending a far higher proportion of its national wealth on defence than most of its Nato allies.

Even the Bush Administration had imposed spending curbs on the Pentagon, well before Britain followed suit. Tom King argues, 'The truth was, it was right to maintain a pretty steady military posture as we watched as spectators. It seemed an anomalous situation at the time in Nato, as our adversary appeared to be retreating but it was too early to start dismantling . . . with hindsight we certainly could have cut earlier, that's true. But we would have been taking a risk. We have to remember certain things had changed irreversibly and certain things hadn't.'

The ebbing of Soviet power and the rise of nationalism seemed to be dissolving the cement that had held certain international relationships stable for forty years. Within weeks of the Nato summit, Iraqi tanks would be streaming across the Kuwaiti desert, Whitehall would be grappling with the realities of that increasingly uncertain world, and the Ministry of Defence would be discovering how much military capability the heavy-spending Thatcher years had really bought them.

Chapter 11

1990 Assault on Kuwait

On 17 July 1990, at a Revolution Day celebration in Baghdad, Saddam Hussein told the Iraqi people that their dispute with Kuwait might soon be settled by force of arms. It was a threat noticed in the intelligence agencies in Washington and London.

Iraq had a number of long-standing arguments with its southern neighbour. Under Ottoman rule, the area which had become Kuwait was part of the same administrative region as Iraq. Bellicose elements in Baghdad had long referred to it as Iraq's 'nineteenth province'. In 1960 Britain had deployed troops to Kuwait at a time of similar threats against the small emirate, an action regarded by many in Whitehall as a textbook case of effective deterrence. In addition to their broad lack of respect for Kuwait's independence, Iraqis questioned the demarcation of the border between the countries, claiming Warbah and Bubiyan, two islands under Kuwaiti control at the mouth of Iraq's narrow outlet to the Gulf. The two countries had an arrangement to share the output from the Rumaillah oil field, which straddled the disputed border, but Iraq accused its southern neighbour of cheating by pumping more than the agreed amount.

Throughout 1990, the simmering ill-will between the two states had focused on this issue of oil production. Kuwait and the other Arab Gulf states had bankrolled Iraq throughout its war with Iran, fearing the consequences of victory by the Ayatollah's regime. After the war, Saddam had carried out only a limited demobilization of his substantial armed forces, and had committed the country to ambitious defence enterprises, such as the development of nuclear weapons and the supergun. These were part of his long-term plan to use Iraq's considerable riches to acquire political leadership of the Arab world – and to back up his threats to 'burn half of Israel' – but they required continued funding.

The end of the Iran-Iraq war in 1988 allowed both countries to step up their oil exports, bringing to a head the issue of Middle East over-production. The Iraqi leader believed that Kuwait was organizing the other Gulf states to oppose increases in Iraqi oil sales, and considered this an aggressive policy.

Kuwait consists of a coastal conurbation surrounded by a desert bereft of natural obstacles. Its featureless frontier was virtually indefensible. The army – just three brigades of poorly-trained troops (a total of 16,000 men) – might have been able to make some sort of stand around Kuwait City, but it was far too small to secure the border. Britain had a long-standing security relationship with Kuwait; a British Liaison Team of about fifty servicemen and women were in the country, advising on training and the tricky task of keeping the country's fleet of elderly Chieftain tanks serviceable.

Kuwaitis had grown lazy on their immense oil wealth. Expatriate workers outnumbered natives; Palestinians, Egyptians, Syrians and Pakistanis had worked there by the hundred thousand, and many envied the riches of which they had been allowed a small share. An experiment in constitutional democracy had been shelved by the Emir, Sheikh Jaber al-Sabah, after mild criticism from an assembly of local worthies. The day after Saddam's Revolution Day speech, the Kuwaiti ruler had placed the army briefly on alert. Positions close to the Iraqi border had been occupied and then relinquished as the Emir and his family decided that even such feeble attempts at self-defence might provoke the Iraqis.

On 24 July, as the Kuwaitis returned to barracks, the USA announced that it had detected the movement of two Iraqi divisions towards the border with Kuwait. The Republican Guard armoured formations (the Hammurabi and Medina divisions) would spearhead the assault. The deployment, consisting of about 20,000 troops with hundreds of vehicles, was spotted by US KH-11 photographic reconnaissance satellites. During its war with Iran, Iraq had benefited from US advice on how to defeat space-based intelligence-gathering, but its generals knew that a substantial invasion force could not be assembled without its being noticed. What they did do, however, was to maintain tight communications security to prevent eavesdroppers from learning of their intentions. The Iraqis had installed a national system of secure land lines, allowing generals to organize the coming operation without UK or US sigint being able to detect it. When giving orders to the troops massing on the Kuwaiti border, care was taken not to send sensitive instructions over tactical radios and so reveal the plan.

Few experts were available to deal with information about the crisis. Intelligence bureaucracies were still very much focused on the Soviet Union. At the Pentagon's Defence Intelligence Agency, there were just two people assigned to Iraq. At the Defence Intelligence Staff, DIA's British equivalent, a slightly larger number of specialists in the Rest of the World Directorate (known within the Ministry as RoW) covered the entire Gulf. Despite the intelligence about Iraq's growing arms industry received from the Matrix Churchill agents, there were huge gaps in their knowledge. As Lieutenant-General Derek Boorman, the former Chief of Defence Intelligence, concedes, the effort 'was under-resourced. There wasn't enough scientific and technical input, and that was shown up by the Gulf War.'

At the Foreign Office, the Iraq desk effectively consisted of one young diplomat, Mark Higson. He says he had failed to grasp the degree to which Iraq had remained mobilized after the war with Iran. MI6 and JIC reports were, in his opinion, 'completely useless – you'd get stuff which you'd actually read in yesterday's *Evening Standard*'.

The low priority assigned to Iraq is easy to criticize in retrospect, but every intelligence agency is limited in the resources it can devote to a particular country, even one as heavily-armed as Iraq. What resources they did have remained, at the insistence of intelligence mandarins, focused on the Soviet Union rather than dispersed across a variety of possible targets around the world.

Whitehall was keen to avoid any repetition of the intelligence failure that had preceded the Falklands invasion of 2 April 1982. The Franks Committee subsequently investigated why the government had been taken by surprise, and although the Committee partially exonerated it – noting the impossibility of reading Argentine intentions – it also showed up many faults in the collection and analysis of intelligence. At the time of the invasion SIS only had a single officer in the whole of South America, GCHQ a single man on duty covering the south Atlantic.

Although indications of the Argentine fleet leaving port had been picked up, these had been misinterpreted in London. Many thought that one key reason why Whitehall was wrong-footed was the fact that diplomatic talks about the future of the islands were still being held at the time. After the Falklands conflict, the resources available to the Joint Intelligence Committee were expanded, and it was removed from the authority of the Foreign Office and given greater independence under the Cabinet Office.

The gathering crisis in the Gulf would test the central intelligence machinery as rebuilt by Percy Cradock and his predecessor Anthony Duff. There were differences between the two crises, of course; Kuwait was not a British possession, and could not therefore be expected to receive the same intelligence priority. There were also similarities, for as Iraqi tanks were unloaded from railway trucks and road transporters around the southern city of Basra, there were diplomatic attempts to mediate the conflict. It would also be a test of the Prime Minister herself, since good intelligence warning is meaningless if there is no political will to exploit it.

As the Iraqi troop movement was publicly announced on 24 July 1990, the Middle East Current Intelligence Group of the JIC met at the Cabinet Office in Whitehall to produce a rapid assessment for ministers. According to those who saw it, the paper was no more than a 'mild warning', suggesting there would be no rapid recourse to force by Baghdad. In referring vaguely to the possibility of fighting 'at some stage', it said little more than could have been surmised about any number of other territorial disputes around the world.

When the full Joint Intelligence Committee, with its representatives from the agencies and the principal Whitehall departments, met on 26 July, there was unease over the tone of the Middle East CIG paper. Many of those present felt that it understated the seriousness of the situation. The JIC minute circulated to the rest of government in that week's Red Book took a more careful line, indicating that there was genuine cause for concern. On the same day as the JIC met, however, the oil producers' cartel OPEC sat in Geneva and produced hopeful phrases about the resolution of the production dispute.

During this period, says one Cabinet Office figure, 'the Americans were frigging about in a very loose way'. There were differences of opinion between the State Department, which stressed the positive outlook for negotiations, and the Pentagon, which took a more pessimistic view. On 25 July April Glaspie, the US ambassador to Baghdad, had given the Iraqi dictator what he interpreted as *carte blanche* to deal with the dispute, telling him, 'We have no opinion on Arab–Arab conflicts, such as your border disagreement with Kuwait.' The Pentagon proved the more prescient, notifying the CIA of a vital change in command procedures. The civilian experts who normally tasked 'national collection assets' – principally the spy satellites – made way for the uniformed operators of the Pentagon's DIA, who were acting on behalf of the Central Command (Centcom), the military headquarters that would have to carry out any US operation in the Gulf. Now that the DIA was running the satellites on behalf of Centcom, it began boosting coverage of the Iraq–Kuwait border area, zooming in from space on the possible invasion force. As more information came in, the Pentagon's concern deepened. It was, said a later Congressional report, 'the first time the Soviet Union took a back seat to another part of the world as an intelligence collection target'.

On Friday 27 July, Percy Cradock sat down at his desk on the second floor of the Cabinet Office to prepare a new minute for the Prime Minister. Having slept on it, he felt that the JIC's paper of the previous day had not gone far enough. Cradock stated that the Iraqis were preparing for some kind of aggression, but that the British and US intelligence communities were uncertain about the timing and the scope of any such action. Many analysts felt that Iraq might simply take the two disputed islands and perhaps the Rumaillah oil field, a limited aggression that would sorely tax Arab and Western political resolve. There was also a feeling – echoes of the Falklands – that Iraq would exhaust all diplomatic avenues before waging war; a meeting between the two states was scheduled for early the following week. The Cradock note to the Prime Minister therefore balanced a prediction that the Iraqi army was preparing for action with questions about when it might happen and how far it would go.

The JIC Chairman's memo was paraphrased in an essay on intelligence aspects of the Gulf campaign in the 1992 Statement on the Defence Estimates, which noted that the troop build-up 'was recognized as a grave escalation of the situation but negotiations between Iraq and Kuwait continued . . . It was not clear what Saddam's precise intentions were, and although eventual hostilities were foreseen, it was not expected that events would develop as rapidly as in fact they did.' According to those who saw them, the JIC minute and Cradock's memo had made one other thing quite clear: the Kuwaiti army would break quickly, and the other Gulf states would be equally incapable of military resistance to an Iraqi attack.

Over the weekend, a reinforced 'crisis cell' in the Pentagon watched events. As more satellite imagery of the border area became available, analysts noted the signs that any commander knows are the prelude to military action: the outloading of ammunition and fuel from supply depots to the forces in the field. This in itself was not evidence that Saddam had decided to invade, but it did tell the USA that he would soon have the capability. On Saturday 28 July President Bush, alarmed by these reports, sent a telegram to the Iraqi dictator saying, 'Differences are best resolved by peaceful means, not by making threats.'

On the morning of Monday 30 July occurred one of the most interesting moments of the Gulf saga in Whitehall. Concerned that he had received no reply from the Prime Minister to his Friday memo, Cradock made further inquiries, apparently suggesting that she should give some public warning about possible Iraqi actions. There was no immediate response.

The Prime Minister had much else on her mind. Her schedule was usually gruelling, but on that day she had learned that Ian Gow, her parliamentary colleague and a close political confidant, had been assassinated by the IRA. The event shocked the parliamentary party, but provided only short respite from the increasingly tense manoeuvrings that were to produce Michael Heseltine's leadership challenge a few weeks later. For Thatcher, personal and parliamentary concerns were both of a particularly difficult kind in the week preceding Iraq's invasion.

In weighing the evidence at her disposal, the Prime Minister may also have taken into account her intelligence adviser's innate caution and the tendency of JIC chairmen to posit 'worst-case scenarios'. In May of that year, for example, the JIC had issued alarming messages about a crisis that had developed between India and Pakistan. Indian troop movements toward the disputed area of Kashmir triggered deep concerns in Washington and London. Richard Kerr, deputy CIA director, later told the US journalist Seymour Hersh that 'we were right on the edge'. The USA felt that the conflict could quickly go nuclear: India had developed atomic weapons early in the 1970s, and Pakistan was believed to have assembled several devices in the late 1980s. JIC minutes echoed the US assessments; an intelligence analyst attached to the Cabinet Office at the time notes, 'Our view was that they were about to go to war.'

The Kashmir crisis provoked secret diplomacy. Robert Gates of President Bush's national security staff visited the region with a message from his leader urging restraint. Given that India's brinkmanship was peacefully resolved, it would be easy to conclude with hindsight that the JIC and the USA had exaggerated the risk of war. Conversely, it might be argued that the incident demonstrated the value of intelligence-driven preventative diplomacy of the type that Cradock was urging over the Iraqi troop movements. Of these two possible interpretations, the evidence suggests that, during those crucial days, the Prime Minister inclined to the former, regarding 'crying wolf' as an occupational hazard for a JIC chairman mandated by Whitehall to be her principal prophet of troubles ahead.

On Tuesday 31 July, Kuwaiti and Iraqi officials met in Jeddah, the Saudi Arabian port. The Saudis were keen to play the role of mediator in the territorial and oil disputes. The meeting broke up with little sign of progress, but with a commitment to meet again a few days later. After the initial concern aroused by the troop movements, Saddam Hussein had the previous week promised President Hosni Mubarak of Egypt and King Fahd of Saudi Arabia that he would exhaust diplomatic channels before taking any other action. Iraq's agreement to further talks therefore lulled these Arab leaders into a false sense of security. Egyptian and Saudi diplomats assured their British counterparts that Saddam Hussein had given his word he was committed to a negotiated solution.

The soothing messages from these two pro-Western Arab leaders were sufficient to sow confusion in the foreign policy centres of Washington and London. The Pentagon drew its own conclusions from the satellite imagery, and the day after the Jeddah meeting declared Watch Condition One (Watchcon One) in its command centre. 'Virtually every national intelligence collection system' in a position to gather information on Iraqi forces was now doing so, according to the later Congressional report.

That morning, Wednesday 1 August, Thatcher left Heathrow for Aspen, Colorado, and a long-scheduled speech to a conference that was also to be attended by President Bush. Saddam's mendacious assurances to his fellow Arab statesmen, she wrote in her memoirs, led her to believe that 'the Iraqi military action was a case of sabre-rattling'. In a minute to the Ministry of Defence written eleven days later, and quoted in her memoirs, she said, 'We thought that Iraq would not move into Kuwait.' This might be a case of Thatcher using the royal 'we'; her minute certainly did not reflect the views of the JIC and, more particularly, her senior intelligence adviser.

Charles Powell, one of her inner circle at Downing Street, adds that the Prime Minister would never have gone to Aspen if there had been a clear warning from the intelligence machinery. He says, 'The most difficult of intelligence to have is that about intentions. In the Iraqi invasion of Kuwait, we knew where every tank was, but we got his intentions wrong because we believed what Saddam told other Arab leaders . . . there was a failure of assessment.'

The notion that the fault lay with the assessment is particularly tough on Percy Cradock, given the reported contents of his warning memo of 27 July. He told me, 'We saw the danger and the prospect of fighting, but could not predict the day or the hour . . . Saddam's immediate intentions remained obscure: they could have been sabre-rattling in order to extract more money from the Kuwaitis, or plans for a limited attack to take an oil field, or full-scale invasion. Or all three in ascending order. The time scale was also uncertain. But there was no intelligence failure.'

Cradock's version of events, with its insistence on the 'prospect of fighting', is validated by the essay in the 1992 Defence White Paper, which was written with access to all relevant documents. Assuming that the phrases 'grave escalation' and 'eventual hostilities were fore-seen' used in the White Paper accurately reflect Cradock's 27 July memo to the Prime Minister, then she alone must take responsibility for the idea that the Iraqi moves were 'a case of sabre-rattling' and that 'we' had decided they would not invade. It is clear that Cradock and the full JIC had been vague about the timing and whether it would be a full invasion, but it is equally obvious the Prime Minister made a personal decision to set aside a reasonably clear warning that the situation might lead to bloodshed, preferring instead to believe in the diplomatic noises emerging from her personal contacts with other leaders and from Foreign Office reports. It was a political judgement of a kind she often made, except that this time it was to prove a particularly unfortunate one, not only because an eleventh-hour US–UK public warning to Iraq might have had some deterrent effect, but also because scores of Britons were about to fall into Iraqi hands.

Cradock and Powell both emphasize the difficulty of guessing Iraqi intentions in those final hours. It had been an axiom of doves in the Cold War intelligence battle that capability did not necessarily equal intention. The Pentagon – which usually took the opposite view, saying that Soviet military capacity led it to doubt the words of the Kremlin – remained true to form on this occasion. They had read the signs of Iraq's impending military action accurately, but US politicians had had to balance that concrete information against the conflicting evidence from the diplomatic arena.

SIS had long regarded the Middle East as a theatre of operations second only in importance to the Soviet Bloc. On this occasion, however, its cupboard was bare, as Cradock and Powell imply and others confirm. None of MI6's agents was able to provide a warning of Saddam's intentions. These were known only to his most trusted advisers.

Sigint was the one intelligence method that might have had a good chance of reading Baghdad's intentions before the attack. As orders are disseminated through an army preparing for action, there are often slips in communications discipline that reveal to the eavesdropper what is about to happen. Iraq's invasion force had grown to such a size – about 100,000 men in seven divisions – that there was every chance information could have been carelessly revealed over the radio. It is to the credit of the Iraqi army, and the experience it gained during its long war with Iran, that this didn't happen.

In the final hours before the invasion, as reports came of growing tension, some airlines decided to divert aircraft due to pass through Kuwait City airport on the way to or from the Far East. A British Airways Boeing 747, however, took off from London's Heathrow airport en route for the Emirate. Why wasn't it diverted? Why hadn't the families of the British Liaison Team in Kuwait been pulled out? The answer appears to lie with the view of the crisis held at the apex of government. One senior intelligence figure blames the Prime Minister, saying, 'There was no action by her – and in those days, of course, there was no action unless the Prime Minister wanted it.'

Early on 2 August 1990 Iraqi troops began to move into Kuwait. The first wave consisted of the Hammurabi and Medina armoured divisions, and the Tawakalna mechanized division, from the Republican Guard. At dawn, helicopters carried commandos into key points in Kuwait City and Iraqi jets strafed the airport runway, narrowly missing the British Airways jet on the tarmac.

Kuwait's armed forces put up no effective resistance. The 35th Armoured Brigade based at Jahra barracks, the only force actually garrisoned between the Iraqi border and the capital, mounted its vehicles and headed in the opposite direction, towards Saudi Arabia. Dozens of its British-made Chieftain tanks did not make it, but broke down. Emir Jaber and his family departed in the same direction, their limousines proving more reliable than the tanks. The Iraqi invasion force succeeded in taking most of its principal objectives in a matter of hours. Hundreds of Britons were trapped, and were to become a 'human shield' for the Iraqi dictator. Washington and London prepared to tackle the crisis.

Whereas the Falklands invasion saw a failure of assessment by the JIC, on this occasion the Committee had at least predicted the likelihood of the Iraqi invasion and the uselessness of the Kuwaiti army, if not the actual timing of the attack. In its report on the crisis and the subsequent war, the US House of Representatives Committee on Armed Services noted that expectations of the intelligence community are often too high: 'Policy makers and private citizens who expect intelligence to foresee all sudden shifts are attributing to it qualities not yet shared by the Deity with mere mortals.' Given the limitations, the JIC's warnings were reasonably precise. The responsibility for reacting to them rested with the Prime Minister.

Chapter 12

1990 Desert Shield

The Iraqi invasion provoked a flurry of diplomatic manoeuvring. Intelligence was soon to play a critical role in convincing Saudi Arabia of the need to deploy Western forces in its own defence, as the Bush Administration was arguing that Saddam was preparing to push on into the kingdom. Western concern about some kind of 'domino effect' toppling the royal princes of the Gulf seems to have stemmed more from a perception of the underlying weaknesses of the countries concerned than it did from any hard information about Baghdad's next move.

On 6 August 1990, four days after the invasion, the Prime Minister sat in on a White House briefing on the situation in Kuwait. She wrote in her memoirs, 'I was never taken into the Americans' confidence more than I was during the two hours or so I spent that afternoon at the White House . . . there were now clear photographs – which the President passed around to us – showing that Iraqi tanks had moved right up to the border with Saudi Arabia.'

In itself, the fact that Iraq's forces had moved to occupy the entire country and secure its southern border said nothing about whether those forces were going to move into Saudi Arabia. The Middle East Current Intelligence Group in London took the view that they were not. Thatcher later wrote, 'The Cabinet Office assessment of Iraq's plans noted that an attack against Saudi Arabia did not seem imminent, because it would probably take a week to assemble the required forces.' A push down towards the main centres of population in the Kingdom's Eastern Province would probably have taken much longer than a week to prepare, since the distances involved were much greater than those within Kuwait.

Prior to the invasion of Kuwait there had been detailed information about the Iraqi build-up, but little was known about their intentions.

In the case of a possible invasion of Saudi Arabia, not only was there no concrete evidence that Baghdad had ordered such a attack, but the satellite pictures also suggested they were not yet ready to do so. But President Bush had taken fright over the failure to deter the invasion of Kuwait, and was determined to get US forces into Saudi Arabia. Ever since the first few days after the invasion, he had realized the need to block Iraqi aggression – and that required a base in the region for US ground and air forces. Dick Cheney, the Secretary of Defence, was sent to brief King Fahd. Spy satellite imagery supposedly showing Iraqi preparations for a push south played a vital role in convincing the monarch.

The Saudi royal family had been in a state of paralysis since the invasion. For more than forty-eight hours after it happened, state television had ignored the Iraqi attack because the House of Saud had not decided what line to take. The King deeply resented being taken in by the Iraqi dictator's lies during the last week of July. Although the royal family had long opposed the stationing of US troops in Saudi Arabia, Cheney's briefing and perhaps some awareness of the weakness of his own forces convinced King Fahd that the moment had come.

Saudi Arabia's rulers had long played a game of divide and rule with their armed forces. The Army was trusted less than the National Guard, which was the modern incarnation of the tribal levies that had imposed the power of the royal house. Army garrisons were deployed away from cities and close to the borders, whereas the National Guard was based near the centres of population where they could stop any attempt at insurrection.

The Saudi Ministry of Defence had made a huge investment – £15 billion according to some estimates – in King Khalid Military City, a large base close to the border with Kuwait. It typified the Saudi approach to defence: lavish barracks for up to 25,000 troops. However, most of the complex was empty, standing by for times of crisis. The 20th Mechanized Brigade, about 5,000 strong, was the only unit based there – and therefore the only force standing between Saddam's Republican Guard and the oil fields of Eastern Province.

After the Iraqi invasion, the 20th Mechanized Brigade was ordered to take up defensive positions along the Kuwaiti border. The journey should only take a couple of hours by road, but one week later the brigade had still not left camp, a senior Western adviser present at the time told me. The road into Saudi Arabia was undefended. Britain and the USA had military advisers with the Saudi armed forces, and a flow of intelligence came in through their embassies in Riyadh. At the critical moment the Saudi army had failed its leaders, so they fell back on their trusty National Guard. The 2nd National Guard Mechanized Brigade, equipped with light armoured vehicles, was ordered to move from its base near the Eastern Province city of Al Khobar to the border, several hundred kilometres to the north. Seven days after the invasion, it formed the first defensive barrier in Saudi Arabia.

On 9 August Britain dispatched a squadron of Tornado F-3 fighters and a squadron of Jaguar bombers to the Gulf; two days earlier, the USA had sent F-15 fighters and paratroopers. This deployment by the RAF was code-named Operation GRANBY, a name produced by an MoD computer and singularly unevocative compared with the US code-name DESERT SHIELD. Once British forces had been committed, the Gulf assumed a higher priority for government and intelligence.

After the invasion and until Margaret Thatcher returned from the USA on 7 August, Geoffrey Howe in his capacity as Deputy Prime Minister had been taking meetings of the Cabinet. Throughout her years at Downing Street, Thatcher had shown a preference for using small, *ad hoc* groups of ministers rather than the full Cabinet or committees of it. The Gulf crisis fell within the purview of the Overseas and Defence Committee, known within Whitehall as OD. The Prime Minister decided to set aside the full OD and go instead for a sub-committee consisting of herself, Douglas Hurd (newly installed as Foreign Secretary), William Waldegrave (Minister of State at the Foreign Office), Tom King (Defence Secretary), Archie Hamilton (Minister of State for the Armed Forces), John Wakeham (Energy Secretary), Patrick Mayhew (Attorney General) and Marshal of the RAF David Craig (Chief of the Defence Staff). This group met frequently, but because of the senior rank of its members, much of the work was delegated to a smaller group of ministers and officials. This other committee met daily, usually under the chairmanship of Waldegrave or King, and prepared much of the agenda for the War Cabinet under the Prime Minister herself. Percy Cradock usually sat in on both committees.

Within a few days of the invasion, the Middle East Current Intelligence Group established the utterly anti-social routine of meeting at three or four a.m. every day. The group produced a daily bulletin of intelligence that took in overnight events. It had to be on Cradock's desk first thing every morning and formed part of the briefing book given to each member of the daily committee meeting. MI6's man on the CIG was David Spedding, its Controller Middle East, a rising star in the Service with a record of working in the Arab world.

Shortly after the Iraqi attack, the Prime Minister told the Aspen conference that the invasion violated every principle the United Nations stood for. She added, 'A vital principle is at stake: an aggressor must never be allowed to get his way.' While public attention focused on the despatch of British forces and on international sanctions, Britain was also taking secret steps to help Kuwait.

Within a fortnight of the invasion, Colin McColl, Chief of SIS, and Cradock were discussing a covert programme of assistance to the Kuwaitis. SIS's plans for disruptive action – in this case, helping to create Kuwaiti resistance cells – were approved by the small committee under Waldegrave's chairmanship and later by the full War Cabinet, according to somebody who saw the relevant minutes. The decision to provide this backing for the Kuwaitis has not previously been revealed.

Disruptive action aimed at supporting the Kuwaitis and destabilizing Saddam would become SIS's principal operational task during the next few months. MI6 had no agents in place who could give worthwhile reports from Baghdad. The idea of quickly recruiting them was a non-starter because of the nature of Iraqi society, and because the cultivation of a high-grade source can take years. The almost complete absence of human intelligence from inside the enemy camp was taken philosophically by those reading MI6's weekly CX Book of agent reports. Tom King reflects, 'Iraq is a police state with awful retribution against anyone who showed dissent. It presented some pretty major challenges. Certainly, when you were dealing with a state as security-minded as it is possible to be, there were bound to be problems in that area.'

SIS sent a veteran officer to run its operation in Saudi Arabia, who I shall refer to only as Mark. He was something of an expert in guerrilla warfare, having served in the Royal Greenjackets, reaching the rank of major, before becoming an intelligence officer. He had served in Oman during the late 1970s, at a time when Britain was giving substantial covert assistance to the Sultan. Mark was in the classic mould of the SIS Middle East specialist – people who, as another officer wryly observes, 'never lose the sand between their toes'. A member of a Foreign Office family who grew up in one of his postings observes, 'Even at the age of twelve I knew he was a spy.' The mission to Saudi Arabia did not require Mark to remain incognito, however. Quickly posted under the flimsy cover of Counsellor to the Riyadh embassy, he headed a team of SIS officers helping to organize the Kuwaiti resistance, liaising with the Saudis, collating reports from refugees fleeing the occupied country, and assisting British forces.

A training camp for Kuwaiti volunteers was set up in eastern Saudi Arabia. Several members of the Special Air Service were attached to the SIS team training them. Britain also apparently provided weapons, mainly Heckler and Koch machine-guns. As with the help given to the Afghan resistance, SIS's effort was a smaller version of a programme being run by the USA and involving Special Forces troops as well as CIA operatives.

Initially, the MI6 bosses in London predicted a wide range of possible tasks for the Kuwaiti volunteers. On 23 August 1990 Saddam Hussein appeared on television with what the Iraqi announcer termed his British 'guests'. Shots of the dictator sitting an English schoolboy on his lap had caused revulsion in Britain, underlining the way he was prepared to exploit hostages both for their propaganda value and as human shields. Saddam thought that Britain and the USA were spineless and that hostages could play a key role in deterring them from bombing. SIS wanted to use the Kuwaiti resistance to find out where the hostages were, as part of a plan to rescue them. It soon became clear that the Kuwaitis were insufficiently organized to take on the task and that the Iraqis had moved the British hostages to military bases within Iraq.

SIS still hoped that the resistance would be able to bring out good intelligence from their occupied country, but that hope proved largely illusory too. Although a Kuwaiti resistance was operating within weeks of the invasion, it consisted mostly of people who had stayed behind. It remained difficult for them to make links with the guerrillas being trained in Saudi Arabia, although those inside Kuwait were able to send out many messages. The team training the volunteers soon concluded that they were unlikely to make effective guerrilla fighters or spies. One person who was involved says the training 'always had limited objectives, and its real value may have been as a long-term political gesture'.

The SIS relationship with other agencies around the world did produce some useful titbits. Data on the Scud missile system was obtained from Moscow, although its capabilities were already fairly well-known from the hundreds of firings in the Iran–Iraq war and Afghanistan. The liaison officer in Tel Aviv later sent a detailed psychological profile of the Iraqi dictator compiled by Mossad and running to several dozen pages. One analyst who read it describes it as 'one of the most useful documents I saw in the entire war. Its basic premise was that whatever challenge you gave him, he would only up the stakes to the point of catastrophe.'

As the intelligence agencies tried to find their bearings, Britain was boosting its involvement in the Gulf. Ground-attack Tornados were committed to Bahrein at the end of August. On 14 September it was announced that the 7th Armoured Brigade group, with 120 tanks, was being sent to the Middle East. Because of this growing commitment, the Prime Minister had to upgrade the command arrangements; two weeks later, Lieutenant-General Peter de la Billière was appointed Commander British Forces Middle East and went out to Riyadh. As he noted in his later book, 'I sought information about Saddam, only to discover at that stage we seemed to possess very little'. The general consulted the British Embassy in Riyadh, which helped with certain information. In what was to become a pattern during the run-up to war and during the conflict itself, the Mossad profile, like much of the best information available to experts in the UK, did not find its way to the field commander.

The commitment of British troops brought a fundamental transformation of role for the Defence Intelligence Staff. From its usual analytical function in Whitehall, the organisation had to change into the provider of hard information that could be used by forces in battle. The Middle East cell in the Rest of the World Directorate was greatly expanded, as was the set-up at RAF High Wycombe, which was chosen as the link between the forces sent to the Gulf and Whitehall. High Wycombe became the Joint Force Headquarters, and its intelligence cell, together with the JIC's Middle East CIG in Whitehall, became the principal centres for collating the most highly-classified reports. The High Wycombe unit processing this information grew from five people before the war to about 150 during it. Air Chief Marshal Paddy Hine, the Commander in Chief UK Air at High Wycombe, became the JFHQ chief, in charge of the global operation in support of GRANBY.

In all aspects of the intelligence build-up US assistance was critical. Pictures from US photographic satellites improved as orbits were altered for better coverage. Few adjustments to the pattern of sigint satellites were needed, as they had already been positioned for near-global coverage. Data from both sources was collated in the USA into a detailed picture of Iraqi military dispositions. The headquarters of particular brigades or divisions could be identified either by the vehicles specifically associated with command elements or by interception of certain types of radio signal. Once the headquarters were identified, the Pentagon analysts extrapolated from information about the standard organization of different types of Iraqi unit to produce overall estimates. These methods were not without fault: some HQs were improperly identified, and the number of troops in the Kuwaiti Theatre of Operations, or KTO (as the allies called the Emirate and the portion of southern Iraq adjoining it), was exaggerated because many Iraqi divisions were not up to full strength. By and large, however, the US intelligence machine was able to produce a comprehensive picture of Iraq's military deployment.

Britain had long maintained a substantial sigint base in Cyprus because of the island's ideal position for listening in to Middle East traffic. It was described by one GCHQ Director as the organization's 'jewel in the crown'. But although the Cyprus station was well placed for the eastern Mediterranean (in which the USA had long shown such interest) and north Africa, Iraq was further away and so represented a more difficult target. In the overall picture, useful sigint from Cyprus was swamped by that acquired from the National Security Agency's satellites. After the initial invasion Iraqi communications experts installed a land line linking Kuwait City to Basra. Much of the high-level military command traffic had become inaccessible to the NSA and GCHQ at this point, but the large deployments in Kuwait still ensured that enough signals were available to plot the battlefield picture needed by the allied forces.

Britain's intelligence relationship with the USA meant an especially high level of 'customer service'. An NSA liaison cell was established at High Wycombe to process British military requests for more specific information or for images from space. Huge quantities of unanalysed sigint gathered by the NSA's satellites poured into Cheltenham. However, British sensitivity about the relationship was such that extreme care was taken in disseminating the material. Any information placed in the most sensitive compartments of security classification – for example UMBRA, the code word for the best sigint material – could not be sent to HQ British Forces Middle East without being 'sanitized', a process that was meant to protect the source of the information but often severely limited its usefulness. The result was that members of the Middle East CIG or the High Wycombe intelligence cell knew far more detail (of limited use to them, given that they were studying the broader picture) than staff officers in Riyadh trying to organize the British deployment. Other coalition partners, including even the French, apparently received only a small proportion of the intelligence assistance given to the UK.

In addition to this stream of (largely US) information coming through the UK, the troops in the field were also plugged into the local US intelligence system. Lieutenant-General Peter de la Billière reveals that General Norman Schwarzkopf, the Commander-in-Chief of US Central Command who was put in charge of coalition military forces, had personally ordered that, 'we not only got access to everything they had, but we had substantial numbers of people blended into their intelligence staff. I never felt the Americans in-theatre were holding anything back.' The French and more minor coalition contributors were not accorded this privilege. Nevertheless, the information going to Britain's field forces reflected their low level in the echelon of command, and there were later to be complaints that it too had been 'sanitized' of much useful detail.

Within two months of the invasion, the coalition-building efforts of the US President who had been a CIA director and a UN ambassador had produced a military and political front that embraced Security Council powers as well as the leading Arab states of Egypt, Saudi Arabia and Syria. With a substantial US force in place and able to defend the Kingdom, President Bush moved towards an approximate doubling of the deployment to provide the forces necessary to take offensive action against Iraq. The initial ground force, based largely on the Airborne and Marines who had been able to get to the Gulf quickly, was to be supplemented by VII Corps, a heavy armoured formation based in Germany. On 9 November the USA announced that it was sending in a new wave of reinforcements: 150,000 soldiers, 1,000 tanks, and more air force attack squadrons.

Lieutenant-General de la Billière had already formed a view about the degree of British influence over allied war plans. While Whitehall spokesmen stressed that the Gulf forces were under national 'command' but US 'operational control', the general realized that he retained a 'yellow card' and could withdraw UK forces from the coalition, but that he had effectively lost control of them in any actual fighting. He rationalized this in his later book by saying, 'We were very much the junior partners of the Americans, whose land and air forces were over ten times the size of ours.'

The general's acute sense of Britain's place in the Gulf scheme of things led him to lobby for an increase in the size of the national contribution as soon as it was known that Washington was going to commit the extra 150,000 troops. Lieutenant-General de la Billière noted that a 'loss of influence' would result unless Britain followed suit. He was keen to ensure that the British Army switched from its initial mission, in support of the US Marines on the coast, to a mission inland with the US VII Corps armour, where the main allied effort – a broad encirclement of Kuwait through Iraq – was to take place. The Cabinet agreed to these military requests.

Following this decision, the 4th Armoured Brigade was added to the 7th, together with strong artillery and Royal Engineer deployments, to make up a somewhat light 1st (UK) Armoured Division (a formation of this kind normally has three or four armoured brigades). Despite the heavy defence spending of the Thatcher years, Britain had chronic logistic problems. Although the Army possessed hundreds of Challengers, it found it could only support a small number in service, so the 4th Brigade had one third the number of tanks of the 7th. Almost all the Challengers remaining in Germany had to be stripped for parts to keep the Gulf force working; within weeks, only seventeen out of the 130 left there were still operational. Although the British Army of the Rhine had only sent about a quarter of its artillery to the Gulf, it did not have enough 155 mm ammunition to supply them, so it embarked on an embarrassing whip-round amongst allies; the Belgians and Dutch declined to help.

The RAF had also been strengthened: it had Tornado bomber and Jaguar squadrons in Bahrein, a Tornado bomber squadron in Tabuk, Tornado fighter and bomber squadrons in Dhahran, as well as many other support aircraft. But the RAF too suffered from the historic under-investment in support and ammunition. The Tornado bomber force had been sent with the prime task of attacking Iraqi runways, so the aircraft were equipped with JP-233, a highly expensive system that dispensed dozens of runway-cratering munitions and mines. The only other options they were prepared for involved either unguided 'iron bombs' or the Alarm, an untried anti-radar missile that had been plagued by development problems.

With this allied commitment to additional forces, the USA went after the most important in a series of UN resolutions: one that would set an ultimatum for Iraqi withdrawal from Kuwait, and would allow for their removal by 'all necessary means' if they had not left. On 29 November, Security Council 678 was passed, setting 15 January 1991 as the deadline.

Throughout November and December, the Pentagon's estimates of Iraqi troop strengths in the Kuwait Theatre of Operations grew. DIS estimates, although occasionally out of synch, followed the DIA ones, as their analysts were relying almost entirely on US information. A Ministry of Defence briefing on 9 November said that there were 436,000 Iraqi troops in the theatre; later in the month it said there were 459,000, then 470,000, and on 7 December that there were 500,000 – and eventually as many as 590,000. These increases in part represented the redeployment of additional Iraqi forces into the theatre, with the analysts simply assuming that each unit was at full strength. In part, they also reflected a political game in Washington. At the 7 December MoD briefing the senior DIS officer told journalists, 'It isn't very clear what the [troop strengths] mean anyway', noting that they were arbitrarily based on projected unit strengths.

As US deployments to the Gulf grew, in pursuance of the plan to acquire an offensive capability, so did DIA estimates of Iraqi troops in the Kuwait Theatre of Operations. British analysts suggest that this was another example of political pressures shaping US assessment. Subsequent analyses would suggest that Iraqi troop strength had been overestimated by 40 to 50 per cent. As US forces built up to the 450,000 mark, they were actually outnumbering the Iraqi forces. Although the USA still fell well short of the three-to-one advantage that some theoreticians regard as prudent for offensive action – and the DIA experts clearly believed in their own estimates of Iraqi strength – there was a desire in Washington to use the most generous possible estimates of Iraqi forces lest US troops should appear to out-number them.

Although the DIS briefing of journalists parroted the erroneous US estimates, it also reflected the quality of some British analysis. On 7 December, for example, the Iraqi dictator's plans for facing the expected air offensive were perceptively described: 'If a war starts, Saddam Hussein will want to preserve strength. The Air Force and Republican Guard may stay out of the fighting and be used as strategic reserves.'

On 28 November 1990, Margaret Thatcher resigned as Prime Minister. In time, the intelligence agencies would notice that John Major took a profoundly different attitude towards them. But the new Prime Minister had stepped into a crisis where issues of security and intelligence were daily receiving the highest priority, and it was not until later that these differences of approach were really appreciated.

During the autumn the US and British authorities turned their attention to psychological operations (psyops) against the Iraqis. In August, Britain's psyops capability consisted of a single man, an officer at the Intelligence Corps training centre at Ashford in Kent. Others were pressed into service to help him, and the British military contribution eventually reached twelve; the US committed its 4th Psyops Group of several hundred personnel. While the military team would concentrate on undermining the morale of Iraqi troops, MI6 stepped in with a modest proposal to destabilize the dictator on the home front. The Defence Advisory Group, a joint military–SIS committee, was set up in London to co-ordinate the plans.

SIS used contacts in Jordan and Turkey to organize the smuggling of video and audio tapes into Iraq. These started with a few minutes of music or innocuous video images, then moved on to seditious messages from Iraqi exiles. The theme was that Saddam was leading the country to disaster and Iraqis would be better off without him. SIS and the CIA also gave assistance to Free Iraq, a radio station which incited the people to revolt; it began broadcasting in December 1990. However, Saudi political sensitivities limited SIS–CIA plans for destabilizing the Baghdad regime. One of the compromises between the allies involved broadcasting Free Iraq tapes from the air rather than from Saudi territory. A modified C-130 transport aircraft code-named VOLANT SOLO was used for the task.

As the UN deadline approached, the allies discussed stepping up these 'psyops', but there was some disagreement about the legality of leafleting Iraqi troops before fighting had begun. Once again, a compromise was reached, and rather than using aircraft – overflights could have been interpreted as an act of war – the first drop of 25,000 leaflets over Iraqi troops took place early in 1991, but before the UN deadline, from a hot-air balloon floated over the border.

Meanwhile, the US Air Force planners under Lieutenant-General Charles Horner's command in Riyadh had drawn up the complex tasking order that would form the blueprint for the opening air offensive. On 24 December Saddam had threatened to attack Israel, so high priority was given to Scud missiles. Sites believed to be involved in developing nuclear, chemical and biological weapons would also be hit. The initial target list also included airfields, key ministries and the strategic communications system. The ground divisions, which the DIA had plotted with some accuracy (where tanks or artillery were concerned, rather than the numbers of troops), would not receive heavy attacks until the strategic targets had been taken care of.

In certain key areas, the target list reflected weak intelligence. Mobile Scud missile launchers had been deployed out of barracks, but analysts using satellite pictures had not been able to follow them. The list of suspected nuclear weapons targets included only about half the major facilities later discovered by UN investigators.

RAF Tornado bombers were to be part of the initial attack, targeting key airfields as part of the campaign to ensure allied air superiority. The information used to brief the crews, like most of that in the hands of army commanders, had come from US sources. A British force of dozens of bombers and 30,000 troops would soon be in action, a more powerful air and ground force than was used in the Falklands. But they were dwarfed by the US contribution – and in intelligence too, as one British analyst says, 'We were just hanging on their coat tails.'

Chapter 13

1991 Desert Storm

Late on 16 January 1991 the coalition forces subjected key targets in Iraq and Kuwait to the first phase of what some commentators have called 'hyperwar'. As flak rounds criss-crossed the night sky, laser-guided bombs, Tomahawk cruise missiles and cluster munitions rained down from above. Through the green or black-and-white light of their targeting sensors, the pilots of F-117 bombers watched their bombs go through the roof of the Iraqi air force HQ. The largest war fought by Western nations since Korea was under way. At British Forces HQ in Riyadh, the contribution to the air offensive was to pose difficult questions of judgement.

RAF Tornados were in action against Iraqi airfields. The British used a variety of weapons against the targets, but were relying on their JP-233 munitions dispensers to do the main damage. The weapons, a hundred of which were used during the war, proved a disappointment. Most of the British targets had to be revisited by US F-111s, which used large laser-guided bombs to demolish the runways properly.

During the first weeks of war Britain lost four Tornados. At first, air chiefs stressed that they had been unlucky and that the losses resulted from the tough nature of the Iraqi targets. They rejected criticisms of the JP-233, later pointing out that only one of the aircraft lost had been carrying the weapon. But US F-111s had also been attacking airfields and none had been lost. The problem was not just the JP-233, but the entire philosophy of low-level attack for which the RAF had trained and equipped during the previous decades. They had flown against the Iraqis at heights of under 100 feet; one of the Tornados had been lost simply because its pilot miscalculated and flew into the ground. The F-111s, on the other hand, had flown in at 5,000 feet, above the Iraqi flak.

Lieutenant-General Charles 'Chuck' Horner, the US officer in overall command of the air offensive, soon expressed doubts about the RAF's tactics. The JP-233 was not popular with the crews, one of them explained to me, because 'it involves flying under heavy fire at 100 feet straight and level for twelve to fifteen seconds with a fireworks display going off on the underside of the aircraft'. Lieutenant-General Peter de la Billière noted in his book on the campaign, 'I could tell that Chuck considered our method of operation a pretty crazy one in this environment.' According to the general, RAF chiefs in London put pressure on Air Vice Marshal Bill Wratten, their senior officer in Saudi, to maintain low-level attacks in order to validate their operational philosophy and the multi-billion-pound procurement decisions that rested on it. Their evaluation of the campaign involved over-optimistic assessments of the amount of damage they were doing to Iraqi airfields.

On 23 January the RAF stopped low-level attacks, switching to the only other bomb it had deployed in Saudi: a conventional 1,000-pound unguided package of high explosive similar to those dropped by Second World War Lancasters. The aircraft switched to medium-level attacks and the results were 'largely ineffective', according to Lieutenant-General de la Billière. It was not until after the allied declaration on 27 January of air supremacy, victory in the battle for the skies, that the RAF decided to obtain laser-guided bombs for its Tornados. Several more days passed before Buccaneer aircraft were sent out and got ready to act in support of the Tornados, directing lasers at targets which would then be locked on to by the bombs. Only now did the RAF Tornados begin making a really effective contribution to the allied effort, destroying bridges, ammunition dumps and command posts. The morale of RAF pilots who had nightly run the gauntlet of Iraqi flak rose as it became apparent they were having greater success. The House of Commons Defence Committee later commented in one of its reports, 'We remain surprised that the RAF were so unprepared for offensive operations at medium level.'

The RAF, in common with the USAF, suffered from delays in Bomb Damage Assessment (BDA). In the case of the British, these made the decisions to move from runway attack to iron bombs to laser-guided bombs more difficult. Later US analyses of the campaign would suggest that those tasking the spy satellites became completely overloaded with requests for pictures within days of the conflict breaking out, making BDA more and more difficult. There was also a shortage of reconnaissance aircraft; satellites were hardly necessary for many of the tasks, given the complete freedom enjoyed by allied air forces within days of Desert Storm beginning. Eventually the USA had 600 people tied up with BDA, but it remained a problematic exercise. As the air campaign moved into the phase where it was primarily directed at reducing the combat effectiveness of Iraqi ground forces in the Kuwait theatre of Operations by 50 per cent, the question of when this target would be reached, clearing the way for the ground war, became the principal intelligence conundrum. DIA estimates would prove to be consistently over-optimistic.

The outbreak of war was accompanied by a witch hunt in Britain itself: the Security Service, Special Branch and the armed forces were involved in what was officially described as the biggest anti-terrorist alert since the war. Alarming assessments by the Joint Intelligence Committee proved critical to the government's reaction. Percy Cradock, the JIC Chairman, was always presenting ministers with the 'worst-case' scenario; many in intelligence argued that this was his job, and that such instincts had served him well in July. But the JIC view of the terrorist threat brought some ministers to near-panic. It suggested that Iraqis could have smuggled chemical or biological weapons into their London embassy, that Iraqi intelligence cells were embedded in the émigré population, and that the Abu Abbas Palestinian faction, long supported by Baghdad, might carry out proxy attacks.

The first response to these assessments was to expel eight Iraqi diplomats and sixty-seven others. It is believed that MI5 officers then entered the embassy to verify that no weapons of mass destruction remained in the basement. What evidence ever existed to support JIC's hypotheses about chemical or biological weapons remains obscure.

An army camp on Salisbury Plain was used to house thirty-five detainees, a measure reminiscent of the Second World War, and a further thirty-three were put in jail near York. Troops appeared on duty at airports, and one of 22nd Special Air Service Regiment's four sub-units, G Squadron, was kept on standby in case of hijacking or sieges.

Some in the intelligence world have subsequently described the alert as highly successful, citing the absence of effective terrorist action during the war. Douglas Hurd, the Foreign Secretary, later revealed, in another episode of the government's worldwide anti-terrorist alert, that information gathered by SIS in a third-world country had enabled them to thwart an attempt on the life of an allied ambassador in Europe. But it must also be said that several countries which did not take such high-profile measures against Arabs did not experience any outbreaks of terror either. Heavy security around ministers and public places was evidently insufficient to deter the IRA from mortaring Downing Street during a meeting of the War Cabinet on 7 February 1991 and bombing two main-line railway stations on 18 February.

Many of the Iraqi detainees complained that they had no connection with the Baghdad regime or any terrorist group, and they were backed by civil liberties groups. A three-member Home Office panel set up under the Immigration Act to hear appeals by some of those due for deportation ruled that the majority posed no threat to national security. An MI5 officer counters, 'The assessments were pretty firm on some, but weak on others; we think it was about 75 per cent right.'

The evaluation of who posed a risk was carried out by G Branch counter-terrorist officers. But the number of experts on the Iraqi community within this arm of MI5 could be counted on the fingers of one hand. Although MI5 had run agents in the community for many years and therefore had some idea of who relayed information about émigré groups to the Iraqi embassy, many of the evaluations were based on slim evidence or hearsay. This did not hinder the Service, as ministers had decided to err on the side of caution. One Cabinet minister at the time told me, 'There was some mistaken information, but most were deported or left quickly. We were anxious that Iraq might be preparing to launch biological or chemical weapons against the West, and in that sort of instance we were inclined to follow a certain line. What was it Churchill said? "Collar the lot."'

In the Gulf itself, soldiers of the Special Boat Squadron had on 23 January 1991 launched Operation MAUDE, probably the most daring British Special Forces raid of the war. Its aim, like that of much of the early bombing, was to disrupt the Iraqi fixed communications network, hindering their control of forces and forcing them into using insecure radios, so increasing the sigint take. Using Chinook helicopters, several dozen SBS men were flown well into Iraq to a point on the main communications land line from Baghdad to the southern theatre HQ in Basra. The highly secure fibre-optic link had been supplied by a British firm. SBS men struck at night just sixty miles from Baghdad, and after finding surface markers for the cable, used pneumatic drills to dig it up.

Efforts like the SBS raid and the air attacks were, in Lieutenant-General de la Billière's words, 'forcing the Iraqis to use their radio network, with the result that we were belatedly starting to pick up useful intelligence'. The general, writing about a period one month after the start of the war, was apparently unaware that sigint had been delivering dramatic results almost since the beginning. Once more, the evidence suggests that good-quality information was being hoarded in the USA and UK because of fears about disseminating it.

According to one person with access to daily sigint briefs, analysts soon came to know Major-General Saleh Abbud Mahmud, commander of III Corps, an Iraqi field force south-west of Kuwait City with a key role in the first line of defence against the allies. Major-General Mahmud was apparently the only corps commander with real fighting spirit, and he was constantly urging the Southern Operations Command to assume the offensive. The general was eventually given permission to try his idea out, and he sent three of his divisions in a thrust towards the Saudi Arabian border town of Khafji. Sigint warned the US forces of his plan and JSTARS, a flying radar station used against ground targets, plotted the moves as they began. Despite heavy bombing of the III Corps units, a force of at least one brigade made it into Khafji and captured the town on 29 January. It was held for about a day before being retaken by the Saudi National Guard's 2nd Mechanized Brigade backed by US Marine helicopters and artillery.

In the days following this drubbing, Major-General Mahmud's forces sustained further air attacks and he again began nagging his commanders by radio. He insisted that some of his men be allowed forty-eight-hour passes to gain some rest from the incessant bombardment. His superiors eventually agreed, but the hapless general soon discovered that many of them went AWOL. According to one allied officer, III Corps had shrunk to about half of its strength by the time the ground war started. As the number of troops deserting and heading for home increased, the Iraqi army became desperate to prevent mass surrenders among those who remained. Soldiers were banned from having white items of clothing, lest they use them to signal their capitulation. In an episode that symbolized the strange mixture of bureaucracy and tyranny in Saddam's state, soldiers in some sectors of the front were told to sign forms permitting their officers to kill them if they attempted to surrender.

Sigint gave good intelligence about the internal collapse of the Iraqi garrison, and this was fed to the allied psyops experts so that they could maximize the effect of their leafleting. During the war they dropped 27 million leaflets on Iraqi units. Lieutenant-General de la Billière's account does mention seeing such intercepts, but only towards the end of the air offensive. Eavesdropping also produced what was probably the most extraordinary intelligence coup of the war – one that has not been described before.

Saddam Hussein was known to rely on a small circle of advisers. In matters of foreign policy, one of the few people whose judgement he trusted was Nazar Hamdoon, Iraqi ambassador to the United Nations. Saddam apparently recognized that Hamdoon understood the Western mind in a way he did not. Several times during the war the Iraqi dictator telephoned Hamdoon in New York to discuss diplomatic strategy. These conversations were intercepted by the National Security Agency.

The method used to obtain this intelligence coup is evidently highly sensitive, and was not revealed to me, but there were several ways in which it could have been done: Saddam may have been speaking over an insecure line in the hope that nobody would pick up the call; the NSA may have broken the Iraqi government cipher; the Americans may have succeeded in tapping the UN mission in such a way as to intercept the signal after it was decrypted (for example, by bugging a line between the cipher room and the ambassador's office); or they may not even have needed to enter the UN mission, using an infinity transmitter to make one telephone on Hamdoon's desk become a live microphone while he spoke to his leader on another.

Intercepts of the conversations were relayed from the NSA to London. They helped to answer some of the mysteries about Saddam's strategy. His decision to send dozens of his best aircraft to Iran five days after the war began, for example, was seen by some as a realization that defeat was inevitable and that he might as well try to save the planes. The intercepts apparently revealed that Saddam did not accept defeat until almost the end, believing that his large entrenched army would be able to impose unacceptable casualties on the allies. These vital reports were kept on a tight distribution, being seen only by certain ministers and officials. One person who did read them says, 'We realized that he was completely out of touch with reality.

His use of language was medieval, from another century.'

For many, the war provided a salutary lesson in the inability of government bureaucracies to keep pace with the speed at which information moved. Situation rooms in Washington were tuned to CNN, in the Cabinet Office there were portable TVs and a Reuters wire machine. When Khafji fell briefly to the Iraqis, correspondents in the battle zone were quickly in contact by satellite phone with their bases and with colleagues in Riyadh. At the daily Central Command briefing that evening (at which I was present), a US brigadier floundered and became obstructive when asked by journalists who knew more than he did what the situation was in Khafji. The hapless officer suffered from the fact that US Marine accounts of the situation were still working their way up the chain of command; the Americans were worried about what they should say, given Saudi sensitivities about the loss of one of their towns.

In the same way that public information in Riyadh could not match the speed of modern news gathering, so secret information also suffered. SIS ran a global programme during the war, trying to speak to mediators such as the Russian Yevgeny Primakov, who had met the Iraqi leadership, and relay their impressions to London. Although this involved dozens of officers at many stations, it produced little of value compared to sigint, claims one analyst: 'The attempt to gather human intelligence from people who had met Saddam could not keep up with events. We could read it in the *Independent* before it came through on the diplomatic circuit. The situation was developing too fast for SIS to cope – it wasn't their type of scene.'

Although there were some contacts between Kuwaiti resistance fighters inside the country and SIS or CIA officers outside, this did not prove very profitable either. Saudi troops had penned hundreds of Iraqi deserters into a camp near the border town of Hafar al-Batin and were interrogating them, but the Saudis were reluctant to allow British or US intelligence officers to share in this work. The Congressional report on the war remarks, 'There were complaints from US intelligence officers about the Saudi military intelligence system . . . it didn't want to share anything.'

All these limitations blunted the SIS contribution during the war, as they had done before it. One observer in Saudi Arabia concluded, 'Human intelligence didn't work – there was very little. It might have worked in a very protracted war.'

Technical methods had their limitations too, and this was nowhere shown more clearly than in the hunt for mobile Scud missile launchers. General Norman Schwarzkopf, the allied Commander in Chief, endorsed faulty intelligence in his briefings, telling correspondents on 18 January 1991 that six Scud launchers had been destroyed. On 20 January he said that 'all of their fixed sites' had been knocked out and 'as many as sixteen' out of an estimated twenty mobile launchers destroyed. Eight days later, Brigadier Buster Glosson of the USAF showed a videotape to another Riyadh briefing, purportedly indicating that 'we have knocked out at least three mobile erector launchers'.

From the second day of the war, Iraq had begun firing Scuds at Israel, heightening the fears of President Bush and other coalition leaders that the Jewish state would retaliate, sowing political disarray in the anti-Saddam front. Military intelligence analysts were dubious about the claims of Scud kills even at the time they were made. One explains, 'People were claiming it left right and centre. Initially you believed it, but bit by bit our faith was undermined in those claims.' There was, however, a political imperative to be seen to be doing something and whatever the reservations of his experts, the Commander in Chief in Riyadh was aware of this.

Within the Israeli government there were some, notably Moshe Arens, the Minister of Defence, who felt that it was imperative to retaliate. But the Cabinet had decided before the war that its response to any Scud attacks would be graded according to the seriousness of those attacks. No retaliation would be forthcoming unless there was a large-scale loss of life.

Iraq never used the fixed launch-sites attacked on the first night, and it soon became apparent that US KH-11 photographic satellites were not going to find the mobile Scud launchers. There were two problems with this venture. Firstly, the narrow aperture of the KH-11's camera made searching the deserts of western Iraq for Scud launchers like 'searching New York by looking through a soda straw', in the words of one US expert. Secondly, the KH-11s swung over the battlefield in a sun-synchronous orbit; they weren't there at night, when most of the missiles were fired, and they orbited, so that an object worthy of further examination on one pass was often not there by the time the satellite next came around. This last problem also bedevilled the BDA experts: a tank might move between orbits, or the flames from a burning tank might go out between one pass and another, leading to it being mistakenly classified as operational.

The only other options for finding the Scud launchers from space were the LACROSSE radar imaging satellite, which did have a slightly larger field of 'view', and the Defence Support Programme (DSP) geo-stationary craft which provided warning of Scud launches. LACROSSE was in high demand over central Iraq and Kuwait; but it could not easily search the western desert, and the ground resolution of its radar images was sufficiently poor to cause many problems with dummy launchers and fuel tankers. The DSP satellites used an infra-red telescope, but although they enabled the development of a reasonably efficient system for relaying warnings about launches to Israel and Saudi Arabia, they too lacked the precision to pinpoint the launchers.

As the missiles continued to fall – eleven landed on Israel in the first few days of war – the resources devoted to finding and attacking them mushroomed. TR-1 aircraft, modified successors to the U-2 spy plane, joined the hunt, as did JSTARS Boeings and RAF Tornado GR-1a reconnaissance variants. Dozens of fighter-bombers were kept loitering over the two principal launch areas: the western desert close to Jordan for firings at Israel, southern Iraq for those directed at Saudi Arabia. Hunting Scuds soaked up more missions than any other type of target in the first ten days of the war.

Lieutenant-General de la Billière was able to turn to his advantage the allied frustration at the inability of spy satellites to find the launchers. He volunteered the services of the SAS to hunt the launchers in western Iraq. SAS observation patrols had moved around there on foot during the early days of the war. The results had been poor: one group of eight, given the call sign Bravo Two Zero, had run into Iraqi forces – three men died, one escaped to Syria, and four were captured. The general's enthusiasm for the regiment he had once commanded was increasingly directed towards persuading General Schwarzkopf, who was known for his dislike of Special Forces, that the SAS could play a vital role.

The Commander in Chief had said in his 20 January briefing, 'Just that area of western Iraq is 29,000 square miles . . . there's not much point putting people on the ground to try and find nine, maybe ten, trucks.' General Schwarzkopf had also described the missiles, which were inaccurate, as 'militarily useless'. But intense pressure from Washington to make the Scuds top-priority targets distorted the general's original plans. Far more air sorties were being devoted to the hunt, so he let Lieutenant-General de la Billière persuade him of the value of the Special Forces deployment.

From 26 January 1991 the SAS was ordered to hunt the launchers, using motorized columns of sixteen to forty men to cross the desert emptiness. The SAS Land Rovers and Unimog trucks were equipped with a variety of weaponry including Milan anti-tank missile launchers. On 29 January a member of the regiment's B Squadron was said to have engaged and destroyed a Scud launcher with Milan; on other occasions, air strikes were called in. The SAS has always been surrounded by mythology, but its campaign in western Iraq took the myth-making to new heights, with stories emerging of troopers attaching explosives to the launchers. Even the Prime Minister endorsed the claims of their success.

In his memoir of the war, Lieutenant-General de la Billière characterized the Scud campaign as 'one of outstanding success'. He noted that 'no effective launches at Israel were made after 26 January . . . the danger of Israel entering the war had receded'.

The evidence for such claims is far from conclusive. After reviewing all the intelligence data gathered during the war, the US House of Representatives Committee on Armed Services report on intelligence aspects of the conflict concluded, 'There is no hard evidence that the great Scud chase destroyed even a single Scud missile or mobile launcher.'

After the war, the UN Special Commission set up to eliminate Iraq's weapons of mass destruction made discoveries that undermined allied claims. From information given by the Russians and seized from Iraqi military offices, the UN established that there had been nineteen mobile launchers: twelve Maz-543 of Soviet manufacture and seven Iraqi-made Al-Nidal or Al-Waleeds. They supervised the destruction of most of these vehicles and inspected others which the Iraqis had destroyed themselves. The investigators used a helicopter to search areas of western Iraq where 'kills' of mobile launchers had been claimed. A member of the Special Commission told me that all nineteen mobile launchers had been inspected and that there was no evidence any were destroyed by allied action. The Special Commission also found at least five dummy missile launchers.

Some time after the war I put these findings to Lieutenant-General de la Billière in an interview for the BBC's *Newsnight*. He replied, 'If you're going to say to me, "Well, how many Scuds did they destroy?" this wasn't altogether the point. They really denied the Iraqi Scuds the capability of deploying sufficiently close to Israel to launch their weapons effectively, and in doing so they undoubtedly destroyed some mobile Scuds . . . I'm quite confident that the Scuds would have gone on operating despite the massive air superiority that we possessed.'

Whatever the general's definition of an 'effective' launch, Scuds did carry on falling on Israel after 26 January: nineteen landed between 27 January and the end of the war. Several fell in residential areas: on 9 February one injured twenty-five people, and on 11 February another hurt seven. A few more landed harmlessly in the Negev desert in southern Israel, but these were believed to have been aimed at the Dimona nuclear reactor.

The SAS and certain US Air Force commanders still insist that some of the mobile launchers were destroyed. These claims cannot be reconciled with those of the UN Special Commission. Either the military men are mistaken, implying that they succeeded in knocking out only dummy launchers, or the UN team got the wrong figure for the number of mobile launchers produced in Iraq. The UN experts are the people who actually looked at the launchers and all the relevant Iraqi papers; they also noted that the dummy launchers were so convincing that one needed to be within twenty metres of them to know them from the real thing. However, Lieutenant-General de la Billière argues that the number destroyed was less important than the pattern of firing.

The generals were right in saying that the huge allied effort disrupted Scud launches, but it cannot reasonably be claimed that the SAS *per se* had any effect on the launch rate. From 17 to 26 January, twenty-one Scuds were fired at Israel and twenty-two at Saudi Arabia; from 27 January to the end of the war (almost one month), nineteen were fired at Israel and twenty-three at Saudi Arabia. Although the SAS, and later the US special operations commando group Delta Force, were hunting launchers in western Iraq during the latter period, there was no concerted Special Forces attempt to track down the launchers in the south of the country that were firing at Saudi Arabia; three small US teams sent on this mission in February were withdrawn almost immediately as there were too many Iraqi troops in the area. In other words, the launch pattern was roughly the same where the SAS were in action and where they were not. Air strikes were used in both of the Scud launching areas and did limit Iraqi firings; having troops on the ground in the western area apparently made no difference.

In an attempt to put the US- and UK-trained Kuwaiti resistance into action, US Navy special forces prepared ten fighters to infiltrate their homeland by sea. According to Rick Atkinson, author of *Crusade*, a history of the war, 'On spotting Iraqi guards on the beach, the Kuwaitis balked and the mission collapsed.'

Britain's 1st Armoured Division continued its training throughout the early period of the air war. Not until 31 January was the division declared operational. Initially, British troops had been sent to support the US Marines, but the decision to expand the UK force in November had been accompanied by a decision to switch the division inland, under the command of the US Army VII Corps.

At Joint Force HQ in High Wycombe, intelligence obtained through the NSA liaison cell had established the disposition of Iraq forces ahead of the British division. One British analyst remarks, 'We knew the position of every last Iraqi tank . . . the overall capability was fantastic.' However, very little imagery from the US KH-11 satellites was actually handed to the British. In most cases, the NSA officers delivered pages of text based on analysis of those images in the USA. Similarly, the decision had been made within Centcom's Riyadh HQ to channel intelligence towards the high-level commanders rather than those on the divisional rung of the military ladder – such as Britain's general in the desert – or below. The result was that Washington's generosity with intelligence brought almost no benefits to field commanders, who yearned to have actual pictures of the Iraqi positions they would be assaulting.

On 21 February 1991, three days before the launch of the ground war, Lieutenant-General de la Billière visited Major-General Rupert Smith, commanding 1st UK Armoured Division, and later noted in his memoir, 'Smith was at last getting some of the intelligence about the disposition of the enemy forces opposite him which he had long been seeking.' This vital data had not come from Cheltenham or High Wycombe but, as the British commander records, from 'unmanned drones equipped with cameras . . . sound-ranging equipment had pinpointed the sites of artillery and mortars. GR-1a Tornados had also been flying reconnaissance sorties over his sector of the front.' Nevertheless, the picture of Iraqi deployments was far from complete – a circumstance that one of Major-General Smith's subordinate commanders would complain about after the war.

When the Coalition divisions rolled into Kuwait and Iraq on 24 February, the opposition in most places crumbled quickly. Weeks of bombardment had cracked the Iraqi will to resist. There was perhaps also some truth in the line that Kuwaiti spokesmen had taken during the previous months of exile: that the Iraqi soldiers did not believe in the occupation, and had no desire to fight. Allied forces soon discovered important limitations to their intelligence. There were fewer Iraqi soldiers in many of the positions than they had expected, mainly because of desertion back to Iraq, and the air campaign had not achieved its goal of reducing tanks and artillery by half.

The Republican Guard divisions on the Kuwait–Iraq border had been the prime target of these strikes. Centcom J-2 (intelligence) had told US field commanders that 388 of the 846 tanks belonging to the three Republican Guard divisions in this area had been knocked out before the ground war started. Subsequent analysis of where and how all of the vehicles had been destroyed showed that between 166 and 215 had actually been knocked out before the ground war; the BDA experts had exaggerated by 100 to 134 per cent.

Allied forces found that the Iraqis were incapable of real resistance. Only two US M-1 tanks were lost to enemy action; none of the 160 or so British Challengers deployed was destroyed. Some accounts even suggest that not one of the Challengers was hit by an Iraqi tank round.

Psyops had played a key role in exacerbating the doubts of the ordinary Iraqi soldier that occupying a patch of another Arab's country was a cause worth dying for. In an attack by the 3rd Egyptian Mechanized Division that I witnessed, several hundred Iraqis immediately surrendered. Fewer than a dozen of those I saw were injured; all clutched the safe-conduct passes or other psyops leaflets dropped by the allies. Some 85,250 of Saddam's soldiers were taken prisoner.

As US armoured divisions closed in on Basra and Nasiriyah, the two principal cities of southern Iraq, in Washington and Riyadh they believed that General Schwarzkopf's encirclement plan had been successful. The Centcom intelligence brief for 27 February said, 'The Republican Guards are encircled . . . they have few options other than surrender or destruction.' But there was another option, and by the time those words were written, several Guard brigades had already taken it. The US encirclement was not complete, and many Iraqi units escaped over pontoon bridges spanning the Euphrates river. The failure to eliminate them was a source of lasting regret to the US Commander in Chief.

Following the destruction of retreating Iraqi units on the Mutla Ridge just north of Kuwait City the previous day, some key decision-makers in Washington, notably General Colin Powell, Chairman of the Joint Chiefs of Staff, had become concerned about the wisdom of carrying on the war. The notion of a 100-hour ground war had appealed to President Bush, who shared General Powell's concerns about overkill. At eight a.m. local time on 28 February 1991 the cease-fire took effect.

In London, members of the War Cabinet arriving at Downing Street learned of the ceasefire. Although President Bush had spoke to John Major the previous day, it had simply been to inform him of the US decision; Britain played no part in it. Someone at Downing Street that morning recalls, 'I came in to be told by Charles Powell that the war was over, that they had called it off. The British were small fry. It was their war.'

Although there was much subsequent debate about why the allies had not gone on to depose Saddam, the same person says, 'There was never any such discussion in Cabinet. We all recognized that we would not carry the Arabs with us if we went on to destroy Saddam.' The coalition built up with such care by President Bush and his Sec-retary of State had been created on the basis of liberating Kuwait. Although the US and UK had added to this prime objective the idea of dismantling Saddam's military might, they believed at the time of the ceasefire that both key objectives had been achieved.

Later that day, Royal Marine Commandos and members of the SBS were preparing to be dropped by helicopter on to the British embassy in Kuwait City. The senior SIS officer in Saudi Arabia had gone into Kuwait in order to link up with elements of the resistance. Shortly before the helicopters arrived at the embassy, I encountered him outside the building with three SBS soldiers. He identified him-self only as Mark (I learned his surname later from contacts), and sug-gested that 'something spectacular' was about to happen that would be worth filming. The symbolic recapture of the embassy – journal-ists had been camped out around it for the previous twenty-four hours – was intended as a final dramatic flourish to the British cam-paign. For many Britons, it was the very fact that the country had been a junior partner in such a great international venture that meant the sight of Royal Marines raising the Union Flag at the embassy could not match the drama of the 1982 re-capture of Government House in the Falklands.

On 3 March General Schwarzkopf and his Saudi counterpart went to Safwan in southern Iraq to agree ceasefire terms with Saddam's officers. Sitting opposite them were the Deputy Chief of the Iraqi

General Staff and Major-General Mahmud, commander of III Corps, whose radio transmissions had provided such enjoyable listening for US and British sigint monitors. The ceasefire terms agreed there concluded the war, but left open a loophole by allowing Baghdad to use its helicopters. In a final demonstration of how accident-prone the intelligence community had become in its estimates of numbers, US officials suggested that up to 100,000 Iraqis had died in the war. Later Pentagon analyses would conclude that the losses, both civilian and military, probably did not exceed 25,000.

The same day as the Safwan ceasefire, a spontaneous insurrection broke out among the Shiite population in southern Iraq. The Shiites were actually the majority in Iraq, and they resented the rule of Saddam and his clique of fellow Sunni Muslim generals, mostly from his home region of Takrit. Heavy fighting erupted in Basra and Najaf, the city containing the most important Shiite religious sites.

By 5 March Kurdish groups at the other end of the country, bordering Turkey and Syria, had joined the insurrection against Baghdad. Kurdish *pershmerga* guerrillas had a long history of struggle against their rulers in Iraq, Iran and Turkey. The rebels sensed that the moment might have come for the creation of a national homeland.

Fearing that these rebellions might lead to the dismemberment of the state, Iraqi generals who might otherwise have been thinking of ways to dispose of a leader with a unique talent for engineering national disasters rallied around him and moved to suppress the revolts. The CIA and SIS had helped to encourage the rebels through their seditious messages and Free Iraq radio station, but they do not seem to have given any direct support to the insurrections. Armoured brigades that had escaped from Kuwait went into action in the southern cities of Karbala and Najaf. Armed helicopters played a key role in attacking the cities too. The Shiite rebels may have believed that the nearby US forces would help them, but they were disappointed. By the end of the month, after heavy shelling in which several thousand people were probably killed, the rebellion was under control. When I asked one senior figure in British intelligence about the earlier appeals for revolt, he replied, 'We hadn't thought it through properly.'

Although the Kurds fared somewhat better militarily, by 30 March Kirkuk, one of the principal cities of northern Iraq, was back under central control. Early the following month John Major's plan for Kurdish safe havens was put to the international community, and British and US forces deployed to Turkey to assist in its execution. A

Kurdish statelet was carved out of northern Iraq and a 'no-fly' zone agreed by the UN Security Council as a means of keeping it safe from Iraqi bombing. A similar ban on Iraqi air operations in the south of the country was later agreed.

Shortly after the war, senior officers assembled in the Queen Elizabeth Conference Centre in Whitehall for a debriefing. It was an occasion attended by almost all the top brass, including the Duke of Edinburgh in uniform. At one point Brigadier Chris Hammerbeck, who had commanded the 4th Armoured Brigade, told his distinguished audience that he had crossed into Iraq 'intelligence blind', not knowing what lay ahead of him. Vice Admiral John Kerr, the Chief of Defence Intelligence, exchanged glances with Air Vice Marshal John Walker, his Director General for Management and Support of Intelligence, who recalls, 'We were not exactly overjoyed by that comment.' Vice Admiral Kerr asked him to look into the complaints.

Walker had earned his spurs flying Jaguar bombers and later commanded Bruggen, the RAF's biggest Tornado station. He was known in his service as a man of strong views, no respecter of received wisdoms. Later that year he was promoted, himself becoming CDI. Walker's verdict on the Gulf War is, 'You had within the intelligence organization an inner intelligence organization. Senior guys had some very good information but everyone else was working in a sort of outer shell.' He adds, 'It was a dissemination problem caused by operational secrecy . . . we paid a very high penalty for operational security.'

Lieutenant-General de la Billière's view is that 'the key problem in the field was that intelligence was so voluminous that it was not manageable'. He says the USA had tried to cope by targeting the information at levels of command above that of Britain's armoured division. The general did not feel starved of intelligence, either by High Wycombe or US Central Command in Riyadh, but points out that 'it's in the nature of the problem that I wouldn't have known if I had been'. Lieutenant-General de la Billière adds, 'You had to accept that there was valuable intelligence being held back to protect the source.'

Despite the scale of Britain's military commitment, there was never any question about who was in charge. Britain remained virtually uninvolved in the central political decisions, such as the one about ending the war. These military and political realities were mirrored on the intelligence plane. SIS and the CIA were not lucky enough to have had any sources of note in the Iraqi regime. Dependence on technical methods of collecting information was near-total.

GCHQ was so sensitive about the information it received from the USA that much of the militarily-significant data which flowed into Cheltenham, High Wycombe or the Cabinet Office was never passed on to the troops in the field. The House of Commons Defence Committee later echoed Air Marshal Walker, noting that there had been 'over-rigorous application of operational security which meant ... dissemination of some intelligence was hindered'. People involved in fighting the war use stronger language and suggest that it virtually nullified the intelligence advantage Britain's special relationship with the NSA could have given, compared with battlefield commanders of other nations such as the French.

The availability of high-level intelligence in London was undoubtedly important in keeping the War Cabinet abreast of the political inside track. The interception of Saddam's conversations with his UN ambassador enabled British leaders to understand that, right up to the launching of the ground offensive, he was not serious about pulling out of Kuwait. The nature of the special relationship awed some of those considering the information and left them wondering what it said about Britain's national capabilities. One of them said to me, 'When you ask "What did the British give?" it's a damn good question. Over 90 per cent of what was in my reports was American material. If we didn't have the Americans, I'd have had nothing to write about. In the intelligence world the Americans have all the cards. Without them, we'd be little better than Belgium. What would we be without the Americans?'

Chapter 14

1991 Moscow Endgame

In the aftermath of the Gulf War, with confrontation with Saddam Hussein rumbling on, unrest in Yugoslavia and signs of growing independence on the part of Soviet republics, relations with Moscow were never to have quite the same centrality in foreign or intelligence policy. But Mikhail Gorbachev's presidency did produce one more moment of high drama in Downing Street.

As the Cabinet got back to normal after the liberation of Kuwait, regulars in the central intelligence machinery began noticing marked distinctions between John Major and his predecessor. There were differences of personality, one mandarin explains: 'He was easier. With a man you joke quite a bit – with Mrs T you didn't make jokes.' Another, a senior diplomat, notes that Major is 'good with foreigners, good at negotiation. He doesn't antagonize people in the way she did. But he's not interested in grand ideas in the way she was.'

Whereas sifting through intelligence reports had been a kind of hobby for Thatcher, the new Prime Minister was conscious of the many other calls on his time, and perhaps of the limited public interest in foreign policy. As Defence Secretary, Tom King watched the transition, and believes that Thatcher was 'always very conscious of her responsibilities on the intelligence side, listened very carefully to advice on that side, and instinctively understood the importance of protecting it . . . John Major took over in a time of war – he had to absorb an awful lot of things very fast. He was certainly not lacking in attention to intelligence matters, but she did indeed have a very special commitment and interest in this area.' A senior intelligence figure adds, 'He was less sold on this particular drug.'

Thatcher had, of course, reserved the right to ignore intelligence advice and rely instead on her political instinct. This had served her well in her relations with Gorbachev, less so in the period of tension leading up to the invasion of Kuwait. Whatever she thought of their assessments, her basic commitment to the intelligence services had remained: its main consequences were substantial funding increases in real terms for the agencies throughout the 1980s, and her many battles against whistle-blowers and others who threatened the veil of secrecy she passionately believed was necessary.

The budgetary consequences of Major's succession soon became apparent; one intelligence mandarin described the post-Thatcher atmosphere as 'New Year's Day with a hangover'. Major's willingness to place SIS and GCHQ on a statutory footing and to allow the services greater latitude in self-publicity was a great relief to those who believed that Thatcher had 'sexed it all up by drawing a veil over everything'.

There was one more important practical consequence for ministers and the staff of the Joint Intelligence Committee. 'Mrs Thatcher didn't like the normal Cabinet Office machinery . . . to the great frustration of Cabinet Office regulars and people who never knew what on earth was going on,' explains one civil servant. 'Under Major, things returned to the proper Cabinet Office way.' Just as the Thatcher approach of having key decisions made by small Cabinet sub-committees, or of using Charles Powell as note-taker in sensitive meetings, had effectively increased her power at the expense of that of ministerial colleagues and certain mandarins, under Major this process was slowly reversed.

In time, a formal Cabinet committee was established to oversee the intelligence services. Mandarins like Percy Cradock, Robin Butler and Christopher Curwen (the former SIS Chief who had become Intelligence Co-ordinator) discovered they had greater discretion over matters affecting the agencies.

During the months of the Gulf crisis, Gorbachev had been busy trying to check the progress of nationalism in his two most persistent trouble-spots, the Baltic republics and the Caucasus region. Relying perhaps on the West's preoccupation with Saddam Hussein, he had tried to thwart the independence movements in the republics. On 11 January 1991 he sent paratroopers into the Lithuanian capital Vilnius to occupy government buildings. This provoked a bloody fracas, causing the army generals who had urged him to take a tough line to insist that such actions were not their job but the Interior Ministry's.

A similar move into the Latvian capital Riga on 20 January was therefore executed by the Omon, an Interior Ministry riot squad.

These attempts at coercion did nothing to stem the nationalist tide. On 9 April the Georgians declared independence. In the Kremlin there was a growing sense of helplessness. Power was not just slipping away from Gorbachev on the periphery of the Soviet empire, it was also being contested at its Russian centre.

Boris Yeltsin was elected President of the Russian Federation on 12 June 1991. He had won multi-candidate elections by standing on a reform platform, beating contenders representing both the old Communist order and the emerging ultra-nationalist one. The election placed Gorbachev at an immense political disadvantage: not only did Yeltsin have a democratic mandate – which it is clear Gorbachev could not get, given how unpopular the economic situation had made him – but the Russian President also stood for a powerful new idea. The Russians as well as the other republics wanted a divorce from the seventy-year Soviet shotgun marriage.

In London, Gloria Craig's Soviet Current Intelligence Group charted events in a series of minutes, some going direct to ministers, others via the Joint Intelligence Committee. Gordon Barrass had been promoted to become her immediate boss, the Chief of Assessments. Barrass, an SIS officer, had attained a position at the same Civil Service rank (Grade 3) as the four directors of his Service, but there were mutterings at Century House about the fact that his Foreign Office cover rank, Assistant Under Secretary, was now higher than that of any other MI6 officer, including the Chief, Colin McColl, whom the Diplomatic List listed simply as 'Counsellor, FCO'. Barrass, the man who had masterminded Gordievsky's debriefing, was an expert on Soviet politics. Although Cradock had been one of his patrons, helping him gain this unusually senior Cabinet Office position, Barrass took a more positive view of Gorbachev than the JIC Chairman, who was of course his superior.

During the summer of 1991, several of the minutes that Craig, Barrass and Cradock sent to ministers warned of the possibility of a military coup in Moscow. As one Whitehall official notes, 'We had a general strategic warning that something would happen.' However, none of the minutes was specific, for example by pinpointing any of Gorbachev's trips abroad or his annual holiday in Crimea as danger points. An intelligence chief concedes, 'I don't know of any evidence that anybody had – something like an intercept, a document or a source which would have constituted real intelligence – about what was going to happen.'

The British ambassador in Moscow, Rodric Braithwaite, sent back a stream of telegrams that were highly regarded in Whitehall, but which betrayed a limited knowledge of internal Kremlin machinations. In any case, these would not have told the whole story, as one of the more philosophical intelligence analysts explains: 'If you've got good embassies abroad and are getting good reports, you're hearing the views of the players. But sometimes the players themselves don't really realize what's going on. The classic case was the move against Gorbachev.'

Yeltsin, it seems, had heard similar rumours and did take practical action. He had appointed both a military adviser, General Konstantin Kobets, and a KGB adviser, Major-General Ivanenko, with the task of creating embryonic Russian, as opposed to Soviet, power structures. Yeltsin ordered General Kobets to prepare a defence plan for his headquarters, the so-called 'White House', and told Major-General Ivanenko to use his professional contacts in the KGB to report any conspiracy against him.

The ministers and Whitehall officials pondering the JIC's generalized warnings had more urgent foreign policy matters to contend with. On 8 May 1991 the republic of Slovenia voted to secede from the Yugoslav Federation. This was followed several weeks later by declarations of independence by both Slovenia and Croatia, where a large Serbian minority set themselves squarely against the process and were claiming their own autonomy in the Krajina region.

At the end of June the nationalist manoeuvrings finally produced bloodshed. The JNA, or Yugoslav People's Army, went into action, sending armoured columns to seal Slovenia's borders, and fighter-bombers to strafe its main airport and roads. The JNA soon found itself in difficulties, its armoured forces held up by Slovenes using mines and anti-tank rockets. These mediocre efforts, like those of the Soviet Army in Lithuania or Karabakh, slowly undermined the position of generals who believed that such actions were needed to save their multinational socialist states, and strengthened those in the general staffs of Moscow and Belgrade who saw things in terms of Russian and Serbian nationalism.

By July, fighting had become intense in the Croatian regions where Serbs refused to accept Zagreb's writ. Although some of the generals who commanded the JNA were non-Serbs, it became increasingly clear that their strategy involved buttressing the Serbian Republic of Krajina rather than the unrealistic goal of reimposing Federal rule throughout Croatia.

Events in Yugoslavia caught out the British foreign policy and intelligence establishments in the same way as the Gulf crisis had. Although there had been many JIC minutes warning of trouble ahead, inertia within the agencies and the impossibility of watching all potential flash points meant that large resources were still focused on the Soviet Union and that there were few people in government who had the specialist knowledge to produce first-rate assessments. Because of the sudden demand for information, a Current Intelligence Group was set up for the Balkans.

Just as the US-led coalition had restricted the UK's room for manoeuvre in the Gulf, so the responses to Yugoslav events were soon being co-ordinated by the European Community. Most senior figures in the Foreign Office, Ministry of Defence and British intelligence regarded the events in Croatia as a civil war. The borders of Croatia were hotly disputed, the government of Franjo Tudjman was evidently unacceptable to more than a third of Croatia's people, and the Federal army was trying to suppress that government: in short, most key officials did not view Croatia as satisfying the usual conditions for recognition as an independent state. But the UK was soon put under pressure to fall in with its European allies.

At Germany's instigation, the EC voted to recognize Croatia. British reservations were set aside, in the hope that the decision might deter the Belgrade authorities from further excesses, and in return for a trade-off: German support for London's position on negotiations aimed at furthering European political union. Far-reaching decisions were made with little thought as to their consequences. Although EC efforts did help to bring a ceasefire in September, the January 1991 decision to recognize Croatia was critically flawed because European nations lacked the will to commit military resources to defend its independence; a Kuwait-style operation was the logical corollary of labelling Belgrade's action international aggression rather than civil war. It was a bluffer's foreign policy: Serbian extremists soon recognized it as such, and this was to produce considerable political, diplomatic and military complications for Whitehall.

When President Bush met his Soviet counterpart on 31 July 1991 to sign the last key arms-control treaty between the superpowers, the diplomatic achievement this represented had become overshadowed by events in the Gulf and the Balkans – as well as by the fact that such deals had now become almost routine. The Strategic Arms Reduction Treaty (START) finally specified the deep cuts in intercontinental nuclear weapons that President Reagan had discussed with Gorbachev in Reykjavik five years earlier. As well as reducing the total of ballistic missiles, it also limited the number of warheads each one could carry. The latter agreement presented a formidable problem of verification, since satellites cannot see inside missile nose-cones. But the Bush Administration had come to trust Moscow and generally placed less emphasis on verification than its predecessor.

As arms-control treaties multiplied, the military intelligence departments of Western nations were obliged to transfer some of their resources into monitoring treaty compliance. In the case of the British Ministry of Defence, this consisted of setting up a joint services arms-control verification team that drew heavily on the expertise of those who had formerly collated information on the Soviet 'threat'. BRIXMIS, the military mission that under the old four-power arrangements had spied legally on the Soviet Army in East Germany, was disbanded on 10 December 1990, a casualty of arms control and German unification. Its officers, many of them skilled Russian linguists, were still in demand, however; Colonel Roy Giles, a one-time deputy BRIXMIS commander, became head of the new verification unit.

US intelligence concerns about the Soviet nuclear stockpile led in February 1993 to an agreement with Moscow to buy 500 tonnes of highly enriched uranium for $1 billion, a measure designed to prevent fissile material falling into the wrong hands. The White House also hoped that this would cushion the rundown of the US nuclear weapons industry, where the Soviet uranium was to be reprocessed. The CIA, however, was uncertain about the size of the problem: its estimate of 32,000 nuclear warheads came with the weighty caveat 'give or take 5,000'. CIA and SIS officials recognized that the recruitment of new Soviet sources could help to stop a dictator like Saddam Hussein buying these weapons, but they had few illusions about the difficulty of the task.

Despite the continued treachery of Aldrich Ames, it was apparent by mid-1991 that SIS had succeeded in recruiting some new sources in Moscow. Their survival was possible because of the way SIS sanitized the CX reports it passed to 'the cousins'. Mikhail Butkov, a KGB officer who defected that year, was probably run for some time as an agent. Vadim Sintsov, a middle-ranking figure in the arms indus-try, was later charged by the Russians with spying for MI6. By mid-1991 a further source was also active, either in the KGB or another department of government, and was to provide intelligence at a crit-ical point that August.

Shortly after the START agreement, Gorbachev left Moscow for a holiday in a sumptuous Crimean villa overlooking the Black Sea. Once he was out of the way, several senior figures, including the Prime Minister, the Deputy Defence Minister and the KGB Chair-man, began to conspire. They believed that the combination of eco-nomic collapse and nationalist unrest had brought the country to the brink, so a state of emergency was needed to reimpose Communist control and remind people of the smack of firm government. A del-egation of the leading plotters flew to the Crimea to persuade Gor-bachev that this was the right course of action. They presented him with a document they had drafted declaring a state of emergency, which he refused to sign. The plotters returned to Moscow and decided to act without him. Gorbachev's communications with Moscow were cut. The interruption of this highly-encrypted signal (which the National Security Agency could detect from one of its geo-stationary eavesdropping satellites but could not decipher) was the West's first indication that something was amiss.

Early on the morning of 19 August 1991, the General Staff ordered several units of the Moscow garrison into the city centre, in contra-vention of the rules that forbade armed troops inside the outer ring road. The Taman Guards Motor Rifle Division, based to the west of the city, provided sub-units involved in several of the critical dramas of the hours ahead. According to the commander of the division, the orders telephoned to him at six a.m. were the first he knew of the coup. Before then, it seems, only a small core of conspirators knew of the plan, which made it virtually impossible for any intelligence service – most importantly, Gorbachev's own – to obtain hard information. Units of the Taman Guards and other divisions began trundling into the city with orders to protect various points; they did not specify on whose behalf, or from whom. A company of twelve T-72 tanks and several other armoured vehicles under the command of Major Sergei Yevdekimov had been given as its objectives the Russian Federation parliament – the 'White House' – and a bridge nearby.

At the Foreign Ministry Press Centre journalists were summoned to a briefing by the main conspirators, members of the self-styled

State Committee for the State of Emergency. They announced several decrees and were cryptic about whether Gorbachev was under arrest. A couple of the Committee members seemed drunk, and it later became clear that the coup had only ever been directed in any real sense for a few hours that morning.

At the Cabinet Office in London, Assessments Staff members watching television pictures of Yeltsin clambering on board one of the Taman division's tanks outside the White House remarked that any really professional plotters would have eliminated him at the outset. Some senior intelligence officers gleefully and prematurely told their colleagues that they had been right about the Cold War not being over after all. In Washington, President Bush perceptively remarked that success for the plotters was far from assured.

Major Yevdekimov, the tank commander, was invited into the White House and asked by General Kobets and parliamentary deputies to give an assurance that he would not fire on his own people. The major agreed to this proposition; in any case, he had received no orders from his superiors apart from the initial command to guard the area. A company of paratroop cadets who also arrived at the White House gave a similar pledge. These actions were mistakenly reported by journalists as evidence that units of the army had 'joined Yeltsin'.

Some senior officers, notably General Yevgeni Shaposhnikov, Commander in Chief of the Air Force, and Lieutenant-General Pavel Grachev, commander of Airborne Forces, had set themselves against the coup from the outset, and were to be rewarded with senior commands when it collapsed. Others, such as General Yuri Maksimov, Commander in Chief of the Strategic Rocket Forces, sat on the fence but took prudent precautions. General Maksimov ordered his ballistic missile crews to assume a non-provocative posture, parking their mobile launchers in view of US satellites.

A 1994 exposé by Seymour Hersh, the US investigative journalist, in *Atlantic Monthly* reported that the NSA had succeeded in tapping into land lines carrying the Soviet Union's highest-level military traffic, presumably in Moscow. Hersh suggested that the NSA had fed Boris Yeltsin with information about the loyalty of different sections of the armed forces during the August 1991 coup. The journalist quoted an anonymous espionage official as saying, 'We monitored every major command and we handed it to Yeltsin on a platter.' If the exposé is accurate, this extraordinary intelligence operation may have explained why President Bush took a sanguine attitude from the outset of the coup.

Senior British and US officials whom I interviewed said that they could not confirm Hersh's story, even under conditions of complete non-attributability. The NSA may have kept Britain in the dark about the tapping operation, but given the intimacy of sigint co-operation this seems unlikely. It is also possible that the NSA did indeed succeed in tapping a Moscow land line but that the content of the traffic through it was not quite as sensational as the journalist's sources claimed. In any case, it is clear from talking to generals and Kremlin officials that once the initial operation of sending troops into Moscow had been carried out, the generals were playing a game of wait and see, providing no significant military support to either side.

By the second day, thousands of people summoned to defend the White House against the anti-reformist forces were manning barricades around the building. The army was effectively paralysed, and KGB Chairman Vladimir Kryuchkov, one of the chief plotters, ordered an élite assault team under his control called Alpha Group to stand by. At the White House, wild rumours circulated of tank movements through the city, even of a submarine approaching up the Moscow River.

At some point, says a senior British figure, an SIS agent warned his controllers about the Alpha Group assault plan. Handling a well-placed source is a complex business that often makes timely communication impossible, but on this occasion, to SIS's credit, it happened. The information went to London, where Percy Cradock told the Prime Minister about it, and then back to Moscow through Foreign Office secure channels.

Rodric Braithwaite, the Ambassador, was told to telephone Yeltsin and warn him. He got through using the normal lines – further evidence of the extraordinary ineptitude of the coup – and passed on the message. Braithwaite himself says that the British warning did not even get through until *after* the violence of that night – by which time the frightened White House defenders thought they had driven off an attack.

Subsequent inquiries suggest that, although Alpha was moved closer to the White House, it never received the order to attack. It would in any case have been difficult for this élite team of about 200 to have taken the huge building without considerable army support. By one of the ironies so beloved of Muscovites, Alpha did get to attack the building in October 1993, on Yeltsin's orders: that later assault involved dozens of armoured vehicles and 2,000 other troops. The fact that Whitehall and Braithwaite considered it worthwhile to pass on this brief, imprecise message casts further doubt on Seymour Hersh's suggestion that all significant deliberations of the Soviet High Command were being relayed direct to Yeltsin by NSA operatives.

Late in the evening of 20 August a column of infantry fighting vehicles drove around the inner ring road, having been told to monitor the curfew imposed by one of the few decrees of the State Committee for the State of Emergency. When the vehicles reached an underpass near the Russian Parliament they ran into a blockade set up by White House defenders, who threw Molotov cocktails at them. Some of the troops dismounted and shot dead three protesters. Some journalists mistakenly described these events as the start of the long-awaited attack, but the armoured column had actually been moving away from the White House when it happened.

The following morning, 21 August, the coup collapsed and the main plotters tried to flee the city. Contrasting the White House events of August 1991 and October 1993, the reformist politician Gregor Yavlinsky said, 'The first began as a tragedy and ended in farce, the second began as farce and ended as tragedy.'

Republics such as Estonia and Latvia took advantage of the 1991 farce to declare independence. Within days, the Soviet Union was no more. Gorbachev, displaying breathtaking political insensitivity, had on his return from the Crimea said that he remained a Communist and expected things to get back to normal. Two days later Yeltsin banned the Communist Party of the Soviet Union and seized all its assets. Although Gorbachev soldiered on, attempting to form a loose coalition of the formerly Soviet republics, by Christmas he conceded defeat – and in an act of personal capitulation symbolizing the only respect in which the Russian Republic remained a great power, he handed the nuclear weapon launch codes to Yeltsin.

A few weeks later in Washington, the Senate hearings to confirm the appointment of Robert Gates as Director of Central Intelligence turned into a trial both of the man and of his organization's failure to read the inherent weakness of the Soviet system more successfully. Gates had been Deputy Director for Intelligence, the CIA's chief analyst, for several years before his appointment as Director.

Analysts called from within the Directorate of Intelligence (DI) attacked Gates for slanting estimates. Melvin Goodman, a Soviet desk officer at the Agency for twenty-four years, accused him of distorting reports about Iran at a time when the Administration was about to begin its covert arms sales. Goodman also said that Gates had skewed a report on the 1985 attempt to assassinate Pope John Paul II in order to point the finger at the KGB. Jennifer Glaudemans, another DI analyst, said that those people working on the Soviet estimate had experienced an atmosphere of intimidation and pressure, leading to the dismissal of some who did not go along with the received wisdom.

Gates defended himself against these criticisms by arguing that the subjectivity of so many intelligence judgements made them easy to criticize in retrospect. Members of the Senate Committee accepted his arguments and voted to support his appointment. Eight months later, Gates gave a speech that did contain a grudging *mea culpa* for the Soviet estimate. He conceded that it was not until early 1989, four years after Gorbachev's appointment, that the Agency really grasped that his reforms would 'unintentionally set in motion forces . . . and bring down the entire political system'. He admitted that 'clear deficiencies in our approach' limited the usefulness of the economic assessments. The professionals had failed to remind 'policy makers and ourselves . . . that from time to time some things are simply unknowable – even to the protagonists'.

It is not the British style to go in for such soul-searching, particularly in public, but criticisms about the assessment process could equally have been made by those who thought Cradock had been an unyielding Cold Warrior. In the case of Britain, after all, these deficiencies had resulted in something more serious than a committee hearing on Capitol Hill: they had led the Prime Minister repeatedly to set aside intelligence advice on a central issue of foreign policy.

On Thursday 29 August 1991, after the regular meeting of the JIC, Cradock summoned the heads of the intelligence agencies and other officials into his office. Champagne and glasses had been made ready. Television pictures of the scenes outside the Lubyanka, the old KGB headquarters, a week before had sealed Cradock's conviction that the Cold War was finally over. 'The decisive point,' he says, 'was to be the aftermath of the 1991 coup and the outlawing of the Soviet Communist party as a national entity. Perhaps most vividly, the television pictures of the crowds pulling down the Dzerzhinsky [founder of the communist secret police] statue outside the Lubyanka.' Cradock made a short speech to his colleagues in which he ironically remarked that the Moscow conspirators had acted as true Marxists and accelerated the course of history. He then invited the denizens of the secret world to toast their victory over Communism.

Cradock's verdict is that 'British intelligence had a good record, from Gorbachev's first reforms on, in recognizing the powerful new forces let loose inside Soviet society. As the changes progressed, the JIC predicted the eventual break-up of the Soviet Union, the likelihood of a coup, and its likely failure. In the early days we and the Americans were alive to the economic weakness of Russia – that it was an Upper Volta with rockets. Perhaps we didn't give this enough weight; but it was masked for many years by the great rise in oil prices, which boosted the Soviet as well as Middle Eastern economies.'

Many would dissent from this view, not least Lieutenant-General Derek Boorman, the defence intelligence chief who was Deputy JIC Chairman as well from 1985 to 1988: he argues that there was a general failure to predict or understand the changes. The last word perhaps belongs to Charles Powell, whose prior diplomatic career and access to the Prime Minister and almost all of Downing Street's foreign policy secrets make him particularly well-placed to judge the performance of intelligence:

> The biggest single failure of intelligence of that era was the failure of almost everybody to foresee the end of Communism. It caught us completely on the hop. All that intelligence about their war-fighting capabilities was all very well, but it didn't tell us the one thing we needed to know, that it was all about to collapse. It was a colossal failure of the whole Western system of intelligence assessment and political judgement.

Part Three

Chapter 15

1991 An Accident of History

Ten days before Christmas 1991 the Home Office announced the appointment of Stella Rimington as Director General of the Security Service. Public statements on such matters were a novelty, part of John Major's policy of more open government, and the fact that the new DGSS was a woman made it doubly of interest to the media and the chattering classes. This was precisely what Patrick Walker, the incumbent DG, Robin Butler and the other mandarins had hoped for when they recommended her to Kenneth Baker, the Home Secretary.

After a couple of years as Director of G Branch (Counter Terrorism), Rimington had been made Deputy Director General for just over a year. Fighting terrorists had proved a black hole for resources, sucking all but a skeleton staff out of F Branch (Counter Subversion) during 1985–8 and about half the officers from K Branch (Counter Espionage) in 1989–92. One former G Branch officer explains, 'We're not talking about devoting more than a few people to each target, but it's such a disparate threat that it consumes a very large proportion of resources.' Rimington and her Board of Directors were convinced that the strategy originally mapped out by Anthony Duff was more valid than ever; if anything, the need for greater resources increased its appeal. By 1994 the counter-espionage, counter-subversion and protective security work (K, F and C Branches), which formed the Service's operational core for forty years of Cold War, had all been so run down that they were amalgamated into a single body with one director, D Branch. An escalation in the IRA campaign in mainland Britain was giving ministers daily reminders of the need for greater counter-terrorist activity.

On 16 December, the day Rimington's appointment was announced, IRA explosive devices went off in shops, the National Gallery and a railway station. From its resumption in August 1988 to 16 December 1991, there had been around sixty bombing or shooting attacks, killing fifteen people and injuring more than a hundred. Despite this, most of the Provisionals' attacks had been designed not to kill but to spread a climate of fear and chaos, to force people in Britain to confront the Northern Ireland troubles themselves. The campaign had developed from actions aimed at killing soldiers – such as the attacks on bands and military recruitment offices in 1989–90 – to bombing public transport in autumn 1991 and fire-bombing stores during the Christmas shopping period; measures designed to inconvenience as many people in London, Manchester or elsewhere as possible.

The IRA's campaign against the British military on the continent of Europe had by mid-1990 fizzled out. Several members of Active Service Units had been arrested, and the gains from their activities had been minimal. There had been numerous 'own goals': an Australian tourist had been shot dead, as had a soldier's wife and the baby daughter of an RAF man. The European campaign could demonstrate no 'spectaculars' such as the 1989 bombing of the Royal Marine Music School at Deal in Kent, which killed eleven, but it had cost the Provisionals dear. In terms of their broader strategy, the IRA had long considered one bomb in London to be worth ten in Belfast, but the shootings and bombings in Germany were not achieving quite the same results. After the killing of a British officer on 2 June 1990 the Provisional IRA Army Council, its high command, therefore abandoned European attacks in favour of a greater focus on Britain itself.

As Director of G Branch, Rimington had fought a Whitehall battle to have MI5 put in charge of all anti-IRA intelligence operations in Europe, and this had happened in 1989. In each theatre where the IRA operated, the balance of influence between the different security agencies was subtly different. In Ireland itself, both the Republic and the north, where MI5 had run agents for the previous decade, displacing MI6 to a purely liaison role, the Security Service had a senior officer at Stormont with the title of Director and Co-ordinator of Intelligence (DCI). But the DCI could not compel the army or the Royal Ulster Constabulary to do anything, and the RUC's Special Branch had in fact become the most powerful of the three agencies running agents in the IRA because it had so many more of them. In practice, the RUC Special Branch and MI5 had evolved a *modus vivendi* in which the locals ran informer networks needed for the counter-terrorist campaign in Ulster itself, and MI5 dealt mainly with sources who could provide information on IRA activities outside Northern Ireland.

In Britain, the picture was even more complex. The Security Service ran agents in loyalist extremist groups, but any warnings from MI5 agents about forthcoming IRA operations were meant to be passed to the Metropolitan Police Special Branch (MPSB). This police intelligence-gathering arm had been set up in 1883 to combat an earlier wave of Irish terrorism. The fight against terrorism – firstly by the Fenians seeking Irish independence, and many decades later by the Provisional IRA – was central to the MPSB's existence, and it had in fact for a time been called the Irish Special Branch. Many of Britain's fifty other police forces had their own Special Branch, but the Met was in charge of national co-ordination. The job of catching terrorists fell to those schooled in a different police tradition, that of the Criminal Investigation Department (CID). Detectives with a CID background therefore made up the bulk of the Met's Anti-Terrorist Unit (known as ATU or SO-13), which sifted bomb sites or arms dumps in the search for clues that could put terrorists in jail.

As the IRA prepared its British offensive, the police network had done reasonably well: five people had been convicted of possessing weapons or carrying out reconnaissance of possible targets. A series of finds between February 1987 and December 1989 had netted 387 lb of high explosive, sufficient for dozens of attacks. But as the Provisionals' campaign had gathered momentum from late 1989 onwards, the police had looked increasingly helpless. Their inability to cope, together with the structural problems of the police system, infuriated intelligence chiefs, one of whom remarks, 'It was outrageous, the number of police forces. It was like something out of Germany in the Middle Ages. If an ASU [an IRA cell] went north, it would affect about half a dozen wretched chief constables, each one a law unto himself, reserving the right to issue idiotic statements.'

Because of the political pressure on the police and MI5 to get results, Christopher Curwen, the Intelligence Co-ordinator at the Cabinet Office, had during 1990 and 1991 written three reports about arrangements for hunting the IRA. One of these actually strengthened the hand of George Churchill Coleman, Commander of the Anti Terrorist Unit, by boosting his ability to co-ordinate investigations of terrorist crime nationally. Although Curwen and his superior Percy Cradock had often considered giving the Security Service the lead, they feared the possible consequences. One civil servant remarks, 'We had the problem of, "Do you want to carry out a revolution in the middle of a war?" We knew the Metropolitan Police would take it very badly.'

The arguments in favour of taking the risk and those in favour of making the existing system work had always been finely balanced, but in mid-1991 the scales tipped. Gerry Warner was appointed Intelligence Co-ordinator in succession to Curwen. Warner had been Director of Counter Intelligence and Security at MI6 until 1990, when he had briefly left the espionage world for a post in the Police Complaints Authority. 'Chris Curwen had a softly-softly approach. Gerry Warner took a more robust view,' notes an intelligence mandarin.

Warner had been convinced by Rimington that the Special Branch only understood how to run 'informers' whereas what was needed were 'agents'. Whereas an informer might be paid by his handlers for information he or she came across, an agent would actively seek involvement with terrorist or political groups on the instructions of case officers. 'Our own rules define an agent as somebody producing secret intelligence while under our control,' says an MI5 man. The Security Service presentation to mandarins such as Warner, Cradock and Butler stressed that a more aggressive use of agents was needed. One Security Service officer summarizes their arguments at this critical moment: 'The aim with the IRA was to destabilize the organization at a strategic level with agents.'

As an ex-MI6 officer, and one who had been in overall charge of counter-intelligence during the latter years of the Gordievsky case, Warner needed little convincing of the value of the well-placed agent. But others, particularly in the police, knew that there were dangers. Brian Nelson, a member of the loyalist terrorist group the Ulster Defence Association, had been arrested in January 1990 by detectives looking into leaks of security forces intelligence material in Northern Ireland. Nelson had been an Army 'offensive penetration' agent, run in much the same way as the agents MI5 wanted to use to destabilize the IRA. He had entered the terrorist nether world on the instructions of his handlers, and his subsequent trial raised many uncomfortable questions about his personal participation in conspiracies to kill people and about the security forces' foreknowledge of certain crimes. The Nelson case created an uncertainty about the agent's role. An MI5 officer remarks, 'It doesn't help if people question the legality without resolving the question.' Ministers wanted results, and those who favoured changing the anti-terrorist arrangements perhaps knew that this could involve fudging some principles.

With Warner convinced, Cradock and Butler soon followed suit, and by the autumn MI5's campaign for leadership of anti-IRA operations had acquired the momentum of a bureaucratic freight train. Although ministers publicly insisted that the issue would have to await the findings of yet another Whitehall paper early in 1992 – this time from Ian Burns, a senior Home Office civil servant – the Permanent Secretaries' Intelligence Services committee (PSIS) approved plans prepared by MI5 and Warner to recruit 300 new staff to take on the new task.

By the beginning of 1992 MI5 had formed T Branch, its domestic counter-terrorism organization. Sections dealing with loyalist terror and Welsh and Scottish nationalist extremism were taken from G branch – which would thereafter focus on overseas threats – and combined with new sections dealing with republican terrorist organizations in Britain. The 300 extra staff were needed for T Branch, for an expansion of A4 – the 'Watchers' surveillance group that played an important role in MI5's plans – and for a small number of extra posts in the Legal Adviser's department. In an attempt to stop these changes, senior police officers began a belated campaign of press leaks, stressing MI5's lack of accountability. In response, Home Office spokesmen insisted that nothing would happen until after the Burns Report. An MI5 officer confirms, a little coyly, that T Branch was formed 'in anticipation' of the changes – but the report had not been written at the time.

I put it to William Taylor – the Met's Assistant Commissioner for Special Operations who was running the ATU, Special Branch firearms unit, as well as other key squads at the time – that changes in MI5 began well before the results of the Burns Report (the fourth Whitehall study on counter-terrorism arrangements in three years) were announced. He says that suspicions were voiced at Scotland Yard at the time, but officials assured the police that the outcome was not a foregone conclusion. Taylor recalls, 'At the highest levels yet another debate was called for. Inevitably questions were posed. Is this a proper review? Is the outcome pre-determined and the review just charade? I must say we were all pretty disappointed it had been opened up again but not surprised by the outcome . . . to say it was pre-determined would be to undermine the integrity of a whole host of people.'

On 6 April 1992 an IRA bomb exploded in London's Soho. It was unclear what the target had been. Commander Churchill Coleman told reporters that the fact that the blast had happened with no warning was 'an act of sheer recklessness . . . we are fortunate indeed that there were no casualties'. This was something of an understatement, since what he had not told the press was that the bomber, James Canning, had been under police surveillance until moments before the blast. Canning was the target of an operation, code-named CATNIP, that the police regarded as their best chance in years of making inroads into the IRA in Britain.

The surveillance continued for a week, when the police raided a house and a nearby lock-up garage in suburban Northolt, recovering six Kalashnikov assault rifles and a large amount of high explosive. Canning had used his lover Ethel Lamb, twenty-three years his senior, as an accomplice, and under questioning she revealed his role as an IRA quartermaster supplying various bombs that had gone off during the previous fifteen months. One of the rifles had been used in the attempt to assassinate the former Governor of Gibraltar. Canning was later sentenced to thirty years, although he was found not guilty of placing the Soho bomb. The police said in court that they lost track of him just before the blast. William Taylor says of the case, 'It is never our intention knowingly to let the criminal prime a viable device and move it, public safety cannot be recklessly jeopardized but some measured risk is necessary.' But whatever hopes the Met may have had that Operation CATNIP might change ministers' minds, it was far too late to preserve the role of Special Branch.

Shortly after the Conservative general election victory on 9 April 1992, Warner, Cradock and Butler went to see Kenneth Clarke, the newly-installed Home Secretary, to obtain his formal approval for the new arrangements. The Commissioner of the Metropolitan Police was summoned to Downing Street, where John Major told him of the new plans and asked him to give full co-operation to the new organization. George Churchill Coleman, the Met's anti-terrorist commander at the time, says, 'There was a lot of understandable unease within the Special Branch. They'd held responsibility for a hundred years. There was some apprehension that perhaps promises being made [by MI5] could not be fulfilled.'

The IRA bomb in the City of London on 10 April 1992 seemed to underline the need for change. The huge device, loaded into a van, killed three people, injured ninety-one and caused at least £1 billion of damage. The next day, another very large device packed with home-made explosive went off at Staples Corner, ruining several stores and damaging a motorway bridge. These attacks demonstrated the IRA's willingness to take lives and cause damage running into billions.

On 8 May Clarke announced the changes in the House of Commons, adding a final insult to the Special Branch by referring to their role in fighting Irish bombers since 1883 as 'an accident of history'. The Home Secretary said, 'The purpose of this change is to enable the Security Service to use to the full the skills and expertise which it has developed over the years in its work on counter-terrorism.' For Rimington, who had taken over as DGSS two months earlier, it was a triumph of Whitehall manoeuvring; for MI5, alone amongst the intelligence agencies, the end of the Cold War meant expansion (from about 1,900 to 2,230 staff) rather than contraction. T Branch would come into effect on 1 October, and then there would have to be results.

Success in Irish counter-terrorism had always been subject to problems of definition. The Security Service stressed that it would only lead in anti-IRA intelligence-gathering. Convicting the Provisionals would still be the ATU's job. But ministerial perceptions of the Met's failure often stemmed from the paucity of convictions – which had very little to do with the recently-announced removal of Special Branch's leadership. Security Service officers preferred to highlight their success in disrupting attacks, using intelligence either to frustrate them or to minimize their consequences, but this was a highly subjective area: the Service itself provided the evidence of all the atrocities that might have happened but for its intervention.

The Burns Report apparently paid tribute to MI5 leadership in Europe, noting that it had been followed by an end to IRA attacks there. But whatever the Service may have achieved in Germany, there was no publicly-available – or even, my contacts suggest, secret – evidence that the Provisionals were still actually trying to mount attacks there. Furthermore, although MI5 officers stressed that convictions were still the province of the police, they recognized that their work would increasingly involve helping to secure those convictions. As Rimington herself subsequently told a police audience, 'When the Security Service plans and carries out intelligence investigations which may lead to prosecution, we must bear constantly in mind the issues of relevance, evidence and disclosure.' In a small number of cases, good intelligence could allow a terrorist to be followed to the point of a crime, so providing meat for a prosecution; and it was on such cases that T Branch would increasingly concentrate its efforts.

Cracking the secrets of the IRA GHQ Staff that ran overseas operations had always been one of the toughest counter-terrorist tasks. The Provisionals' England Department drew people from a variety of backgrounds. It had the pick of the IRA units in Ulster: for example, two young terrorists who accidentally killed themselves with a bomb in St Albans in November 1991 were attached from the Belfast Brigade. Others were recruited in Britain, including, it would later emerge, some non-Irish left-wing activists. The IRA tried to use 'lily whites' – people without criminal records – particularly when setting up its support network of arms caches and safe houses; an English accent was also a distinct advantage in this work. Operations such as the mortar attack on Downing Street required experienced Northern Ireland specialists to come over for limited periods under assumed identities. In general, terrorists chosen for work in Britain were assumed to be those with the least likelihood of being security forces informers.

Penetrating the GHQ Staff was problematic for MI5 or the RUC Special Branch. Clearly, whoever was in charge in London the key intelligence came from across the water. Churchill Coleman notes, 'Everything in terms of operations, planning and direction happens in Northern Ireland or the Republic. Much depends on who has the finger on the pulse over there.' Occasionally somebody on the IRA's fringes might provide a tip-off – like that which began the Gibraltar operation. At other times, the disappearance of known bomb-makers or snipers from their usual haunts might prompt an alert in ports and airports. The Security Service had long singled out IRA quartermasters, who were responsible for storing and dispensing weapons, for special efforts at recruitment. Intelligence of the arrival of an arms consignment was vitally important: it could allow the Service to follow the people who received it. Under certain circumstances, it could also enable MI5 technical officers to tamper with bomb-making materials in order to prevent devices exploding.

T Branch officers understood all these operational techniques, but now it was a question of putting them into practice. They were helped not just by the substantial extra resources given to MI5, but by the fact that the IRA had so escalated its operations in Britain that it could no longer select its operatives with the same care. The chances of MI5 finding a first-rate source or exploiting mistakes were growing.

As T Branch and A4 members readied themselves for the counter-terrorist campaign, Scotland Yard trained them in the techniques of gathering evidence for court cases rather than for intelligence reports. A measure of the ill-feeling which persisted was the fact that members of the Met leaked reports about how unused their new trainees were to getting the kind of information that would stand up in court. Ian Burns, the Deputy Under Secretary at the Home Office, later told a Commons committee that the change-over had been 'as smooth as possible in the circumstances . . . It would be a mistake to claim there have not been difficulties; of course there have been difficulties, but both teams are putting their shoulders to the wheel and have been successful.'

Shortly after the 1 October 1991 change-over, an operation took place that highlighted both the merits of MI5 involvement and the doubts that some police and civil libertarians harboured about its techniques. The operation involved a cell of the Irish National Liberation Army, a republican offshoot that, compared with the Provisionals, had a reputation for factionalism and poor discipline.

A long-term MI5 agent named Patrick Daly had infiltrated an INLA group that was planning a bombing campaign in Britain. In 1989, under instructions from his controllers, he had gone to Galway in the Irish Republic to join the INLA. Daly had been associated with its political wing, the Irish Republican Socialist Party, for years, and had been 'talent spotted' as a potential MI5 agent while living in Bristol, after some years as a comparatively low-level informer for the Avon and Somerset Special Branch.

At the later trial, Daly said that he had been asked by the INLA Chief of Staff to find explosives for a campaign in Britain. In February 1992 there was an operation to steal some from a quarry in the West Country. T Branch officers had substituted fake explosives and hidden several armed police around the store. Two INLA men, Martin McMonagle and Liam Heffernan, were arrested at the site, and a third escaped. McMonagle and Heffernan were subsequently convicted.

For MI5, the case was a textbook example of their operational principles: a small fish had caught two bigger ones, and months of effort by a wider circle of INLA members had been wasted on an operation that would never come to anything. McMonagle's lawyer had claimed, however, that Daly was actually the leading light in the conspiracy, an *agent provocateur* who spurred the others on. The cost of using Daly had been high: whereas Special Branch informers in Ulster often received no more than a few thousand pounds, the price of paying and resettling Daly had been revealed in court as almost £400,000.

The DGSS responded to these criticisms in a later lecture: 'Agents within target organizations are run according to strict internal Service guidelines to counter the defence that they have been deployed as *agents provocateurs* or that they have planted incriminating material.' Despite the confidence with which Rimington expressed her position, within the Service there was much debate about the legality or otherwise of certain actions by MI5 sources, and about whether changes to the law were needed to protect such people from prosecution.

Those in the police who resented the way MI5 had elbowed Special Branch aside knew that Gower Street had relied on two negative perceptions on the part of politicians and officials: that law enforcement had itself been too slow to deal with problems that cut across force boundaries, and that the victors in the counter-terrorist battle had benefited from a certain class-based or education-based prejudice against the losers. That senior police could not match wits with the brighter graduates in MI5's General Intelligence management stream or in the command element of the IRA was a perception not easily challenged.

The police recognized the need for national information-gathering structures, and in April 1992 the 300-strong National Criminal Intelligence Service was formed. The aim of NCIS was to collate data on organized crime, including drug-dealers, and on certain other types of criminal conspiracy, such as football hooliganism. Some senior policemen had tried to convince the Home Office that NCIS, or a similar organization, could be expanded to deal with terror. Their failure owed much to their lack of understanding of the Cabinet Office central intelligence machinery and the role it would play in furthering the MI5 cause.

Arguably, the main consequence of Gower Street's machinations from mid-1991 to April 1992 was to bring many more resources into the fight against the IRA. Many of the staff of T Branch now applied themselves to the problem, and A4 units backed up police surveillance sections. It amounted to a near-doubling of the people directly assigned to the task. Police sources admit that they could never have convinced Whitehall of the need for such an increase. By the end of 1992 IRA operators in Britain were being hunted by hundreds of people in T Branch, A4, Met Special Branch and ATU.

As the number of intelligence officers available for analysing reports grew, so did the surveillance of those suspected of being linked in any way with terrorism in Britain. Government figures show that whereas 412 telephone intercept warrants had been approved by the Home Secretary in 1988, in 1991 the figure was 670 and in 1992 it had reached 756. Thomas Bingham, the Interception of Communications Act Commissioner charged with regulating this activity, reported in 1993 that the growth was 'very largely due to an increase in the number of warrants issued in terrorist cases to the Security Service and the Metropolitan Police Special Branch'. Each warrant could be used to cover several phones that a targeted individual might use.

In addition to this regulated form of surveillance, there were other areas where Special Branch and the Security Service needed no specific warrants. The newer telephone exchanges allowed analysis of the numbers called by a particular subscriber over several months. By courtesy of bank security departments, suspects could be followed through their use of cash or credit cards. The spread of security cameras produced several leads, and government scientists worked on ways to get automatic vehicle number-plate recognition from police traffic monitoring cameras.

The strategy begun by Anthony Duff to restructure the Service from a Cold War instrument into what was effectively the national counter-terrorist unit had come to fruition under Rimington. By 1993 counter-terrorism was consuming three-quarters of its effort. Because of the change, the Security Service had managed to grow, while MI6 and GCHQ sat nervously awaiting Treasury pruning.

Internally, members of the Service were given a new sense of purpose; few could doubt the value of working to stop bombs going off on British streets. Whereas the 1980s had brought forth Massiter, Wright, Day and Ingram, no G or T Branch officers now rushed to tell the story of civil liberties trampled underfoot in the fight against terror. The absence of whistle-blowers, coupled with the achievement of another Duff strategy – low-key public relations efforts by the agency – gave the DGSS greater control over how MI5 was presented publicly.

Rimington began lunching newspaper editors, resuming the practice stopped by Margaret Thatcher. It had been restarted in the mid-1980s without ministers' knowledge, but Ken Clarke later magnanimously defended it by saying, 'There are so many who believe in conspiracy theories in this area of a somewhat bizarre kind, that it is helpful to have a Director General who is a living, walking, moving human being who can be met by people, who can be trusted to talk to newspaper editors.'

The relationship between Rimington and the media was not an entirely happy one; she was forced to move house after one newspaper revealed her address. Distrust of MI5 remained, and not just on the Left. When William Rees-Mogg, former editor of *The Times*, wrote that the Service had bugged telephone calls by members of the Royal Family, many people were ready to believe him. Press leaks by police disgruntled at the way MI5 had taken over IRA matters reinforced the perception that it was an underhand, sinister organization.

MI5's publicity campaign eventually produced a glossy brochure giving considerable details of the Service's structure and some of its activities. It contained a postal address for anyone seeking to contact the Service – a half-way house to Patrick Walker's ambition of having MI5 in the telephone directory. The agency even went in for one of the image consultant's favourite devices: it introduced its own logo.

In 1984 the former K Branch officer Miranda Ingram had predicted that objections to greater accountability would come 'from those who revel in their secret world and who want to hang on to the glamour'. When Rimington accepted an invitation to deliver a televised lecture on the BBC ten years later, she confessed, 'I must admit that it is with some hesitation that I set out to shed some daylight – I have a sneaking feeling that the myths may turn out to be more fun than the reality!' The reforms of Duff, Walker and Rimington were upsetting some who believed that secrecy did glamorize the work, but evidently the MI5 Board accepted that this openness was a price worth paying for positioning their agency as a no-nonsense modern organization that hunted terrorists – something that most members of the public could agree was a good thing – and kept its real operational secrets safe.

Issuing photos of the Director General, publishing its postal address and acquiring a corporate logo did not, however, excuse MI5 from facing the issue of parliamentary accountability. The decision to give it the leading role against the IRA had exacerbated the issue. Even solid Tory loyalists such as John Wheeler, then Chairman of the Home Affairs Committee, had bought the police argument that MI5 control in this area removed from parliamentary oversight something that had previously been subject to it. The Home Secretary, summoned by Wheeler's committee in November 1992, argued, 'I do not believe that it would be right to make the Security Service accountable to a select committee of this house.' The MPs begged to differ, stating in their later report, 'The Committee believes that the value for money of the Security Service and its general policy are proper subjects for parliamentary scrutiny.'

The arguments in favour of a Parliamentary Committee grew. Clarke's line with the Home Affairs Committee – that any supervision of intelligence service policy would soon draw in operational matters – had been one of the government's last attempts at the 'slippery slope' argument so beloved of Thatcher. During the Home Affairs hearings, Clarke got MI6's official name wrong, a sign of ministerial ignorance about even basic intelligence matters. In private, many in the Cabinet realized that it was an unhealthy state of affairs. Tom King, who had been Defence Secretary until 1992 and was to play a key role in establishing greater Parliamentary supervision, notes that 'when this whole thing was conducted behind a wall of secrecy, that was not the best basis for ensuring that it was proper value for money. I can remember one public expenditure survey meeting where we were all sitting around, and it really was very difficult when half of the people didn't know what the other half were talking about or how much it should cost.'

The arguments about accountability were eventually replayed in a debate on the Intelligence Services Bill. On 6 May 1992 the Prime Minister confirmed to the House of Commons that MI6 existed and that it was the government's intention to put it and GCHQ on to a proper legal footing. Although the Security Service had won a famous Whitehall victory in 1992, its foreign intelligence counterparts faced a quite different climate, one of uncertainty and financial pressure.

Chapter 16

1992 Into the Balkan Quagmire

In June 1992 Percy Cradock stood down as Chairman of the Joint Intelligence Committee. The Chairman's job was attached to that of Prime Minister's Foreign Policy Adviser, and its incumbent moved in several planes, being Whitehall's senior assessor of all intelligence, someone whose counsels on broad issues of overseas policy were heard in Downing Street, and a central participant in the budgetary process of the intelligence collection agencies.

Cradock had, in the words of one analyst, 'completely dominated the intelligence community by sheer force of intellect', and was 'a man with whom you hesitated to argue'. His intense *gravitas* in meetings with the Prime Minister or when chairing the JIC had impressed many; he stood for the importance of intelligence. In areas where his job description was imprecise, Cradock had exploited that imprecision to build himself a greater role in the Whitehall process. His unusually long tenure of seven years had allowed him to consolidate his position.

As he stood down, the JIC Chairman had many concerns about the maintenance of what President Bush called the New World Order, and Britain's place in it. Cradock worried that the Gulf War had been too easy; trouble spots such as the former Yugoslavia had already shown themselves to be messier. Victory in the Gulf had created high public expectations that other problems might be solved with the same speed and laser-guided precision. US leadership in the Gulf had allowed comprehensive sharing of intelligence, but what of the areas of the world where London had an interest and Washington did not? The US presidential campaign was coming to a close, with signs that a Democrat victory would be followed by a period of intense introspection. Bill Clinton had managed to turn President Bush's prowess in foreign affairs into a liability, equating it with an abrogation of his responsibilities towards the sagging US economy.

Cradock's successor was Rodric Braithwaite, the British Ambassador in Moscow. Braithwaite's two postings in Moscow, totalling eight years, gave him impressive credentials for analysing the growing chaos in Russia, which was regarded as the top priority for national intelligence. He also had a string of economic jobs to his credit, and they too seemed the right qualifications for an age in which, according to the pundits, economic competition would supplant the nuclear arms race as the primary focus of international rivalry.

Braithwaite, whose physical appearance and nervous energy reminded many of the actor Denholm Elliott, inspired loyalty among his Foreign Office colleagues, who saw him as a man whose lively intellect frequently undermined Whitehall's received wisdoms. He made no secret to his friends that he wanted the Number 10 foreign policy adviser's job, but he had mixed feelings about the JIC chair that went with it. Braithwaite did not regard intelligence with reverence, sharing the belief of many diplomats that the Red Book and other assessments seldom added much to media reports. He quickly offended the SIS by calling much of its political agent reporting 'soft intelligence', and implying that such work was really the preserve of the Foreign Office.

The British intelligence system aimed to provide a quality service to the small group of ministers and officials at the top of the national power structure: Prime Minister, Foreign Secretary, Cabinet Secretary, JIC Chairman, Foreign Office Permanent Under Secretary and so on. But as the incumbents of these key posts changed, interest in intelligence waned. John Major was 'less sold' on it than his predecessor; Braithwaite believed in its value, but within a more restricted field. Douglas Hurd, who had established himself as Foreign Secretary in the run-up to the Gulf War, was enigmatic in his approach to the agencies.

Publicly, the Foreign Secretary demonstrated a heady enthusiasm for MI6 and GCHQ, which were both under his supervision. He told a press conference marking the launch of the Intelligence Services Bill, 'No week goes by without having drawn to my attention examples of where the work of one or the other of these agencies . . . actually protects British interests and saves British lives.' But as a former diplomat who had long hankered after the Foreign Secretary's job, Hurd also shared many of the King Charles Street attitudes towards intelligence. Many diplomats respect the professionalism of the MI6 colleagues with whom they share diplomatic missions, but regard the task of political reporting as theirs alone. People who have worked with Hurd suggest that, in private, he is interested in agent or sigint reports carrying the highest security classification, particularly when they concern forthcoming diplomatic negotiations, but not in the bulk of intelligence reporting. 'I know for a fact,' says one former intelligence mandarin, 'that Hurd very rarely reads JIC assessments; he doesn't find them useful.'

Like the new Prime Minister, the new Foreign Secretary had much less appetite for ploughing through day-to-day intelligence reporting than Howe or Thatcher had. Hurd preferred diplomatic telegrams on political matters, and was increasingly fascinated by the role television news had in informing the political agenda on issues like the former Yugoslavia.

Britain had in June 1992 committed 300 non-combat troops, mostly from the Royal Army Medical Corps, to Croatia as part of the United Nations Protection Force or Unprofor. The Croat–Serb war had been frozen by a European Community-brokered ceasefire, only to be succeeded that spring by war in Bosnia Herzegovina. The Sarajevo government, under its president Alia Izetbegovic, had tried to move the republic's multinational population towards independence. Although Muslims made up the largest slice, they did not form a majority, and had relied on a political alliance with Croats and some Serbs to outflank the 35 per cent of the republic's population, almost all Serb, who wanted to remain part of the Yugoslav Federation and boycotted the referendum on independence.

A declaration of independence by Bosnia Herzegovina on 27 March 1992 was followed by European Community recognition on 6 April. The EC foreign ministers had repeated their mistake of recognizing an embattled new republic without being ready to defend it. In the case of Bosnia Herzegovina, the international legal problems of defining the new state were even more difficult than they had been in Croatia.

Since the Ottoman occupation centuries before, the settlement pattern in the region had been that the Serbs lived mainly in villages and the Muslims in towns. Although the JNA, the Yugoslav People's Army, had actually fought in Croatia – an action that the Zagreb authorities could describe as international aggression – in the new conflict the JNA had turned over huge stocks of weapons to the Serbs and left. In Bosnia Herzegovina, therefore, there were many besieged pockets of Muslims and Croats, making it harder to draft a ceasefire, and the forces that surrounded these enclaves were mostly local Serbs (although others from Krajina and the Serbian republic did join in) and therefore not 'external aggressors' under international law.

Whatever the Sarajevo authorities might say about external support for the Serbs, the conviction that this was a civil war was central to Ministry of Defence advice on the conflict during its early months. Senior officers had a horror of committing British troops to the Balkan quagmire. Throughout the spring and early summer, Cabinet ministers publicly insisted that the UK was not prepared to put combat troops into the former Yugoslavia. Malcolm Rifkind, the Defence Secretary, energetically told sessions of the Overseas and Defence Committee of the Cabinet that such a commitment could well be endless, involving considerable losses. But ministers like Rifkind were swimming against a tide of televised images of suffering. Shots of half-starved prisoners in Serb detention camps roused uncomfortable echoes of the Holocaust; an attack by Serbian snipers on a bus taking children out of Sarajevo further touched public sympathy.

British diplomacy tried hard to rise to the challenge of the first European war since the defeat of Nazism. Peter Carrington, the former Foreign Secretary and Secretary General of Nato, tried to mediate between the warring parties. He was succeeded by David Owen, another former Foreign Secretary and leader of the defunct Social Democratic Party. Hurd wanted to add the British government's support to these efforts. When Britain's turn to take the rotating Presidency of the EC came around that summer, he saw it as the perfect opportunity to demonstrate British diplomatic skills and launch an initiative to stop the slaughter. One of those at the centre of the Whitehall debate notes, 'The trigger for getting a policy was television and the fact that we were taking over the Presidency on 1 July.' That policy would involve not just efforts at peacemaking, but the commitment of British combat troops to Unprofor.

The Foreign Office focused on convening a conference, to include the warring parties, the UN Secretary General Boutros Boutros Ghali and European nations, to be held near the end of August. As the bureaucratic head of steam built up behind this initiative, the Overseas and Defence Committee of the Cabinet agreed to commit a battalion of British troops to Bosnia, together with Royal Engineers support and reconnaissance troops. Unprofor had called for national contingents, as it planned to establish a fully-fledged operation in the republic, UN Bosnia Herzegovina Command or BHC. On 18 August 1992 the government announced its readiness to send 1,800 soldiers. France had earlier committed 1,100 troops to the BHC; it already had troops in Unprofor supervising the Croatian ceasefire. Spain and Canada also joined in. By long-standing Whitehall convention, the deployment of combat troops made Bosnia a top priority for national intelligence.

From the outset the Bosnian deployment was quite different from actions such as the Falklands or Gulf wars. Its purpose was to deliver humanitarian aid, not to coerce one side or another into relinquishing its conquests. In Bosnia there were major restrictions on the collection of intelligence and its dissemination. The UN itself did not empower its peacekeeping or humanitarian forces to compile intelligence. As Air Marshal John Walker, the Chief of Defence Intelligence, explains, 'Intelligence is a dirty word in the United Nations. The UN is not a thing in itself, it's an amalgam of 183 sovereign nations. If it does intelligence, it will be doing it against a sovereign UN member, so it's incompatible. But you need a military intelligence job to protect your troops. If you don't, you pay for it in body bags.'

On previous missions the UN had turned a blind eye to member states gathering intelligence under arrangements euphemistically called 'operational information' or 'military observation'. The absence of the USA from Unprofor deprived it of the enormous intelligence-gathering resources used in the Gulf. British commanders soon realized, however, that mechanisms were needed to collate the information gathered by outposts of the different national contingents. To this end, intelligence cells were established at the national support headquarters in the Croatian port of Split and later at the BH Command initially at Kiseljak in central Bosnia, later in Sarajevo itself.

Army Intelligence Corps troops wearing blue berets swapped information with their colleagues, particularly the French and the Canadians. It was, however, an operation mainly designed to collate data, making the most of the soldiers' information-gathering skills to prepare briefings for higher commanders or visiting politicians. Any channelling of sigint or agent reports from GCHQ and MI6 to troops in Bosnia Herzegovina was constrained by the intelligence community's strict rules about dissemination. Nervousness of this kind had resulted in much useful information being held back from troops in the Gulf, where the command arrangements had been almost ideal. In the former Yugoslavia, where Russian and Ukrainian officers played significant roles in the Unprofor command structure, there was little chance of any intelligence – except that which had been sanitized to the point of near-uselessness – being disseminated from London. The British evolved a special means of sending sensitive data, for example the raw eavesdropping intercepts which under the UKUSA Treaty system were marked 'Handle Via Comint Channels Only', to Lieutenant Generals Michael Rose and Rupert Smith when they were commanding the UN in Bosnia. A small cell of British soldiers under an Intelligence Corps major was established at the UN residency in Sarajevo with highly secure communications equipment. Each day it received secret intelligence which was then used to brief the generals.

The 1979 Lancaster House Conference, at which the parties to the Rhodesian conflict had agreed to settle their differences under HMG's mediation, was regarded in Whitehall as a textbook fusion of diplomacy and intelligence-gathering. All of the main protagonists, including Joshua Nkomo and Robert Mugabe, were under SIS surveillance. Hotel rooms and those used by the delegations for meetings within Lancaster House itself had been bugged. Daily reports were made to the then Foreign Secretary, Peter Carrington, as he prepared for each negotiating session. The talks paved the way for the successful transformation of minority-rule Rhodesia into Zimbabwe.

Delegates assembling for the 1992 London Conference on Bosnia Herzegovina were also bugged by MI6. The conference, which ended on 28 August, was, *The Times* breathlessly announced, 'a triumph of international diplomacy'. On paper, the final declarations seemed impressive: UN supervision of Serb heavy weapons; the setting-up of a war crimes tribunal; banning military flights; lifting the sieges of Sarajevo and other towns. But the protagonists were not ready to accept these measures in practice, and all of them would undermine their implementation. The cynicism of Serbs, Muslims and Croats was something good intelligence could chart but not alter.

Whereas the role of GCHQ and MI5 in the Gulf disappointed many analysts, Bosnia was a long-term commitment in which they would have ample opportunity to develop their sources of intelligence. Captain Jonathan Cooke, one of the top DIS officers, ran the directorate which included the former Yugoslavia. He says Britain's espionage agencies 'had a bit of trouble getting up to speed. It wasn't a priority they could quickly get good at. SIS and GCHQ needed to improve their expertise in the language. On the frequencies [to be intercepted], GCHQ had to start almost from scratch. The quality at the beginning was a bit iffy, it was never exceptionally good.'

SIS did succeed in making several significant agent recruitments in the former Yugoslavia. One analyst, who digested these CX reports in London, notes, 'The problem in the Balkans is that too many people say too much, so we had a wealth of intelligence but some trouble separating the wheat from the chaff.'

After the subsequent imposition of a no-fly zone, more sophisticated intelligence-gathering technology was deployed in the Balkans. US, Nato and Royal Air Force E-3 Awacs radar aircraft were all eventually used to enforce the ban. These aircraft were capable of picking up electronic intelligence, helping to pinpoint the radars for surface-to-air missiles and fighter aircraft in flight. This operation is co-ordinated by Nato in Italy.

The troops sent to deliver aid required two basic types of information: about local conditions, including the state of roads and the personalities of warlords, and about the wider picture, such as a forthcoming Bosnian Serb offensive or illegal Croatian arms imports. The local picture came from soldiers on patrol, from informal contacts with aid organizations, and from liaison meetings with the belligerents. In Sarajevo, the UN deployed British and other artillery-locating radars, enabling it to make its own judgements about who had broken which ceasefire.

British warships patrolling the Adriatic were used to gather signals intelligence. Their mission was to enforce the UN arms embargo, but they were also able to detect radio signals and radar emissions. Data on Serb air defence radars, for example, could be passed to the Nato pilots operating over Bosnia. British forces also deployed certain sigint and electronic warfare troops in the former Yugoslavia under cover of its UN mission. A perusal of back copies of *The Wire*, journal of the Royal Signal Regiment, indicates a steady stream of postings to the Balkans of operators from units trained in the collection of such information, such as 9 Signal Regiment in Cyprus. The main purpose of these deployments was, it seems, feeding back sigint to Britain rather than to Unprofor. The sigint take increased as the foreign military involvement deepened. One analyst had told me that conversations between General Ratko Mladic, Commander of the Bosnian Serb Army, and his subordinates were regularly intercepted. Later in the war, according to the expert, these intercepts provided dramatic insight into the general's 'depression, paranoia and growing mental instability'. During the period 1992-3, however, Mladic's army suffered few battlefield losses and usually held the initiative.

Those intercepting the Serb military traffic soon discovered, however, that sigint could rarely provide warning of forthcoming offensives. One of them notes, 'A lot of communication is done by [secure] land line or face-to-face. Mladic likes to be there in person during a big operation.' Captain Cooke maintains that these factors, as well as Bosnia's mountainous geography, conspired to ensure that the GCHQ/NSA take on Bosnia was not as comprehensive as that on Russia during hostilities in Chechnya, for example. The flow of intercepts and agent CX reports into the Balkan Current Intelligence Group in Whitehall was often sufficiently for good general briefings to ministers, but the usual rules on the dissemination of sensitive reports further limited what was given to troops serving in-theatre.

British and other UN commanders on the ground often felt short of information about the wider picture. Details of the kind of weapons obtained by Croatia, for example, were largely pieced together from freely-available military publications and other media digested by the British int cell in Split or by the Rest of the World Directorate of the Defence Intelligence Staff.

By mid-1992 John Major's policy of loosening the public purse-strings slightly had combined with a fall in tax revenues caused by the recession to produce a growing gap between government income and spending. It was becoming clear to intelligence chiefs that, bereft of Thatcher's protection, their budgets could not be preserved indefinitely. At about the same time, the decision was announced to extend the tenure of Colin McColl as Chief of SIS beyond his sixtieth birthday in September 1992. MI6 colleagues suggest that McColl stayed on 'against his personal wishes', largely to oversee the move to a highly expensive, extravagantly designed new headquarters in London's Vauxhall and the introduction of the Intelligence Services Bill in Parliament. Although these factors were undoubtedly important – the new HQ was linked to the wider financial question as it had gone substantially over budget – the politely-phrased announcement concealed one of those curious rounds of manoeuvring among Whitehall mandarins that characterize the selection of intelligence service bosses.

The decision to keep McColl had parallels with the appointment of Anthony Duff to the Security Service eight years earlier, in that the Cabinet Secretary played a key role after selection boards had failed to produce a suitable successor. In the case of MI6, there was concern among senior Cabinet Office officials that, in the increasingly tough public spending climate, a new Chief might be unable to fight for his Service as well as McColl could.

Keeping McColl in post must have meant considerable disappointment for Barrie Gane, the Director of Requirements and Production, who most people at Century House assumed would succeed. Gane was interviewed for the job, but the mandarins running the selection did not feel he could match McColl as an impresario for the organization.

Shortly after the April 1992 election the Cabinet Office issued a list of senior ministerial groupings that included the newly-formed Intelligence Services Committee. A government information pamphlet noted that its role was 'to keep under review policy on the security and intelligence services', and its creation was one of the achievements of the policy of more open government. But in reality, Cabinet ministers had little time to give to running these agencies. As with most appointments of intelligence chiefs, the Prime Minister's announcement that McColl was staying on was essentially a ready-made decision referred for signature. One senior Whitehall official observes, 'There was no proper successor. The feeling was that we didn't have the right sort of person to take over . . . The Prime Minister knew precious little about it; there was no political element.'

Several developments during the last months of 1992 disturbed those in Whitehall who believed in the Atlantic alliance as the cornerstone of Western security policy. On 3 November Bill Clinton had won the US presidential election. The advent of George Bush four years earlier had caused concern to many, since it had meant a tilt away from the UK towards Germany as the primary partner in Europe. Now, the president-elect publicly chastised the British Conservative Party for supporting his defeated rival, and declared that he wanted to turn the page on Bush's foreign policy-based presidency.

The Bush Administration continued until the New Year, and geared itself up for one last foreign adventure. Bush and Boutros Ghali, the UN Secretary General, had been publicly flirting with ideas about 'peace enforcement' or 'pre-emption of hostilities'. Both men argued that many more lives could be saved if the UN got involved in conflicts earlier and did not have to rely on a consensus among the warring parties about how the mission should be defined. The idea of having one's hands tied behind one's back did not appeal to the Pentagon, so President Bush was seeking different ways to involve his country in UN missions. The Secretary General had publicly stated his concern that the Western preoccupation with Bosnia was taking attention away from many other conflicts where there was also enormous suffering. The USA and UN chose to join forces – unwisely, as it transpired – and experiment with these concepts in Somalia.

Tribal conflict in Somalia had by late 1992 turned this east African state into a bloody anarchy. The Pentagon endorsed the idea of sending in US troops to push through aid and disarm the bands terrorizing the country. The Chairman of the Joint Chiefs of Staff, General Colin Powell, whose philosophy of the use of force had seemed so right in the Gulf War, famously described Operation RESTORE HOPE, the Somali mission that began on 9 December, as 'sending in the cavalry'. In fact the mission violated almost all of his principles about the use of US troops, being essentially an intervention in an internal conflict (no internationally recognised borders had been violated as in Kuwait), an open-ended commitment and one in which the objectives were over-ambitious. UN forces withdrew three years later leaving the country little better off.

Britain declined to take part in RESTORE HOPE. Some in the Foreign Office liked the idea, seeing it as another chapter in the country's history of supporting US military ventures, but the Ministry of Defence was strongly opposed. Service chiefs felt that their forces were already overstretched in Bosnia and elsewhere, and they realized that, even more than in Bosnia, this was a civil war into which outsiders ventured at their peril.

When the Clinton Administration took over, it used air power in an attempt to influence the Balkan situation without committing ground troops. This policy caused considerable disagreement with Britain and France, whose ministers argued that their troops on the ground would suffer in retaliation for US air strikes. The US refusal to commit troops to Bosnia and the British refusal to get involved in Somalia showed the growing transatlantic differences about security in the post-Cold War world.

The government booklet entitled *Central Intelligence Machinery* published in 1993 asserts the value of having intelligence agency representatives in foreign countries: 'It is important to be able to share information so that decisions can be taken on the basis of a common perception.' Nowhere were there more British representatives engaged in such work than Washington: three SIS officers, two from GCHQ, two from MI5 and a representative of the JIC itself. But by the end of 1992 it had become clear that, in the absence of the old rallying cry of anti-Communism, neither intelligence co-operation nor diplomacy between the formerly intimate allies could bridge the gap between their perceptions of when it was worth risking the lives of one's soldiers and when it was not.

Britain's interest in Bosnia evolved in fits and starts. Ministers and generals found themselves dragged towards commitment, despite a deep-rooted feeling among decision-makers such as Hurd, Rifkind and Field Marshal Richard Vincent (Chief of Defence Staff and later Chairman of Nato's Military Committee) that Britain should not get sucked in. The JIC had been recording its concerns about the instability of the Yugoslav Federation since 1988. Many of its minutes were explicit about the dangers of conflict and the possibility of it spreading into neighbouring countries. One intelligence chief suggests that the Foreign Secretary in particular put little faith in these JIC predictions: 'He always considered them too pessimistic.' The reluctance of politicians and officers to throw lives and money into what might be a never-ending commitment conditioned their response to the intelligence forecasts. Here is Air Marshal Walker's verdict:

> Bosnia is not a million miles from Vietnam. The first Americans despatched were sixty-four advisors. They pulled out with 539,000. Bosnia crept up on us. There was a complete lack of a national strategy, and largely because of that there's been a spillage beyond the conflict. It has driven a coach and horses through any idea of a new German 'Bismarckian' foreign policy, badly damaged the chances of any European security policy, driven a wedge between Europe and the US over policy, and damaged perceptions of us in the Islamic world.

Chapter 17

1992 Time for Revenge

On 8 August 1992 a telephone call to the Kingston upon Thames home of Michael Smith, an electronics engineer working for GEC, summoned him to a nearby phone box. The caller, an MI5 officer putting on a Russian accent, told him, 'I am George speaking. I am a colleague of your old friend Viktor; do you remember him?' Smith replied that he did, then agreed to go to a call box where a meeting would be arranged. 'Viktor', or Colonel Viktor Oshchenko, a KGB officer specializing in scientific and technical intelligence, had defected to Britain shortly before. Smith walked into a trap. When he arrived at the telephone box, Special Branch officers arrested him and bundled him into an unmarked car.

When Special Branch officers searched Smith's house, they found £2,000. There was also a letter dating from 1990 that government lawyers subsequently produced as evidence of Smith's 'reactivation' as a Russian spy. Notes and classified papers were found hidden in his car.

Smith at first denied the charge of espionage, but his story changed from one day to the next as Special Branch interrogators revealed the extent of their knowledge. By the time of his trial in autumn 1993, Smith's defence involved admitting to receiving payments of £19,000 for confidential information, but claiming that he believed he was acting on behalf of a commercial competitor rather than a foreign power. The court did not buy this argument; he was found guilty and sentenced to twenty-five years in jail, which was reduced to twenty years on appeal. The case prompted much newspaper hype: the London *Evening Standard* labelled Smith as 'the most treacherous spy since Blake, Philby, Burgess and Maclean'. The whole affair seemed an unpleasant flashback to the Cold War spy game that many people assumed had ended.

By some accounts Oshchenko recruited Smith as far back as 1972, when the KGB officer had been working at the London *rezidentura*. He was an ideological spy, who had joined the Kingston Young Communists. Claims at his trial that he had done so to meet girls produced howls of laughter. From 1976 Smith had worked at Thorn-EMI on classified projects such as developing the trigger mechanism for Britain's WE-177 nuclear bomb. Two years later Smith's security clearance was pulled after Special Branch discovered his Communist links. During his time on classified projects, Smith had travelled to Portugal; it was claimed at his trial that this was for training in KGB spycraft.

Smith tried to regain his security clearance, but failed, and when he joined the GEC Hirst Research Centre in 1985 he was confined to non-sensitive work. In May 1992 GEC made Smith redundant.

The case posed several questions, notably how long the Security Service had known about him. If Smith had been a KGB asset since the late 1970s, wouldn't Gordievsky have known about him? Spokesmen for Russian intelligence implied that they believed Oshchenko to have been a British agent before his defection. The Security Commission report on the case, completed in July 1995, indicated that if Oshchenko had betrayed him, it was not during the agent's early career. Smith's security clearance was only withdrawn in 1978 after notes about his Communist Party membership were found in MI5. They had been placed in the organization's registry seven years earlier in a different Michael Smith file. Despite the disastrous potential of this error it is unlikely that the loss of the information on the WE-177 fuse, essentially a low-tech device, represented a grave national blow. Far from being a superspy, Smith was a sad case who thought he could get away with selling useless material to support his hobbies: much of his KGB money went on a synthesizer and a computer. It was a measure of the KGB's shortage of quality agents that they were prepared to pay him.

The court was informed by the prosecution that the Hirst Centre operated at the 'leading edge of technology', but there was some doubt about whether the case was suitable for trial under the Official Secrets Act. To questions as to whether his client could be tried under the Act, Rock Tansey, Smith's barrister, quoted Thatcher as saying that Russia was no longer an enemy. An equally good case could have been made that the low-grade civilian material Smith supplied was not damaging to national security. In the event, however, the security establishment wanted their prosecution and they got it, with a heavy sentence thrown in for good measure. Smith's trial formed part of a wave of arrests, defections and expulsions that marked an outbreak of Cold War spy fever.

Following the 1991 Moscow coup the KGB was broken up. The overseas espionage arm, the First Chief Directorate, was made into an independent service, the SVR. The sigint arm was also given independence, leaving the internal role of the old KGB to a new Ministry for Security or MBR. The military intelligence service, the GRU, remained unchanged. Russian intelligence chiefs stressed that they wanted international co-operation against drug traffickers, nuclear bomb smugglers and Islamic fundamentalists. In September 1992 Yevgeni Primakov, head of the SVR, described budgetary cuts in his organization and offered a 'no-spy' deal to Western countries. Such offers presumably did not include Aldrich Ames, Primakov's best (and probably only) agent in the CIA.

As a concession to the changing times, MI6 even declared one of its Moscow-based officers to the authorities. Controller Sovietbloc, one of its six geographic divisions, was no longer Sovbloc but Controller Central and Eastern Europe; in the Service, both the individual holding the post and the division itself go by the same acronym, in this case CCEE. The name may have been changed to reflect the collapse of Communism, but attitudes at the top of the organisation had not. Colin McColl, Chief of SIS, and his fellow senior officers, sensing their advantage, responded to Primakov's outwardly friendly noises by pursuing the crumbling Russian foreign intelligence service with renewed aggression. One SIS officer notes, 'They were obsessed with the idea of revenge for Philby, and they got their chance.'

Oshchenko's real prize was a spy ring in France; he had been working at the Paris *rezidentura* up to his defection. Several well-placed agents were uncovered, including an engineer at a nuclear research establishment who had been passing details of French atomic bomb tests. During 1991–2 a series of defections enabled Western counter-intelligence services to roll up many of Moscow's spy networks. SIS played a central role in this.

In addition to Oshchenko, Mikhail Butkov, a senior SVR officer in Oslo, defected to Britain during 1991, and in 1992 a GRU officer who has not yet been named came across. It is also thought that a couple more Russian intelligence officers remained as British agents in place. Butkov's information lay behind a threat made by Douglas Hurd during a visit to Moscow late in 1991 that mass expulsions would follow if Russian spying in the UK was not reduced. Viktor Konoplyov, another SVR man, defected to the Americans in April 1992.

These agents and defectors brought substantial amounts of information which led to the expulsion of four Russian diplomats from Belgium, as well as the arrest of several suspected agents there (on Konoplyov's information); Denmark's unannounced banishing of Sergei Konrad, an SVR man, in March 1992 (presumably as a result of a Butkov tip to the British); Michael Smith's arrest in August; Norway's unannounced *persona non grata* of GRU station chief Viktor Fedik from Oslo in October (also possibly related to SIS information); France's expulsion of four SVR men in October; and the expulsion of Colonel Alexander Zobkov, believed to have been GRU station chief in Washington, at the beginning of 1993.

Did these arrests and expulsions signal a new wave of Russian espionage, or were they simply the remnants of the old? Almost all authorities agree that it was the latter. Oleg Kalugin, former head of KGB counter-intelligence, says the SVR is 'too demoralized' to be effective in Western countries. He adds, 'Only a very foolish man would work for such a heavily-penetrated organization.' In its 1993 public information pamphlet the Security Service stated, 'It is a fact that the old threat no longer exists, but it is equally true that spying continues.' The size of that continued threat, or at least MI5's perception of it, could be gauged by Stella Rimington's statement in 1994 that the resources available for counter-espionage had been cut by half between 1990 and 1994. Robert Gates, the Director of Central Intelligence from 1991–3, says that the activities of the GRU remain 'aggressive', and that it and the SVR are now primarily engaged in scientific and technical intelligence, trying to help Russia's lumbering economic enterprises as they struggle to find a place in world markets.

McColl and his four SIS directors took great pleasure in the success of their counter-intelligence campaign against their historic adversaries, despite the fact that Russia had ceased to be a Communist power. In 1993 a jubilant senior SIS officer told me, 'We've taken them apart, absolutely screwed them.' At the same time that MI6 was disrupting Russian espionage, it was also carrying out its own espionage; the end of ideologically-based international rivalry meant that it was sometimes hard to tell the methods of the different agencies apart.

After the Cold War ended, the Russians were not the only service looking for economic information. France had long sought to improve its international competitiveness through intelligence-gathering; and the USA's increasing preoccupation with its economy led to political pressure on the CIA for greater activity in this area. For the SIS, the principal areas of interest were Russia's weapons of mass destruction, her arms sales and a new mission added by the JIC machinery: the activities of the increasingly powerful criminal gangs commonly referred to by Russians as 'mafia'.

It was economics of the personal kind that motivated spies in the early 1990s. James Woolsey, Gates's successor at the CIA, damned Aldrich Ames as a man who had betrayed agents to the firing squad 'because this warped, murdering traitor wanted a bigger house and a Jaguar'. When I asked one British intelligence officer, 'What on earth –', he cut me short with the word 'money' before I had even finished my question about why anyone still spied for Moscow. The SVR excoriates its defectors with similar language: for example, SVR spokesman Tatiana Samolis said that Vladimir Konoplyov had gone to the CIA 'for material gain'.

While some SIS officers still try to cast their agents as acting out of principle, others admit that cash has become a major factor, particularly in eastern Europe and the former Soviet Union. The stream of former Soviet spies and officials who headed for Western publishers, hoping to cushion their retirement with reams of hard currency, has its unseen mirror image in the secret world. MI6 officers suggest that they are now highly selective, turning down many offers from Russians on the basis that 'resettling an agent can be a highly expensive business. We only want to do it for top-grade information.' Although Gordievsky spied in the early 1980s because he disliked Soviet ideology, the would-be Russian traitor of the early 1990s had to convince SIS he was worth his pension plan.

The US government did go into partnership with the Russians in initiatives to reduce the danger of Russian nuclear warheads going adrift. During 1992 tactical nuclear warheads, shells and land-mines – generally the smallest of nuclear weapons – were removed from outlying republics into storage areas within Russia itself. This step was designed to place these most-easily stolen of devices under secure Russian protection. The Department of Energy was committed to shipping hundreds of tonnes of Russian uranium to the US under the deal signed in February 1993.

Germany's intelligence service, the Bundesnachrichtendienst or

BND, also stepped up its liaison with the Russian security authorities in an attempt to prevent the smuggling of nuclear bombs or materials. A German newspaper subsequently ran a story suggesting that Iran had succeeded in buying three Soviet nuclear weapons in the republic of Kazakhstan. Although this was hotly denied in Moscow, an increasing number of reports in European newspapers demonstrated public anxiety over possible 'nuclear smuggling' and the readiness of certain Russians to offer radioactive materials, real or imagined, to investigative reporters.

This German and US co-operation over nuclear security recognized that the weapons were still under the control of a functioning Russian organization – and that, however many dozens of intelligence officers Western agencies might throw at the problem, Moscow was still deploying the weapons by the thousands. SIS did not enter into any of these collaborative arrangements, beyond declaring a small number of its officers to the Russians and holding some exploratory talks.

US–UK attempts to counter the proliferation of weapons of mass destruction and to verify arms-control agreements continued to focus on biological weapons. In April 1992 Boris Yeltsin confirmed the existence of the offensive weapons programme and signed a presidential decree banning it. The initial visit of a UK–US delegation to the institute controlled by the covert Biopreparat programme in St Petersburg (formerly Leningrad) in January 1991 had only heightened anxieties. Officials of Biopreparat consistently refused to admit that they had been engaged in weapons research, although some admitted that the plants had been working on 'defensive' military projects.

Following the defection of Vladimir Pasechnik, the SIS and the CIA needed to be sure they knew what was going on inside Biopreparat. There had been an additional defector, and there is evidence that the agencies succeeded in keeping at least one agent in place in the organization. Western concerns were listed in a letter from Douglas Hurd, the British Foreign Secretary, and Lawrence Eagleburger, his US counterpart, to Andrei Kozyrev, the Russian Foreign Minister, on 24 August 1992. The letter was not released publicly, owing to the need to avoid damaging rows with Moscow while the West was seeking to retain their goodwill on arms and nuclear warhead agreements, but I obtained a copy of it in Russia and it reveals much about the post-Cold War anxieties of Western governments.

Hurd and Eagleburger welcomed the Yeltsin pledge to get rid of biological weapons but noted, 'Recent information we are providing with this letter suggests that work on the offensive programme may nevertheless be continuing.' In 1990 Margaret Thatcher and Percy Cradock had argued over whether Mikhail Gorbachev was aware of the programme. The Yeltsin declaration had convinced people in SIS and the Foreign Office that the new leader was determined to come clean about the work, but that elements in the military-industrial complex were obstructing the elimination of Biopreperat. Hurd and Eagleburger expressed concern that 'some aspects of the programme which President Yeltsin acknowledged as having existed, and which he banned in April, are in fact being continued covertly and without his knowledge'.

The meat of their letter concerned the attempts by Biopreperat staff in St Petersburg to disguise what went on there during the January 1991 visit; this information had evidently come from the later defector or an agent in place. There were claims that a new plant was being built at Lakhta, near the city, for the large-scale production of germ warfare agents. The letter suggested that the Russian declaration to the United Nations acknowledging the programme 'presented an incomplete and misleading picture'.

Despite the public support for Yeltsin's reforms from Britain and the USA at the time, the August 1992 letter also contained language that underlined the subject position of the former Soviet superpower. Hurd and Eagleburger asked the Russian Foreign Minister to add to his country's UN declaration, or else 'we will be obliged to explain publicly our reservations in this area'. It explained that 'questions have arisen on this subject in the US Senate', and that these would have to be answered, with possible consequences for US aid to Russia. 'In sum, this issue could undermine the confidence in the US and UK's bilateral relationships with Russia,' they warned.

The US–UK letter finished by spelling out the measures Washington and London wanted Moscow to take in connection with a list of suspect facilities. It was strong stuff, explicitly suggesting that the writers had a better idea of what was going on in certain Russian institutes than the Kremlin did. Intelligence had been the driving force in convincing the two foreign secretaries that their letter was justified. Were the charges fact or speculation?

My own visit to the St Petersburg Biopreperat institute with a BBC team late in 1992 produced blanket denials by Yuri Tsventitsky, the Director, that the plant had ever been involved in biological warfare. He maintained this line even when told that Russian Foreign Ministry officials had confirmed that references to St Petersburg in the government's UN declaration on germ warfare alluded to his institute. A scientist at Biopreperat who I was able to talk to alone confirmed that there had been such research and that Tsventitsky knew all about it, but did suggest that it had stopped. Further evidence was produced that the research had finished, in the form of photographs showing that the Lakhta site mentioned in the Hurd–Eagleburger letter was an unfinished shell.

An article in the newspaper *Komsomolskaya Pravda* in September 1992 contained evidence both that the Biopreperat executives had been dishonest and that the Western intelligence agencies might have been overstating their case. The story, a shining example of the kind of investigative journalism possible in the new Russia, drew on interviews with Biopreperat scientists. Although they were unnamed, the authoritative content of the article spoke for itself. The *Komsomolskaya Pravda* journalist wrote that in 1989, after Pasechnik's defection, 'it was decided it was time to cut back.' He suggested that Biopreperat had stopped military work and was trying to turn itself into a civilian money-making enterprise in the biotechnology sector. Managers who had overseen the biological weapons programme were, however, struggling to keep the different institutes and factories together as one functioning business rather than selling them off – which might have been as much a sign of the desire of the factory bosses to get rich in the new Russia as it was of any subterfuge. The article suggested that as long the organization remained under these individuals, 'it is too imprudent to ignore the danger of this work being resumed'.

In the light of this previous dishonesty by management, the idea of continuing the intelligence-gathering on Biopreperat evidently struck Hurd or the mandarins of the Cabinet Office as sensible. Efforts to this end by MI6 or the CIA carried the risk of detection, but as the Hurd–Eagleburger letter made clear, London and Washington considered themselves well within their rights to spy on Russia in pursuit of this kind of information, however iniquitous they might label the SVR or GRU's activities in their own countries.

SIS's work on drugs and terrorism had by 1992 led to the formation of a new section dealing with organized crime. In places like Colombia, where drug barons blew up airliners and controlled billions in investments, all these activities fitted together well. McColl had convinced his Whitehall 'customers' that this work merited the attention of MI6 rather than the Serious Fraud Office, Customs and Excise or any other law-enforcement body. Within SIS the new section was nicknamed 'funny money'. The drugs, crime and anti-proliferation functions of SIS Requirements were combined in a special new department called Global Tasks.

At a 1993 press conference marking the publication of the Intelligence Services Bill, the Chief of SIS gave an extended explanation of why such work fell within the remit of his organization. McColl said that 'individual law-enforcement agencies can sometimes benefit from the wider look and the further reach that a foreign intelligence service has when it comes to uncovering illegal networks which operate across frontiers', and added, 'There is a tendency, I think, for bad men to operate where they think they are safe, and if we can help to reach out into some of those places we can help the law enforcement agencies in not only this country, but in other countries as well.'

Unlike the MI5 men and women deployed against the IRA in Britain, SIS officers were not envisaged as gathering evidence for prosecutions. Instead, the Cabinet Office hoped that the Service might assist agencies such as Customs and Excise with warnings about specific individuals or shipments, as well as helping to maintain UK influence with foreign governments. The absence of SIS evidence in court cases – MI5, by contrast, was increasingly involved in terrorism trials – makes it hard to measure the value of MI6's 'funny money' work. One success story leaked to the *Observer* involved the breaking of a cocaine-smuggling ring.

In 1991 SIS apparently learned of a group of Czech former intelligence officers whose yen for free enterprise led them to become major drugs importers, shipping cocaine through the Polish port of Gdansk. SIS passed its information to the relevant authorities, and it was reported that this led to the arrest of a member of the Cali cocaine cartel in Colombia as well as the Czech conspirators. This new development for MI6 was not without its opponents, although it seems to have generated only a small proportion of the friction caused by MI5's expansion. SIS managers claim that the emergence of powerful criminal networks in Russia is a potential danger to the UK. But officers of the National Criminal Intelligence Service, the police body set up to tackle organized crime in Britain, stressed in a number of briefings to journalists that there was no evidence of substantial Russian mafia activity in this country. From 1992 onwards, MI6's new role and the residual bad feeling from MI5's take-over of Irish terrorism prompted numerous expressions of concern and leaks by senior police officers about the intelligence services taking over responsibility for more of their turf.

Operations against organized crime gangs in Russia, as against nuclear weapons proliferation, involved an element of co-ordination with the local authorities that did not sit easily with the desire of SIS management to 'take apart' and 'screw' Moscow's intelligence services. One Whitehall observer with access to MI6's CX reports during this period says that their primary preoccupation remained with neutralizing their professional opposition. He notes, 'Most of the coups of any intelligence agency are coups against the opposing intelligence agency.'

The successes of 1991–3 did indeed lead McColl and his Director of Counter Intelligence and Security at Century House to channel more of their resources against the espionage services of other countries. According to one officer, Iran had by the end of 1992 become SIS's number two counter-intelligence target. Considerable MI6 and MI5 resources had been devoted to disrupting plans to assassinate the author Salman Rushdie, who had remained in hiding since Ayatollah Khomeini's edict ordering his execution. Several teams of Iranians were tracked trying to hunt him down, says an MI6 man. Although there was a broad stream of corruption in Iranian life, their espionage personnel were very difficult to recruit; unlike the Russians, they still believed in their ideology.

Station officers the world over remain the spearhead of MI6's long-term counter-intelligence plan. One explains, 'My job involves getting friendly with Russians, Iranians, North Koreans, Iraqis and some other Arabs. Whereas most British diplomats avoid such people, particularly the intelligence officers among them, I seek them out, which means most of them soon know exactly who I work for. My message to them is simply, "If you're ever interested, this is where to find me." I tucked a business card into the breast pocket of an Iranian once at a reception and he nearly died of embarrassment.' The successful recruitment of an Iranian or a Russian in some obscure country may only pay dividends years later when he goes on to some more interesting job in his capital or elsewhere.

After the August 1991 coup in Russia, Britain's intelligence and foreign policy establishment decided that old-style mass expulsions were no longer possible, given the improvement in relations between the two countries – although this did not mean that individual SVR or GRU officers might not be quietly ordered out of Britain. At the same time, SIS exploited the general decline in morale of Russia's intelligence services to recruit several promising new agents and to step up its own activities inside Russia against targets such as the biological weapons programme.

Publicly, the Foreign Secretary saw no apparent contradiction between his 1991 representations to Russia's Foreign Minister about the continued level of Russian intelligence activity in the UK and his letter of August 1992 to the same minister which implied that Western intelligence had a better idea of what was going on in certain institutes than President Yeltsin. From being a state that had to be spied on because its ruthless Communist grip on power made it dangerous, Russia had become one which was spied on because its absence of a proper grip on power made it dangerous. For those at the intelligence coal-face, it was even more basic than that: there is always a difference between the targets set by the hierarchy and the areas where agent recruitment actually makes headway (as any spy who has attempted to recruit a North Korean will testify). The end of the Cold War presented the SVR in particular and Russia in general as a prostrate foe that held out a begging bowl to the world. The managers of SIS, schooled in the Cold War battlegrounds of Warsaw, Vienna or Geneva, could not resist taking advantage of that weakness.

Chapter 18

1993 Intelligence, Power and Economic Hegemony

The appointment of James Woolsey as CIA Director by the Clinton Administration intensified a debate within US intelligence that had its parallels in the other major Western powers. In February 1993 Woolsey told a Senate Intelligence Committee hearing to confirm his appointment that economic intelligence-gathering 'is the hottest current topic in intelligence policy'. He announced the setting-up of an Agency task force to inquire into the collection and uses of such information. Some within the Washington intelligence community regarded his actions with cynicism, noting that Denis DeConcini, the chairman of the Senate committee, was one of the few genuine believers in the idea that the CIA should be helping US firms to win a bigger slice of the world economic cake. They predicted the internal review would come to nothing, since most people at the CIA did not see it as part of their duty to pass information to corporations so that they might use it to make money.

Two years after Woolsey's remark, France expelled five US intelligence officers following a twelve-month operation by the Direction de la Surveillance du Territoire or DST, the French internal security service. In a leak to *Le Monde*, sources at the Interior Ministry let it be known that the US officers had paid a French official for details of the national negotiating position in the forthcoming GATT (General Agreement on Trade and Tariffs) negotiations, as well as paying a manager in the national telecommunications firm for information on export bids, and bribing several other people in the economic sector. How far had US intelligence realigned itself to economic priorities? Had British agencies been following the same agenda?

Economic intelligence-gathering has always been subject to

problems of definition. The CIA Directorate of Intelligence had long compiled statistics and forecasts about matters ranging from Soviet oil production to how the world sugar price affected the stability of Fidel Castro's regime in Cuba. Within Whitehall's Joint Intelligence Committee, this had its counterpart in the work of the Economic Unit, a semi-detached element of the Assessments Staff formed in the late 1980s. The Unit was staffed by members of the Treasury and Bank of England on attachment, and circulated reports to those organizations. Its papers also sometimes found their way into the Red Book. It was a kind of Current Intelligence Group for economic trends.

Both the USA and UK also conducted eavesdropping and agent-running in support of diplomatic negotiations, be they arms-control talks or economic talks. Robert Gates, Director of Central Intelligence from 1991–3, notes that such activity has been 'a legitimate subject of US intelligence for thirty years'. In this sense, the CIA officer who offered money to the official from the French Prime Minister's office to find out about GATT was doing nothing new. SIS also carried out such operations and had formed an Economic Section in its Requirements department in the late 1980s.

From the early 1990s a growing number of US voices, both Democrat and Republican, were demanding activities which went beyond this. They spoke about 'creating a level playing field' for US companies in world markets. Their ire was focused on Japanese companies such as Mitsubishi and European ones such as Airbus Industrie who had, they believed, respectively dumped goods on the US domestic market or won international contracts by virtue of being subsidized. The pressure from politicians like Denis DeConcini was for some form of counter-attack in the field which CIA officers called commercial or industrial espionage.

The early shots in the Washington debate were fired shortly after the fall of Soviet communism in August 1991. The following month the *Washington Post* published details of a CIA analysis called 'Japan 2000', which discussed the global rivalry between US and Japanese business. This was followed by a more influential essay by Stansfield Turner, CIA Director 1977–81, in the journal *Foreign Policy* setting out a post-Cold War agenda for the US espionage community.

Turner argued, 'We must redefine "national security" by assigning economic strength greater prominence.' He wrote, 'There is no question that friendly foreign countries make use of their intelligence services against US businesses' and advocated the USA stepping up such activities too, but warned, 'We will not want to be caught by friends in the act of spying.' The answer, in Turner's view, to spying on those 'to whom we turn first for political and military assistance in a crisis' and not getting caught was to do it through 'those impersonal technical systems, primarily satellite photography and intercepts'.

Gates disagreed with Turner on almost every aspect of the argument. 'The issue is whether we should steal the technologies of foreign companies, and that's what I'm dead against,' he said. Turner's emphasis on technical systems also rankled with Gates, who said, 'I have never believed that you could get adequate intelligence wholly through technical means.' Gates and others argued that there could be more help given to US companies to stop others stealing their secrets and to the government to fight unfair trade practices, but that commercial or industrial espionage for the benefit of national companies was a non-starter. These responses gave some comfort to the columnists and writers who kept the issue on the US political agenda throughout 1991–4, because they at least conceded that more effort was needed in the global struggle for markets.

US anxieties over economic intelligence-gathering became particularly focused on the French. In September 1991 Pierre Marion, head of the Direction Générale de la Sécurité Extérieure (DGSE) from 1981–5, told a US television programme that he had set up a special section within the organization and that US businesses had been among its targets. The Franco-American row got worse. In April 1993 a US news agency was leaked (presumably by the CIA) a French intelligence document which listed US firms and institutions targeted for spying. In the resulting furore, several large US firms pulled out of that summer's Paris air show and Claude Silberzahn, then head of the DGSE, was sacked, presumably because of the French government's embarrassment that the USA had obtained the document. British defence firms such as Rolls-Royce, British Aerospace, Westland and Vickers, as well as several financial institutions, were also on the French list.

The French had recast their post-Cold War intelligence-gathering in a particularly Gallic fashion. Silberzahn told *Le Monde* in March 1993, 'Political counter-espionage isn't a real priority for us because the political spy rarely wants to crack the decision-making systems of the great democracies, which anyway can be read about in open sources. Today's espionage is essentially economic, scientific, technological and financial.' The DGSE felt freer about disseminating its economic intelligence than the CIA or SIS because, even in the early 1990s, many of France's largest defence and other contractors remained in state ownership and certain executives retained a high-level security clearance.

In Britain, the issue of whether the end of Cold War should mean a redirection of intelligence effort towards boosting the national economy received almost no discussion, either publicly or within the central intelligence machinery. British politicians did not register any public anxieties about the worsening trade balance with Japan, as their US counterparts did, and realism combined with diplomatic decorum limited any fuss over the French.

Within SIS, the professional culture defined economic intelligence as unglamorous. 'It doesn't really excite people, and anyway we've few officers who have a really detailed knowledge of finance or industry,' one MI6 officer told me. Instead, the bosses maintained their struggle against Moscow's espionage agencies as well as pushing hard for counter-proliferation work – even fighting drug traffickers was deemed sexier, more worthwhile.

At the centre of government, the demand for economic intelligence is limited. The principal bodies analysing it are the Economic Section of the JIC Staff and the Overseas Economic Intelligence Committee (OEIC). One person who sat on the OEIC in the 1980s told me that it was frequently given Blue Book raw sigint which clearly originated from bugging embassies in London, but adds, 'It was all pretty unimportant in terms of its contribution to policy, and I ended up feeling it was all a waste of time.' This ex-OEIC member's own experience of sensitive international negotiations on behalf of Britain suggests, 'Embassies are simply not informed about these things. We didn't tell ours what we were doing, so we'd be unlikely to find out things by bugging other people's.'

When it comes to passing on their product outside Whitehall committees, British intelligence officers share the uncertainty of their US colleagues about the appropriate channels for economic data. A former MI6 man explains, 'There is the problem if you get useful economic information: what are you going to do with it? You might find out what OPEC were doing, so that would be of direct use to the Treasury. As for passing it to industry, that's a completely different matter. Most of industry is not governed by the Official Secrets Act, and because you get information which is dangerous to the people who provided it, you can't guarantee their safety.' MI6 and GCHQ had long pursued economic information for certain government and commercial interests.

Britain did exploit intelligence in some of its arms export deals. This was particularly true of government-to-government ventures such as the Al Yamamah contract with Saudi Arabia. Under Memorandums of Understanding signed in 1985 and 1988, Britain picked up business in excess of £20 billion supplying dozens of Tornado jets and Hawk trainers, as well as entire air bases, missiles and minesweepers, to the Kingdom. One official linked with the project suggested to me that Britain had beaten France's rival bid by gaining intelligence about which Saudi officials they intended to bribe (as well as the size of the 'commissions') and by outbidding them. Daphne Park, a former SIS station chief, told a BBC *Panorama* programme in 1993 that officers in the field did sometimes let British businessmen know what the foreign competition might be for a particular contract.

GCHQ was the principal gatherer of economically-useful intelligence. Much of it came in inadvertently through the trawling of international telex and telephone lines. Robin Robison, a JIC clerk who handled sigint material in the late 1980s, later told a newspaper that he had read intercepts of the tycoon Robert Maxwell's phone calls.

According to one former GCHQ officer, there were no official mechanisms for disseminating commercially-useful information direct to industry, but it did happen. He says, 'There were no rules. If you take the right decision you get all the credit. If you make the wrong one you'll get all the blame. If you play golf with the chairman of [a major public company] for example, and you think there's something he should know, then you take that decision, but the protection of future intelligence is paramount.'

Managers at Cheltenham 'reacted swiftly after 1991 to move to new targets', says one Whitehall intelligence mandarin. It expanded its activities in support of counter-terrorism and counter-narcotics. This often involved eavesdropping on data exchanges between banks. As early as 1989, US media reports suggest, the NSA – GCHQ's US counterpart – was intercepting financial transfers over the Clearing House Interbank Payment System (Chips), a computer network used for transactions between finance houses in dozens of countries. NSA's aim in trawling through Chips was to trace money used by Colombian drug barons and terrorist groups. Under

UK–USA arrangements, GCHQ was party to much of this data.

Financial transactions, like digital telexes or faxes, can be trawled at very high speed by supercomputers searching for key words or numbers. GCHQ was extensively tasked by SIS's Global Targets section in connection with its inquiries into drugs, guns and bad money.

The traditional closeness of the Anglo-Saxon sigint allies posed some problems as economic targets came into view. Where arms sales were concerned, for example, the Gulf War was followed by a number of bruising encounters as the military allies became commercial competitors seeking to cash in on the insecurity of the Arab sheikhdoms. UK Ltd was usually the loser.

The USA announced the $9 billion sale of seventy-two F-15 fighters to Saudi Arabia in September 1992, limiting the chances of further Tornado sales under the Al Yamamah deal. Two months later, a US firm beat Britain's Vickers over a contract to supply 236 tanks to the Kuwaiti army. British businessmen complained of heavy political pressure from Washington. A further tank contract in the United Arab Emirates was lost to the French. London took only limited comfort from a contract to supply armoured personnel carriers to the Kuwaitis. Defence sales was an area where intelligence had traditionally been used to help British competitiveness, but there was little sign of it in the critical Middle East market.

Some GCHQ officers began wondering whether the US access to almost all information gathered at Cheltenham might not be used against the interests of the UK's European allies. They spoke of Britain as 'an intelligence Trojan horse in Europe'. The CIA, by long-standing convention, sat in on the weekly meetings of the JIC, as did the Australians and sometimes the Canadians. It is not usual for the French or the Germans to do so. The Cabinet Office tried to get round the problem of the USA picking up secrets with the 'UK Eyes Alpha' classification by dividing up the meetings: there was a session with the outside observers, and then, in the ironic words of one participant, 'We would pretend we had finished and wait until they had left before carrying on.'

References to sensitive intelligence about European allies – for example, on a negotiating position to be adopted at some future date – always oblique in any case, were confined to that second session. The proportion of information the USA and UK would not share with each another had begun creeping up in the mid-1980s and continued to do so in the early 1990s.

For John Adye, Director of GCHQ since 1989, the early 1990s were a period of considerable anxiety over the sigint relationship. Whatever the divergent political interests in Bosnia or Somalia, Adye's organization was electronically and financially joined at the hip to the NSA. Britain was paying a substantial slice of the cost of the new US geo-stationary sigint satellite system, the Menwith Hill station in north Yorkshire had been expanded (an investment on which the USA would want to see a long-term return), and secure transatlantic data links allowed analysts at the NSA headquarters at Fort Meade, Maryland, to dip into Cheltenham's intercept databases.

Adye was anxious that the Intelligence Services Bill to be put before Parliament in 1993 should not damage the NSA relationship. The draft legislation allowed for the setting-up of a committee of parliamentarians to oversee MI5, MI6 and GCHQ. At GCHQ's insistence, the Bill contained a clause preventing the disclosure to the committee of 'information provided by, or by an agency of, the Government of a territory outside the United Kingdom where that Government does not consent to the disclosure of the information', In other words, nothing the NSA told GCHQ could be passed on to MPs without Washington's agreement. What did this mean in practice?

One intelligence officer reveals, 'When I went there, I thought of GCHQ as a great British institution. But the managers themselves told us that 95 per cent of all sigint handled at GCHQ is American.' Although Adye and other Cheltenham mandarins might quibble at the figure of 95 per cent, I have encountered no one who disputes that most of the intercepts seen there were actually collected by the USA. Not only did the Intelligence Services Bill rule that the bulk of Cheltenham's sigint raw material was beyond the new committee's automatic reach, but it was also misleading about the nature of some of Britain's interception work, stressing that GCHQ's powers:

. . . shall be exercisable only (a) in the interests of national security, with particular reference to the defence and foreign policies of Her Majesty's Government in the United Kingdom; or (b) in the interests of the economic well-being of the United Kingdom in relation to the actions or intentions of persons outside the British Islands; or (c) in support of the prevention or detection of serious crime.

No mention is made of interceptions in support of US foreign policy, but Adye and any other GCHQ officer of significant rank knew that they were frequently carried out – a symptom of the organization's deepening anxiety about whether it was pulling its weight in the Anglo-Saxon sigint alliance. In 1994 the *Guardian*'s Richard Norton-Taylor obtained a copy of a staff manual which spelled this out. It told GCHQ employees that the organization's contribution to the relationship must be 'of sufficient scale and of the right kind to make a continuation of the Sigint alliance worthwhile to our partners' and added, 'This may entail on occasion the applying of UK resources to the meeting of US requirements.'

Michael Herman, former GCHQ division head, weighs up what is at stake in the relationship and concludes, 'It's bound to get somewhat less close. For years it survived on the personal relationships struck up in wartime. But there was a side to it which was hard bargaining. There was, though, a general rule that when the US budget was under threat there'd be more co-operation; it is more threatened now, of course, so [the relationship] can't wither quickly because of the joint projects in which so much has been invested.'

From the US perspective, there were good reasons to maintain the close tie with Britain. Lieutenant-General William Odom, Director of the NSA 1985–9, is scathing about the size of the British contribution to the sigint partnership, but believes that the agency needs its facilities in Britain both for relaying the take from its geo-stationary satellites and for listening to neighbours. Lieutenant-General Odom believes that 'even though we get ripped off [by Britain], as long as we're in Europe we need the access, so we go along with it . . . it's the logic of the common good. We're better off with you putting in your little bit than if we threw you out.'

When I put Lieutenant-General Odom's remarks to Morton Abramowitz, former head of the State Department Intelligence and Research agency, he remarked, 'If the Director of the NSA thinks, "Jesus Christ, the Brits should put up more money", that's a testimony to the success of your people. Bill can gripe, but ultimately he kept going to dinner with you guys, didn't he?' Abramowitz concedes, however, that Britain's ability to continue benefiting from the enormous US intelligence resources is essentially a success of the style – he notes, 'You have superb intelligence diplomats' – rather than the substance of its contribution.

Lieutenant-General Norman Wood, an air force man who finished his career running the US intelligence community's programmes in the early 1990s, and was therefore party to discussions about Britain's future usefulness, lists his reasons for continuing the partnership: 'They're a European power, they understand Europe better than we do; their human intelligence apparatus is better defined than ours; the ability to operate economic intelligence gathering inside Europe, which we could not do.' When I put it to him that the USA was using Britain as an intelligence Trojan horse inside the European Union, he replied, 'You may call that an intelligence Trojan horse. I wouldn't use that term, but the concept is broadly right.'

What links Lieutenant-General Wood, Lieutenant-General Odom and Abramowitz is that they base their views on a cold calculation of US interests in which the *quality* of the British input into the relationship – which successive generations of GCHQ and SIS managers have argued within Whitehall was critical – is not in fact paramount. Instead, they believe that geography, wider security interests and the perceived trade rivalry with Europe make it worthwhile to maintain the tie with Britain. Lieutenant-General Odom ranks Britain in the same category of 'geographic' usefulness as Australia; the implication must be that the UK and Australia have about the same value to the NSA, even though the Antipodean intelligence input must be considerably smaller.

Politicians seem to accept that the absence of European alternatives to the GCHQ–NSA partnership means that sigint will remain an exception to the rules applying in most other areas of diplomacy or security policy. Geoffrey Howe says, 'As long as Britain can go on enjoying the best of both worlds, then it's the best thing to do. It is one of the fields where it remains more difficult to establish effective partnerships with European neighbours, unlike diplomacy generally. I doubt whether the intelligence link between France and Germany, for example, is stronger than ours with the US.'

One reason for maintaining the transatlantic arrangements is that they seem to offer the agencies a sanctuary from each other's espionage. The 1947 UK–USA sigint treaty is said to include a promise not to intercept the other signatory's communications. It is known, for example, that Britain did intercept US signals between 1939 and 1941, when the USA entered the Second World War. Everyone I spoke to believes that the 1947 agreement was honoured during the Cold War and that the NSA, for example, did not use its UK bases to spy on Britain. Morton Abramowitz says, 'I know for sure that we do not read British communications. I have never seen intercepts of that kind.'

During the mid-1990s there are signs that the US–UK compact is under increased strain. British intelligence believes that the US intercepted conversations in 1994 between Lieutenant-General Michael Rose and British troops acting as forward air controllers in the Bosnian town of Gorazde. The incident came at a time of great tension between Washington and London over whether the use of Nato airpower should be escalated in the Balkans. Captain Jonathan Cooke, Director of the DIS division which included Bosnia at the time, told me, 'We certainly believed the Americans tapped into communications of that sort . . . the Americans interpreted the threshold for airstrikes differently to us. They could use those sorts of interceptions to say the UN knew the Serbs were doing something and didn't react.'

The interception of the conversations of Lieutenant-General Rose appears to have represented a true crossing of the rubicon, a change in a convention almost fifty years old. Captain Cooke notes, 'The people may have been mainly British, but we were talking about the UN', a distinction which may have proved important to the eavesdroppers in justifying their action within Washington's secret bureaucracy.

Transatlantic differences also resulted in problems with the usually intimate sharing of intelligence. Captain Cooke says, 'They more or less admitted they were holding stuff back from us, not everything but really the bits relating to the most pronounced political divide. They didn't feel we took their information about Serb atrocities seriously enough. We felt they weren't taking evidence of Muslim or Croat atrocities seriously enough . . . they pushed the stuff which favoured more punitive action against the Bosnian Serbs.' By the summer of 1995, Washington's view had prevailed. The British and French agreed first to a substantial programme of Nato airstrikes and, following the conclusion of the Dayton peace accords, to the ending of the UN mandate and its replacement with the US-led Peace Implementation Force.

Spying by agent between the US and the UK was never quite as regulated as sigint and is likely to have continued at a low level (albeit surrounded by various bits of agency doublespeak) throughout the Cold War. One SIS officer suggested that the CIA's Clandestine Service or Directorate of Operations maintained a cell of twenty people whose task was to analyse British agent reports in order to work out who the sources were, possibly with a view to poaching them. 'We don't know why they feel they have to do this, but we know that they're up to it,' he says. When I asked a former senior member of the CIA Directorate of Operations about this charge, he denied it and said that the analytical desk which processed MI6 reports anyway consisted of only two or three officers. Whether or not the allegation is true, it is an interesting example of the rivalry which exists even within one of the world's closest intelligence relationships.

Although the CIA and SIS follow a convention of not running agents in each other's bureaucracies, this is very much a matter of subjective definitions. To circumvent the agreement, an agent can be described as a 'contact' or 'source'. The senior CIA officer comments, 'You're always asked, "Are you really spying on the Brits?" The answer is no, because there is really no need. Our access to government is first-rate.' Few in the British agencies doubt that the CIA London station has a good many contacts, ranging from politicians to journalists.

Just as UK–US stresses over Bosnia may have undermined long established signals intelligence practice, so other issues appear to be shifting the ground on the running of agents. One senior MI6 officer says, 'We do not spy on America because the JIC does not set us that task. But you can ask whether they should be setting us that task; there are various issues today, for example relations between Washington and Sinn Fein, which you could argue we need to know about.' When asked whether the CIA might, in the light of the 1995 French expulsions, be running agents in the UK, a top MI5 officer told me, 'I don't know if they are. I'd like to think they would think very carefully before taking the risk of getting caught spying on us, but presumably they went through that thought process in the case of France.'

SIS officers may talk of their concerns about US activities, but equally many of Britain's traditional allies are the target of MI6 agent recruitment. One officer told me about an agent he ran in a Commonwealth country: 'Every so often, sometimes as often as once a week, we would meet in a hotel room which I had booked under a pseudonym. He would produce minutes from Cabinet meetings which I used a small hand-held scanner to copy.' India and Pakistan are regarded as particular targets and among the few places in the world where standards of tradecraft need to be almost as high as those in Moscow.

Officers in SIS or GCHQ agree that operations against the French or other European Union partners are a common occurrence. Peter

Wright's book *Spycatcher* explained how the French embassy in London was bugged during 1960–3. The operation succeeded in circumventing French codes by tapping a line carrying telex traffic before it was encrypted. It is clear from talking to SIS and GCHQ staff that similar operations have continued to this day, including those against European allies. It was perhaps to these operations that the former Foreign Office Minister of State David Mellor, generally a sceptic on the value of espionage, was referring when he told me, 'The one thing I did find really interesting was the diplomatic intelligence on some of our allies, which revealed in some cases a quite staggering dishonesty.'

SIS's Controller Europe department and GCHQ's K Division are the principal sections that target allies. Most of their work is aimed at trying to give Britain an advantage in matters such as the talks preceding the Maastricht Treaty that accelerated European integration. One former K Division officer says, 'We're all spying on each other. You need belts and braces, collateral on collateral. It would be as vital today to know where your European partners are coming from as it used to be to know the order of battle of Soviet forces.'

Although the MI5–GCHQ efforts of the early 1960s described by Wright involved simple taps and cable relays to a room in the Hyde Park Hotel, near the French embassy, today's operations are of a different order of sophistication. An example of the kind of operation mounted by the UK–USA sigint partners against diplomatic missions emerged in 1995. It took place in Australia and primarily involved the NSA and the Australian Security and Intelligence Organisation or ASIO (their equivalent of MI5), with some additional help from GCHQ.

The Chinese embassy in Canberra was moved in 1982 to a new purpose-built complex. In the late 1980s the NSA operation got under way, producing so much material that there were often thirty US personnel in the Australian capital handling it. The NSA and ASIO had filled the embassy with high-tech monitoring equipment. The connections between the various surveillance devices were made with fibre optic cables buried in the embassy walls. In this way, the NSA ensured that it could receive a large volume of information (including TV pictures as well as sound) and at the same time defeat Chinese counter-surveillance experts, who would be searching for tell-tale electromagnetic radiation. British experts are believed to have assisted in routing the signals from the embassy to a monitoring station.

Although details of the NSA's take from the Canberra operation remain highly secret, it is believed to have included monitoring the setting of codes in the cipher room, so allowing the NSA to break Chinese messages from all around the world on any given day. Following revelations of the operation by an Australian newspaper and TV station in 1995, Gareth Evans, the Australian Foreign Minister, said there had been 'great damage' to national security. The *Sydney Morning Herald* suggested that similar collaborative operations had been mounted against the Japanese, Malaysian, Indonesian, Russian, Iranian and Iraqi missions in Canberra, in breach of the Vienna Convention setting out diplomatic immunity. It would be surprising if the US eavesdropping agency did not exploit its relationship with the UK to mount similar operations in London.

For GCHQ managers, however, trying to maintain standards in the face of technological change was proving highly expensive.

Chapter 19

1993/4 Very Huge Bills

During the 1980s the Whitehall debate on the funding of GCHQ had focused on the cost of satellite espionage, but by the early 1990s it was centring on how Britain's technical spying organization might remain viable in the face of two new challenges: the growing use of fibre optics in global telecommunications and the spread of more advanced encoding systems. In many places, including Britain, fibre-optic lines between population centres had succeeded the microwave systems of the 1960s and 1970s.

During the late 1980s Britain installed a military fibre-optic trunk system code-named BOXER that connected 200 sites. BOXER cost £130 million, but had major advantages over the previous Backbone system of microwave links: it could handle more data, it stood a better chance of surviving a nuclear war, and it was highly secure. MoD planners were so impressed by its capabilities that they began funding projects to link computers in the network of national military and political command bunkers to provide a new 'Doomsday' system for managing the country. At the same time Mercury, a civilian telecommunications company, began installing fibre-optic links between major cities and offering its services to the business world.

The experts from GCHQ's Communications and Electronic Security Group who were involved in the new MoD projects were able to brief their colleagues in GCHQ's interception side on the potential of the extraordinary new medium. GCHQ and NSA managers had recognized since the mid-1980s that the advent of fibre optics could undermine their multi-billion-dollar investment in sigint satellites. GCHQ's biggest research project of the late 1980s and early 1990s explored ways of attacking the traffic which travelled down the glass threads as streams of light. The former head of one British intelligence agency says that GCHQ's research on fibre optics 'dealt with a huge problem and produced a very huge bill'. The money went to a variety of projects looking at different aspects of the problem, but one rough estimate is that Cheltenham spent £100 million on fibre-optic research over several years.

Despite the size of the bills, GCHQ's investigations did not produce any simple answers: there was no way that light running through buried cables could be picked up from afar in the same way that microwave signals could be caught in space by the parabolic dish of a CHALET satellite. Instead, the research effort concentrated on other methods of attack. The booster stations required every few dozen miles on fibre-optic trunks were identified as a weak point, as were the junctions at each end with the conventional telecommunications system. It was discovered that the fibre-optic lines themselves could be cut and the signal intercepted; according to one expert, 'You can bleed a signal out of it under certain conditions.' But all these methods required a physical intervention, which was the same problem the sigint agencies had faced for years with the Soviet Union's system of buried land lines.

During the Cold War there had been several successful attempts to intercept Soviet communications lines. During the 1950s tunnels were dug into the Soviet zones of Vienna and Berlin to tap into phone cables; the Berlin action was exposed to the Soviet authorities by their agent in SIS, George Blake. The investigative journalist Seymour Hersh claimed in 1994 that during the 1991 coup in Moscow the NSA intercepted land lines carrying military traffic. However, attacking underwater cables particularly attracted intelligence operators during the 1970s and 1980s, because it was easier to do so undetected than to dig underneath the streets of Vienna, Berlin or Moscow.

In Operation IVY BELLS in the late 1970s, the NSA and the US Navy succeeded in attaching a tapping pod to a Russian line off the Pacific coast. By 1981 IVY BELLS had been compromised by Ronald Pelton, an NSA man who had become a KGB agent. The tap was attached to the cable by an US submarine and although the operation was complex, involving the recovery every six months of receptacles holding tape cartridges, it succeeded in intercepting a large volume of military messages sent either uncoded or in weak ciphers. The success of IVY BELLS prompted US Navy intelligence chiefs to propose options as ambitious and expensive as running a submarine cable from Greenland to tap into Russian lines off the Arctic coast, so removing the need to recover tapes – an option which would have cost more than $1 billion.

Britain's desire to copy the USA led to an extraordinary defence and intelligence spending débâcle. In 1978 the Ministry of Defence approved the construction of HMS *Challenger*, a unique ship referred to as a Seabed Operations Vessel. During subsequent years the Royal Navy described *Challenger*'s mission variously as submarine rescue and the recovery of nuclear warheads or other sensitive materials. In fact, as one admiral revealed to me, 'There was a very strong intelligence element to the Challenger programme.'

The ship's primary role was to ensure that the Soviet Union did not mount an IVY BELLS-style operation against Britain. Naval security experts were particularly concerned about communications cables and the possibility of devices being deposited on the sea bed to monitor the comings and goings of submarines. There were, however, those in GCHQ and the Royal Navy who advocated that *Challenger* be used to attach British listening devices to the undersea communications links of other nations.

At 7,800 tonnes displacement and 134 metres long, *Challenger* represented a huge investment. She had a system of thrusters able to keep her stationary even in heavy seas. Her saturation diving equipment meant that frogmen could operate below 1,000 feet. In addition, *Challenger* was equipped with a diving bell able to descend to 20,000 feet and an unmanned submersible.

Problems with wiring and the diving system meant the ship was a disaster. She ended up costing £211 million instead of the planned £71 million. Between her launch in 1981 and her disposal early in 1993, *Challenger* was only operational for about three years because of a series of refits. She was sold for a hundredth of the price she had cost the taxpayer.

By the time *Challenger* was taken out of service in 1990, the threat of Soviet intelligence operations in British waters was perceived to have lessened considerably. It is not thought that GCHQ's research into fibre-optic interception had delivered workable solutions by this time. But a question mark remains over whether, during her brief and expensive life, *Challenger* was used to install underwater eavesdropping devices on non-fibre-optic cables. The Royal Navy's decision at a time of defence cuts to discontinue operating this highly expensive vessel may, however, have come shortly before British, US and Soviet experts began making progress in intercepting messages sent by light through undersea links.

Early in 1995 Rear Admiral Michael Cramer, Director of US

Naval Intelligence, publicly drew attention to the fact that Russia was continuing to build sophisticated miniature submarines. He told a US newspaper, 'I think they recognize that future communications and technology, particularly with undersea [fibre-optic cable] offers very interesting opportunities . . . they are building submarines that have the capability to exploit things on the bottom of the sea.' The paper estimated that there were around 10 billion undersea fibre-optic channels in use around the world in 1995, rising to around 100 billion by 2010. The admiral's remarks were a rare public glimpse into the world of US and Russian technical espionage and the direction of its evolution in the late 1990s. They imply a clear belief on the US side that the technical problems of intercepting undersea fibre optic trunk cables have been, or will shortly be, overcome.

During the Cold War, the Cocom (Co-ordinating Committee for Multilateral Export Controls) group of seventeen Western nations had prevented the export of high-quality communications technology, including fibre-optic lines, to the Soviet Bloc. Shortly after the 1991 Moscow coup AT&T, the American telecommunications giant, tried to sell fibre-optic lines to Moscow but was blocked by the US government. The issue soon found its way to the House of Representatives Foreign Affairs Committee. In September 1991 Christopher Hankin, Deputy Assistant Secretary of State, told Congress that 'our intelligence capability requires us to block some things that could be very helpful for the Soviets'. Any large-scale switch to fibre-optic trunk lines in Russia would undermine the effectiveness of the NSA's CHALET and MAGNUM satellites, designed specifically to exploit the weakness of Moscow's microwave trunk system.

As this exports-versus-intelligence debate continued on the Hill, a German firm was winning a similar Russian contract. The Germans circumvented the Cocom restrictions by using Carl Zeiss Jena, an East German firm, to make the sale. Early in 1992 the National Security Council bowed to commercial pressure from one of the USA's largest corporations, and on 5 March announced a change of rules. An agreement between Cocom's eight leading members allowed the sale of fibre optics to Russia, but still bound member nations not to install such systems across Siberia, where they might be used to provide secure links between air bases or ballistic missile sites.

From GCHQ's perspective, the only silver lining so far to appear in the cloud cast by fibre optics is the possibility that the lines may be used to send unbreakable codes, boosting the security of British communications. In the mid-1990s a GCHQ-financed project and a commercial one run by British Telecom were both exploring the possibility of using the quantum properties of light to send unique codes of unbreakable complexity, where any interference with the fibre-optic highway itself would be detectable in the message at the other end.

Neither GCHQ nor the NSA, with its greater resources, can afford to minimize the long-term implications of the global move to fibre optics and improved cryptography. Both developments force the agencies to go for physical interception of the communications system rather than picking the signals out of the atmosphere. In cases like the Syrian involvement with the 1986 Nezar Hindawi bombing attempt in London, or (probably) Saddam Hussein's conversations with his UN ambassador in New York during the Gulf War, this physical intervention may involve breaking diplomatic immunity. In cases where fibre-optic junction boxes are tapped, there are the attendant problems of placing the device without being caught and ensuring it remains undetected. All these techniques deny to the eavesdropper the simpler ways to avoid getting caught – those 'impersonal, technical systems' that Stansfield Turner mentioned in his 1991 essay on post-Cold War intelligence.

Although there was much controversy – on Capitol Hill, at least – about whether intelligence agencies should be deployed for the economic good of the country, other developments after the end of the Cold War gave business new freedoms to move in directions profoundly harmful to the agencies.

Since the 1970s the NSA has been trying to check the development of codes by academia or industry. The US author David Bamford describes in his book *The Puzzle Palace* how they struggled to control academic debate on cryptography and its commercial exploitation. IBM's Data Encryption Standard (DES), a cryptographic system aimed at big business, has been downgraded by Federal authorities to ensure that it is still crackable. The deal NSA tried to strike with industry was that it should retain the ability to read this commercial traffic, but that the encryption should be strong enough to stop virtually anybody else from doing so.

By the early 1990s computing developments meant that DES was becoming obsolete. Owen Lewis, a former government sigint officer who became a communications security consultant to industry, explains, 'When it appeared, for a cost of about $20 million you could have built a machine which would take twenty-four hours to decode a message. Now you could build a decoder for $1 million which could break DES in minutes.' Partly as a result of the UK–USA sigint shift towards economic targets, partly as a result of the cryptographic world's own dynamic, a demand for what the experts call 'strong cryptography' emerged, and products were developed to meet it.

Mathematicians at the Massachusetts Institute of Technology and the Weizmann Institute in Israel developed a cryptographic system that relied on public key. This allowed the code for sending a message to be openly published, while only the receiver held the formula to unlock it. Public Key Cryptography, as it became known, was an advance because it made the dissemination of an encryption code easy: for example, all branches of a bank could have it and would not have to keep it under lock and key, but only head office could make sense of their encoded messages. The mathematicians eventually produced the RSA algorithm (after the initials of its three inventors), which has not yet been cracked by the world's mathematicians and their computers.

The RSA system had its drawbacks, notably that it took a long time, even with powerful computers, to encrypt a message. Phil Zimmerman, another amateur US code-builder, took a more conventional 'symmetrical' cipher, which relied on both parties knowing the algorithm, but added the RSA code to it: the first part of the message used RSA and contained the codes needed to unlock the rest. In this way, the new cipher system – called Pretty Good Privacy or PGP – acquired the cryptographic strength of the public key system and the speed of more conventional ones. Zimmerman distributed PGP free, claiming that he was giving back to ordinary citizens the ability to communicate privately that they had been robbed of by the interception of telecommunications. Any reasonably powerful desktop computer can run PGP, so housewives, professors, drug barons or terrorists can use it to communicate via telephone modem.

Throughout the Cold War NSA and GCHQ had never broken the high-level Kremlin ciphers. Now, PGP and similar systems developed by the manufacturers of code machines extended strong cryptography to anybody who wanted it. Lewis explains, 'Certain governments do not want to allow systems which they cannot read themselves. That wall has been maintained for forty years. It has broken down now you can get extremely good crypto programmes on your desktop. This means governments are losing control, and they don't like it one bit.'

For years, rumours have circulated in the worlds of mathematics and intelligence that the NSA or GCHQ have done deals with the makers of crypto machines to allow them certain 'trapdoors' that will break the codes. Everyone I spoke to in GCHQ denied that the agency had any such advantage. Instead, they simply use large computers and some of the country's best mathematicians to break the codes. The advances in processing power and the development of cryptography have worked to government's disadvantage. Martin Kohanski, a mathematician and businessman who has given much time to trying to break new codes, thinks this is inevitable because 'it's several orders of magnitude harder to decode than to encode. A PC can encode at several thousand characters per second, but you'll need several weeks on a very good supercomputer to decode it.'

In Britain, the Department of Trade and Industry (DTI) is responsible for licensing the export of crypto machines. During the early 1990s the DTI's list of foreign-made machines that required licences for re-export grew, as more models became available which were, to all intents and purposes, uncrackable at Cheltenham. There were no laws to stop British firms using these codes, although things like secure telephones did require licensing. Where it had the power, for example in its regulation of radio frequencies, the government blocked these secure systems. Owen Lewis explains, 'A strong, digitally-encrypted system will not get a licence. Those who wish to do it illegally will do it anyway, and those who apply will be refused permission at the administrative stage.'

The NSA tried to persuade business to use an encryption system called Clipper which would be programmed with a 'back door' allowing the US government to crack the code. Their lukewarm response was evidence that corporate USA was doubting the wisdom of allowing the NSA to 'read its mail' at a time when the agencies were increasingly interested in economic data. US crypto manufacturers had the same anxiety about Clipper as the British ones had about similar GCHQ proposals: domestic laws might force businesses to use 'secure' systems with built-in 'trapdoors' for the NSA or GCHQ to listen in, but why should export customers buy such equipment, when (as anybody with access to the DTI's export restrictions list could see) many German, Italian and Swiss systems promised greater security? In the end, the Clipper project foundered when an expert at the AT&T phone company showed that the chips could be reprogrammed to prevent the Federal authorities from decoding messages.

Greater public demands for privacy, stemming from incidents such as the interception of the Prince and Princess of Wales's conversations with their respective lovers, led to the introduction of a cryptographic system in the Europe-wide GSM cellular phone system. Signals from the phones are decoded as soon as they enter the phone system proper, the aim being to defeat the amateur or commercial eavesdropper. British intelligence agencies could use a normal telecommunications interception warrant to tap a GSM conversation at the exchange. What the widespread availability of technology such as GSM phones did do was to create one more obstacle to the 'trawling' of cellular telephone signals picked up by the sigint agencies. While the algorithm used is weak and easily broken by NSA or GCHQ computers, the multiplication of this task by thousands (when many lines are being searched rather than a specific number intercepted) poses one more problem for sigint managers.

Commercial pressure has also changed the rules governing the sale of satellite imagery. Once again, US firms cited the foreign competition: France's SPOT operation and the availability from May 1993 of Russian satellite images. Many corporations, from mineral prospectors to those planning major construction projects, seek such pictures. The SPOT system has a ground resolution of ten metres – so even an object the size of a Boeing 747 appears only as a rough cross shape. The Russian KFA-3000 satellite has a 0.75 to 1.50 metre ground resolution, which means things like tanks show up. In one press article published in 1994, the pictures from this system were sufficiently good to show the storage bunkers for Israel's Jericho ballistic missiles.

US firms like Lockheed lobbied for a change in policy. Leading their campaign was James McMahon, a former Deputy Director of the CIA, who told Congress that market research suggested a global market of $5 billion to $7 billion for information from aerial and satellite photographs. In March 1994 President Clinton announced a 'one metre imagery' policy, clearing the way for firms such as Lockheed to sell images of that resolution. Three US groups plan to launch payloads with one-metre resolution cameras during the late 1990s. Administration officials argued that systems like the KH-11 CRYSTAL satellite would still have the advantage, with their reported ground resolution of ten centimetres. The new policy called into question France's major investment in the HELIOS imaging satellite, since it offered about the same quality of picture.

President Clinton's policy also means any nation can buy these photos from a US operator or, subject to export clearance, buy a photographic reconnaissance satellite of their own. Press reports in the USA suggested that Saudi Arabia, the United Arab Emirates, the Republic of Korea and Germany were among the nations expressing an early interest in such a purchase. The imaging spy satellite may soon be a tool of middle-ranking European powers or rich Gulf states. Israel has gone its own route, for example by launching in 1995 the third in its Ofeq series, believed by experts to be a photographic intelligence payload. As a result of decisions made in 1987, GCHQ remains locked into the NSA's sigint constellation. The British intelligence community may join the many other customers for future imagery marketed by the US consortiums poised to take advantage of the new policy.

Signals intelligence is a constant battle between offence and defence, the code-maker and the code-breaker. Although GCHQ (or more likely the NSA, with Cheltenham sharing the product) may in the future produce some mathematical answers to public key cryptography or some technical answers to fibre optics, the trend in the early 1990s was for technology to beat the eavesdropper. Lieutenant-General Derek Boorman, Chief of Defence Intelligence 1985–8, confirms that 'our take from signal intelligence must be reducing'.

One British intelligence mandarin says, 'With the advance of information technology, the quantity of information, the use of fibre optics and new cryptography techniques, you have to run very hard to stand still.' In this context, 'running' means spending large sums of money. The problem for the shadowy figures of the sigint world was that their budgets were being cut, not increased. In the summer of 1993 Congress took $1.2 billion out of the US intelligence community's budget. A similar struggle was going on in Britain, and GCHQ was about to lose it.

Chapter 20

1993 The Axe Falls

During the summer of 1993 the intelligence services came under renewed Treasury attack as part of a drive to cut government spending across all departments, a move made necessary by the spiralling public sector debt. The agencies were caught at a particularly bad moment by this cash crisis. Not only did the end of the Cold War make many people believe that economies were sensible, but the agencies, particularly MI5 and MI6, were also bogged down in substantial overspends on new headquarters – a highly-visible focus for public comment – and on an area that remained classified and therefore invisible to all but a few in Whitehall: the introduction of information technology.

The site for the new SIS headquarters, overlooking the Thames at Vauxhall Cross in south London, had been bought for £130 million in 1989. Terry Farrell, a post-Modernist architect whose buildings typified 1980s corporate Britain, designed the substantial construction of green glass, ochre panels and wide lobbies. Inside, there were specially-planted trees and luxurious fittings that aroused envy in other, more cash-strapped Whitehall departments. SIS had insisted on substantial modifications to the building, including the fitting of triple glazing – a measure designed to defeat bugging systems that pick up sound by laser through the vibration of window panes.

The government subsequently admitted that these modifications to the building had substantially increased its cost. By 1993 this was estimated at £240 million. The new HQ became the subject of Whitehall jokes: it was variously dubbed the Aztec Temple, the Transpontine Babylonian Palace, Ceausescu Towers and the Mighty Wurlitzer.

The Security Service, by contrast, had opted for a more restrained corporate embodiment: Thames House, a substantial stone-built block of the 1930s just north of Lambeth Bridge. The new MI5 building was intended to bring under one roof employees previously scattered in Curzon Street, Gower Street, Euston Tower and elsewhere. Like the MI6 building, it was designed to accommodate computer systems.

The modifications to Thames House destroyed most of the building except the façade, causing a minor outcry among conservationists. One feature was retained, however: a not quite full-sized squash court. MI5 staff who later worked in the building joked that it had only been left because Robin Butler, the Cabinet Secretary, was a keen squash player. The refurbished interior also contained a 'staircase to nowhere' in the staff restaurant. Early estimates of the cost of the new HQ of around £85 million made it a bargain compared with the Aztec Temple. However, by 1994 it was up to £227 million, a figure that seemed to have absorbed the substantial expense of the Service's information technology programme.

The cost of the new buildings, equivalent to around eighteen months' budget for each of the two espionage services, caused many murmurs in Whitehall. One mandarin remarks, 'At the time they were planned, the new buildings may have seemed logical enough, but by the time they were ready for use, the political and public expenditure climate was so very different.'

Some were reminded of Cyril Northcote Parkinson, whose study of the Royal Navy from its time of imperial greatness to the 1950s produced various axioms about bureaucratic behaviour. His most famous observation, Parkinson's Law, stated that 'Work expands to fill the time available for its completion.' The new MI5 and MI6 headquarters brought to mind another Parkinson discovery, that the Royal Navy's HQs seemed to grow in size and splendour as it declined. 'A perfection of planned layout is achieved only by organisations on the point of collapse', Parkinson had written. 'During a period of exciting discovery or progress there is no time to plan the perfect headquarters.'

In addition to searching for perfection in bricks and mortar, the agencies had also been substantially overspending on the introduction of information technology. Almost all areas of government were to find that computerization involved a costly learning process, but in other agencies such as health authorities or the Department of Education and Science these disasters became public knowledge.

The Defence Intelligence Staff was the first intelligence organization to attempt a comprehensive IT programme. The plan to put computers on the desks of many of its analysts was code-named TRAWLERMAN, and work began on the new system during the late 1980s. Lieutenant-General Derek Boorman, Chief of Defence Intelligence when the project started, concedes that it 'ran into major problems. We tried to be too advanced.' The difficulty with TRAWLERMAN, he explains, is that it was planned as a centralized system with a mainframe computer, and that by the time it was in service there was a general move towards decentralized networks.

One senior officer familiar with TRAWLERMAN, which had been installed by 1994, describes it as 'absolutely useless'. Problems with software and integration meant it could not perform the tasks originally intended, he says. The cost of the Ministry of Defence's learning process was around £65 million.

SIS started on the IT road slightly later, but its plans were even more ambitious. Until the late 1980s MI6 remained largely uncomputerized. In the early 1980s it transferred its tracing system of agents around the world from thousands of index cards to a mainframe in a heavily-shielded room at Century House. The Soviet Bloc empire had its own small database of personalities behind the iron curtain. The new plan involved creating a system called ATHS/OATS, which stood for Automatic Telegram Handling System/Office Automation and Telegram System. The eventual aim was to enable SIS stations worldwide to send their reports by secure means into the new system, and for all significant departments in London to have access to them and other materials (such as databases or financial figures) on desktops.

Managers at Century House had seen other organisations stumble with IT and were determined to avoid their mistakes. A Foreign Office telegram-handling system called Folios had gone over budget and been cancelled after about £15 million had been spent. The CIA had bought several thousand Wang desktop machines for its HQ in Langley that were billed as 'non-radiating' terminals. SIS acquired several of the computers and ran tests with what one participant calls the 'little grey van' of GCHQ's Communications and Electronic Security Group (CESG) parked outside. The boffins in the van discovered that they could read the text on the Wang screens.

CESG pinpointed the two danger areas as the monitor screen and the dot matrix head in the printers. Their grey vans contained enhanced TV detector technology; within a few hundred yards of Century House, the radiation from the TV tubes in computer screens or from the printers was sufficiently strong for the contents of files to be read. ATHS/OATS became possible when gas plasma screens were developed for laptops and laser or bubble jet printers arrived on the market. Because the project was considerably more ambitious than TRAWLERMAN, involving data links as well, its price was correspondingly higher: between £120 million and £150 million was spent from 1988 to 1992. Predictably, perhaps, they were still spending in 1994, and the overspend may have been in excess of £20 million. By 1995, however, ATHS had delivered results, with SIS stations around the world using it to send their reports into London.

MI5 had, perhaps wisely, waited longer. The Service's greater openness led to it mentioning in its 1993 public information brochure that 'more sophisticated intelligence databases using the most modern technology are now being introduced'. Since the 1970s MI5 had had a computerized index of its suspect files called R2. The aim of the new project was to expand the index, as well as offering other office automation functions to staff. It is a substantial project, probably costing around £100 million, but at the time of writing it is too early to assess whether it will be completed within budget.

The difficulties with IT at MI5, MI6 and GCHQ were compounded by the way they chose to buy their systems. The Ministry of Defence, for example, had during the 1980s decided to renegotiate all contracts where it was the main contractor: the aim was to transfer the responsibility (and therefore the risk) for integrating all the elements of complex weapons to industry rather than keep it within the department. The MoD also made more use of fixed-price contracts. The use of such procedures on TRAWLERMAN meant that an overspend of several million pounds had to be met by the contractor rather than the public. Costly mistakes across Whitehall led to new procedures, but only some seem to have been applied by the other intelligence agencies. One manager from a firm which sold computer systems to government says, 'The highly secure ends of government tend to be a law unto themselves. They place numerous small contracts with different firms, and act as the main contractors themselves. It's done in the interests of security, but leaves them with the risk.'

The cost of buildings and IT for MI5, MI6 and GCHQ can be conservatively estimated at £700 million during 1988–94. As late as the autumn of 1992, spending on these services was still rising quickly because of these major commitments. The so-called 'secret vote', the budget heading for some of the agency spending (it went mainly on

MI5 and MI6 wages), rose by 8.5 per cent to £185 million for 1992–3. This figure excluded most of the money spent by GCHQ, which came under the Ministry of Defence budget, as did a multitude of other expenses including MI5's phone bills. Other government departments also carried some of the costs, including the Foreign Office, Transport and the Environment. As measured by a revised estimate, the 'real cost' of the three agencies in 1993–4 was revealed in the 1994 spending figures as £974 million. The DIS is not included in this figure, and in 1994–5 cost around £60 million.

During the summer of 1993 the Treasury gathered its forces for an assault on the secret budget. It always considered that the agencies had escaped proper financial scrutiny. The issue was apparently considered by the Cabinet Committee on the Intelligence Services, which heard various papers from officials such as Gerry Warner, the Intelligence Co-ordinator. Kenneth Clarke, the Chancellor, went into the meetings with a determination to get cuts, according to one participant who paraphrases his message to the agencies as 'Come off it!'

There was consensus among ministers that the intelligence establishment could not escape the 'equal misery' formula dictated by the public spending crisis. This dismayed Air Marshal John Walker, the Chief of Defence Intelligence, who observes, 'At the end of the Cold War, the intelligence task actually increased and that was a very difficult argument to get over to people . . . if you're going to expand the number of nations where you might have to commit troops and if you are also cutting back your forces then the one area you cannot make economies in is intelligence. Whitehall, however, operates on the basis that everyone must make savings.'

Treasury officials adopted standard management procedures and decided to focus the economies on the most expensive item in the budget: sigint. A memo from John Adye, Director of GCHQ, to his staff, a copy of which was obtained by the *Guardian*, indicates that the Treasury initially sought to cut 5 per cent from the organization's budget each year for three years. Given that Cheltenham had become used to real rises year on year for almost fifteen years, economies on this scale would have been painful indeed. Adye's memo suggested that his pleading managed to reduce the cuts to between 2 per cent and 4 per cent for each of the three years.

Because of GCHQ's spending on technology – a substantial slice of their £500 million or so spend for 1994 was going on ZIRCON and other long-term investments – much of the saving would have to come from staff cuts. The civilian staff was to be reduced from 6,500 to 6,000 over the three years. Early in 1994 government figures revealed it had already gone down to 6,228. Changes to the support structure in 1995 were designed to cut another 600 jobs.

There were also unannounced cuts in the military eavesdropping organization working for GCHQ. A careful reading of *The Wire*, journal of the Royal Signal Regiment, and of *RAF News* reveals changes to the military structure. During the Cold War the Army had deployed two 'radio' regiments on GCHQ's behalf: 9 Signal Regiment in Cyprus and 13 Signal Regiment in West Germany. The primary mission of the latter was to detect changes in Soviet Army radio transmissions that might presage an assault on West Germany. In March 1995, 13 Signal Regiment was disbanded; roughly two-thirds of its strength went under the cuts, and the remainder of its soldiers returned to the UK to man sigint facilities at RAF Digby in Lincolnshire. With other changes, it is apparent that the services of at least 500 Army and RAF members (out of around 3,000 in mid-1993) were lost to GCHQ.

SIS was also forced to take cuts. At the press conference to launch the Intelligence Services Bill in November 1993, Colin McColl explained, 'After the Falklands War, when we were quite clearly seen to be too thin – not just there but in other areas as well – we increased our numbers during the 1980s. We are now on a declining path, and I think over the next two or three years we will be back to where we were before the Falklands War – that is, very roughly.' The chief of SIS added, 'We are having a difficult time.' Although official figures have not been given, the MI6 cuts mean a fall from around 2,400 in 1993 to about 2,150 in 1996. Early in 1994 the government said that 2,303 worked for MI6.

The decision of McColl to stay on, the search for a new chief, and the infighting caused by the agency's financial situation caused a stream of early retirements that in some cases amounted to dismissals. Some officers refer to a 'night of the long knives'.

Barrie Gane, Director of Requirements and Production, left in 1993. He was not due to retire until September 1995, and most people had expected Gane, as number two in the organization, to succeed McColl. He had even sat an appointments board for the job at the Cabinet Office, but McColl's two-year extension had left Gane with no future; the Chief wanted to pass the leadership on to someone from a younger generation.

The boards to decide on who would succeed McColl were apparently held in the second half of 1993, and they resulted in the selection of David Spedding, Controller Middle East during the Gulf War. Spedding had been in pole position for the job since taking over from Gane as Director of Requirements and Production. His career, with postings in Beirut, Abu Dhabi, Amman and Santiago, suited the post-Cold War priorities of the agency. An officer describes Spedding as 'the first Chief not to have come up through the "master race" as we call it – the Soviet Bloc'. The new Chief took over in September 1994, which gave him eight and a half years to serve before retirement age.

McColl's selection of new leadership for the Service caused a considerable turnover in higher management. Not only had the three directors taken early retirement, but there were other officers in their late forties or early fifties who realized they could no longer expect to reach the highest levels of MI6 and left. It is believed that twenty officers from the Service's Intelligence Branch management stream (around 5 per cent of the total) left as part of the changes. The turbulence was felt in most parts of the organization: after Spedding gave up the job of Controller Middle East, for example, it had three incumbents in two years. An MI6 station officer who observed events from a far-off posting could not keep track of the changes and remarks, 'We were sitting out on a limb, shouting at a black hole.'

As the Cabinet Office handed out the cuts, it appointed Michael Quinlan to carry out a review of spending, administration and policy. Quinlan had been Permanent Under Secretary at the Ministry of Defence. He was a respected figure in Whitehall, known principally as a 'theologian' of nuclear strategy: he had been on the Cabinet subcommittee that chose the US Trident ballistic missile system. Quinlan's review was in two parts: the first examined the new financial accounting system for GCHQ, SIS and the Security Service; the second was restricted by his terms of reference to an examination of foreign intelligence-gathering operations. The Security Service was not included in this section and the DIS was subject to a separate review.

Air Marshal Walker felt that this subdivision of Quinlan's review was mistaken, pointing out that his DIS was the largest centre for analysis of the raw information gathered abroad by GCHQ and SIS. 'To look at collection without looking at the analysis didn't seem sensible,' he says. 'It didn't seem a natural marriage.'

Whatever the intrinsic merits of his approach, therefore, Quinlan's report was not the overall strategy document that some in Whitehall and intelligence wanted. There had long been suspicions at the Treasury, for example, that counter-intelligence work at MI6 overlapped with some counter-espionage tasks at MI5, or that military attachés reporting to DIS might be making similar reports to MI6 stations.

Quinlan's findings in part two of his study are paraphrased by Air Marshal Walker as 'an endorsement of what was being done'. There were no proposals for radical change, more a recognition that the broad range of tasks required of the agencies meant they had limited room for manoeuvre. Captain Jonathan Cooke, one of Walker's directors in DIS at the time of the review, comments, 'It didn't grasp nettles it circled the nettles. For example, SIS got an easy ride and they do have some fundamental questions to answer in terms of what they're achieving in terms of resources to results.'

At the Ministry of Defence, the review of DIS was part of a wider process by which teams examined all aspects of operations under the Defence Cost Studies (DCS) programme. The results of DCS were announced in July 1994, but some of the reports caused considerable bad feeling within the organization.

The Defence Cost Study team on the Defence Intelligence Staff was headed by Derek Boorman, the former general and a member of the Security Commission. Boorman came to the conclusion that the DIS management structure needed to be 'flattened' and that more resources needed to be put into multi-disciplinary teams capable of switching quickly between crises or points of interest. His inquiry brought him into conflict with Air Marshal Walker, the CDI, who made it clear to senior officers and officials that he resented his predecessor's approach and conclusions.

When Boorman had been Chief of Defence Intelligence in the mid-1980s, his organization had had four major subdivisions, each headed by a service officer of two-star (major-general, for example) rank or the equivalent civil service grade. Before leaving in 1988 he had abolished one of these divisions, the Directorate of Economic and Logistic Intelligence, and spread its staff among the others.

The Defence Cost Study paper was a chance for Boorman to finish the job. He recommended a restructuring of management that would leave just one official at two-star rank. The paper, which aimed to improve efficiency and deliver savings of £20 million over five years, also involved retiring several of the DIS's older experts in the Scientific and Technological Directorate. This last measure prompted a leak to the press attacking the proposals. Boorman's aim was to prevent the DIS doing small amounts of analysis on a large number of topics and instead to focus his multi-disciplinary groups on a limited number of targets of current interest.

Prior to the backbiting provoked by these studies, the Chief of Defence Intelligence had come to the conclusion that publicly-available information was the answer to many of the DIS analysts' questions. Ministry experts had calculated that there were 8,000 databases around the world, ranging from on-line newspaper services to medical or engineering services, of use to the intelligence analyst. The CDI referred to it as a 'data deluge'. The shortcomings of the TRAWLERMAN computer system and cash limits mean that Britain has yet to give the subject the treatment many intelligence chiefs believe it deserves.

During McColl's tenure as Chief, SIS also tried to redeploy some of the staff freed by the closing of certain stations to 'fire brigade' duties, ready for dealing with sudden crises. The reductions in its overseas stations – mainly in the formerly Communist east European countries and certain African states – were limited, leaving around sixty stations reporting to six regional controllers in London. Although the geographic organization remained largely the same, the functional organisation had expanded because of the creation during the previous decade of the terrorist, narcotics, proliferation and finance requirements sections within the Global Tasks branch. With staff cuts under way, SIS therefore had more chiefs and fewer Indians.

The new, younger board of directors installed at SIS by the end of 1993 had more radical views about the need for change. David Spedding, the new Chief, was aware of the 'know nothing' syndrome of spreading shrinking resources over too many regions and topics. Throughout 1994 the SIS management studied how the organization might be changed. Early in 1995 a wholesale reorganisation of SIS was implemented, probably the most important since that which followed the Second World War.

The organization had functioned for many years with six geographic controllerates: one London-based, the others covering Middle East, Far East, Western Hemisphere, Central and Eastern Europe, and Africa. Under Spedding, Africa and the Middle East were merged, as were the Western Hemisphere and Far East controllerates. The Global Tasks part of the organization was made into a fully fledged controllerate, as was Operational Support, a department that existed mainly to assist officers in overseas deep cover operations. The changes were meant to make the organization less geographically minded, better suited to transnational phenomena like drugs or proliferation.

At GCHQ there was a long-term decrease in staff – it may have been as high as 7,000 in the mid-1980s and was coming down to 6,000 – but the management structure was left essentially intact. GCHQ officers saw little change except for a shift in resources between the two big sigint processing groups, J Division (the Soviet Bloc unit) losing some staff relative to K Division, which dealt with all other regions.

MI5, like MI6, showed a long term trend of creating more management, although in its case this was mitigated by the increase in staff. Between 1985 and 1995, the Security Service added three new posts at Grade 3, the tier below Director General. At the next level down, the heads of sections within branches, my rough estimate is that eight additional posts appeared, an increase of around 20 per cent.

The consequences of the structural problems in foreign intelligence-gathering were, in the words of one Cabinet Office observer, 'that our concerns were more and more diffuse but we knew less and less about each subject'. This caused frustration to some; Field Marshal Peter Inge, the Chief of the General Staff, noted acerbically in a lecture early in 1994, 'In the intelligence community I am told that the threat is now called multi-faceted or multi-directional, which actually means that we are not very sure what it is or where it's coming from.'

Some believed that the loss of the Soviet focus had left the intelligence establishment increasingly accident-prone. There were many examples to quote.

The peace deal between the Palestine Liberation Organisation and Israel in September 1993 had taken Britain by surprise. It had not figured in Middle East Current Intelligence Group papers. Iran and Iraq were the top Middle East priorities, and the lone SIS officer stationed in Israel relied on his meetings with Mossad and military intelligence officials for information. They had been kept in the dark about the secret talks by their Prime Minister, so the British government, dependent on the liaison relationship, had known nothing. A team from the BBC TV programme *Panorama* had, however, uncovered the 'Norway channel' and filmed the final stages of the negotiations.

The withdrawal of North Korea from the Non Proliferation Treaty in March 1993 provoked a crisis over the inspection of its nuclear facilities, which the CIA alleged were making atomic bombs. As tension built during the year, British ministers needed briefing. The issue was due to come before the United Nations Security Council, where the UK was determined to hold on to its permanent seat, and Washington had climbed several steps up a ladder of diplomatic escalation that might have involved a Gulf-style military coalition against North Korea. An official party to JIC discussions on North Korea says that Britain was 'almost wholly dependent on American intelligence' on the subject.

In the absence of a clear threat, maintaining the Security Council seat in the face of suggestions that Japan or Germany better deserved such a mark of great power status had become a foreign policy goal in itself. Meetings of the Cabinet intelligence committee in 1993 had underlined the conflict between a desire to make savings and the need to gain a wider range of intelligence in support of a global foreign policy. One senior figure in intelligence notes that the Cabinet was never tempted to make deep cuts in the establishment, because 'no minister is ever going to say, "We're a small power and we don't need all that stuff." It's politically and psychologically impossible.' They were hoping that Quinlan might produce findings that would resolve these contradictory aims and give clearer direction to intelligence work.

The Intelligence Services Bill was published on 24 November 1993. Its most significant innovation was the creation of an oversight committee. After some final attempts during 1992 to side-step this development, the government had floated the idea of a committee of privy councillors. The deliberations of the committee would be governed by the rules of this ancient royal body, which prevent members from divulging anything to outsiders. Many in the Commons had wanted a select committee drawn from the main parties with certain powers over officials. The six-member panel appointed by the Bill was a compromise between the two proposals. Although the Home Secretary had told the Home Affairs Committee a year earlier that it would be impossible to separate 'policy' from operational secrets, in November 1993 the Foreign Secretary stated, 'Policy is quite wide, but there is a distinction in real life between policy and the details of operations, and I think that is one that both the agencies and the committee would want to respect.'

The Intelligence Services Bill said that members would 'examine the expenditure, administration and policy' of the agencies, but the members would be appointed by the Prime Minister rather than by the usual parliamentary process for select committees. The committee would hold its sessions *in camera* and the Bill conceded the agencies broad swathes of sensitive information they could refuse to divulge.

The Bill also contained safety mechanisms that could prevent committee members or even the heads of the espionage services from doing what the judge in the Matrix Churchill case did: making public politically-embarrassing intelligence material. It gave the Prime Minister the right to excise anything he defined as prejudicial to the agencies' functions from any committee reports, and provided for a blanket veto on information if 'the Secretary of State has determined that it should not be disclosed'. The legislation therefore aimed to allay agency concerns about sources or methods being compromised while giving broadly-defined powers to the PM and Cabinet ministers responsible for the respective agencies to keep certain things from the committee. Given ministerial workloads, it left much of the task of deciding what was or was not suitable for release in the hands of the 'permanent government' of departmental civil service chiefs and its head, the Cabinet Secretary.

Parliamentary oversight had been conceded, but as Douglas Hurd said, 'Certainly this committee will be within the ring of secrecy.' One of Whitehall's intelligence mandarins says, 'Open intelligence is a contradiction in terms. What I can do with you is take you behind the curtain. But if I really speak to you openly and frankly, you will never be able to come out again.' Another senior official suggests, 'We may simply have transferred the problem from one between MPs and government to one between MPs who are part of the committee and the rest of their colleagues.' By late 1994, the members had been appointed under the chairmanship of Tom King and the committee prepared for its first sessions. The prospect of an MI5 branch director or an SIS station chief going before Members of Parliament to explain their actions had become real.

The spy chiefs realized that the arrival of greater parliamentary scrutiny would be accompanied by greater contact with the press. As with more substantial operational matters, however, each agency made its own judgement about far such contacts should go. The Security Service proved the most open: Stella Rimington gave public lectures, and was even made available for a photo opportunity at her desk. Since their beginnings in the mid-1980s, MI5's press contacts had been handled by the DG's Legal Adviser, a senior figure with a seat on the Board of Management. The volume of press and parliamentary liaison had grown to the point where several officers in the DG's secretariat were assigned to it. They began to operate more like a normal Whitehall press office, responding to inquiries but almost always on a non-attributable basis.

SIS had briefed dozens of editors and journalists in the run-up to the Intelligence Services Bill, but now decided that its priorities were different. McColl, says one intelligence officer, 'had come to the conclusion that mystery and secrecy were essential to recruitment'. This attitude led to inconsistencies in the agency's public profile. Although Spedding had been publicly named as Chief of MI6 by the government, he described himself in the 1995 edition of *Who's Who* by the customary cover title 'Counsellor, Foreign and Commonwealth Office'.

MI6 contacts with journalists usually took place in plush restaurants off Piccadilly and were governed by strict rules of non-attribution. John Simpson, the BBC's Foreign Affairs editor, did however manage to persuade them that he should write about one of these occasions in the *Spectator*.

These SIS briefings imparted one principal message: that the Service had vital new tasks to perform, that it was still relevant. There was also a strong desire to tell reporters that SIS was only in the business of *gathering* intelligence. The analysis of CX reports or other material rested with the Joint Intelligence Committee machinery, and SIS could therefore not be blamed for any 'intelligence failures'. This message was somewhat undermined by the Service's occasional willingness to bring its in-house analysts to these lunches to brief reporters on particular points of interest. Beyond promoting a general awareness of the lie of the land from SIS's point of view, the management had more limited objectives in its press relations than MI5.

SIS's attitude to the press was complicated by the fact that it sometimes wanted to use the press for its own purposes. An MI6 section called Operational Information, consisting of about twenty staff, is the Service's centre of expertise in planning psychological operations. Briefings by officers from this section, usually involving foreign rather than UK press, are deemed to require specific ministerial approval; general briefings on the Intelligence Services Bill did not. Like agent runners, Operational Information staff use pseudonyms when briefing their contacts. Major themes of briefing by this SIS section during the early 1990s were: the need for continued surveillance of Russia; instability within Iraq; and IRA connections with foreign states.

GCHQ took the most conservative approach. Its Director never got beyond holding a few lunches for the editors of national newspapers. GCHQ was highly reluctant to brief journalists on specific issues, apparently because it felt such meetings would take its officers on to dangerous ground where sigint techniques might be compromised.

McColl, Adye, Butler and Hurd joined forces for a unique 'on the record' press conference on the day the Bill was launched. Journalists assembled on one side of a room in the Foreign Office, intelligence officials on the other. MI5's Legal Adviser was present, as was SIS's Director of Security and Public Affairs and a host of other officers. Mindful perhaps of the strict 'deniability' of many of their previous meetings with the journalists, not to mention the suspicion with which reporters with intelligence services contacts are regarded by some of their colleagues, the two camps sat pretending they did not know one another until after the press conference had ended, when some cautious handshakes broke the ice.

During the meeting, McColl projected himself with all the self-confidence of a man who knows how to work the Whitehall system and has taken the lead in Foreign Office amateur dramatics. He did, however, make it clear that there were strict limits to his openness, so that while his voice was being recorded, cameras had been banished from the meeting. Asked why he would not be photographed, the Chief of SIS explained:

> Secrecy is our absolute stock in trade, it is our most precious asset. People come and work for us, risk their lives for us sometimes, risk their jobs often, because they believe SIS is a secret service . . . It is also very important for the people who help us abroad – and there is a difference here, I think, between us and the Security Service because our most important constituency is abroad . . . I am very anxious that I should be able to send some sort of signal to these people that we are not going to open up everything, we are not going to open up our files, we are not going to allow ourselves to be undressed in public with their name as part of our baggage.

McColl dominated the proceedings, although deferring to Hurd. John Adye, controlling three times the budget and staff of MI6, sat uncomfortably throughout. His few remarks – 167 words during the one-hour conference – betrayed in his voice and body language the signs of stress. Adye praised the Bill for providing 'more open accountability and public reassurance while still preserving the secrecy which is essential to the discharge of our work'.

Any journalist who hoped that the conference might be the first of many was to be disappointed during the following years. John Major's policy of more open government had borne fruit, something that none of those who had been able to cross-examine Colin McColl on the record could easily deny. But the agencies were determined that this unprecedented public statement, which ministers believed was necessary to support the Bill, should not in any sense become routine. Some had deep misgivings about any contact with the media. Others more open to the idea believed that it was necessary to mend fences after the Thatcher years, when press discussion of intelligence matters risked responses ranging from court injunctions to a raid by the Special Branch. One senior civil servant says, 'We sexed it up by drawing a veil over everything.' The agencies were hoping the whole subject would become as unsexy as possible. As journalists and intelligence officers shuffled out of the Foreign Office meeting, one MI6 man remarked, 'My definition of success would be to call a press conference to which you would all be too bored to come.'

Chapter 21

1992/3 Irish Intrigues

Between MI5 taking the lead in the anti-IRA intelligence effort in October 1992 and the Downing Street Declaration by the British and Irish leaders setting out peace terms for Northern Ireland in December 1993, secret peace negotiations and the counter-terrorist campaign became interwoven. Senior intelligence officers played a key role in government policy, and there were signs that the establishment of MI5's T Branch (Irish Counter Terrorism) with substantial resources was having an impact on the IRA.

The government had spent some years trying to signal to the IRA its views about the future of Ulster. As Northern Ireland Secretary, Peter Brooke had attracted the attention of many republicans by the statements he made in an interview in November 1989. He said it was 'difficult to envisage a military defeat' of the IRA, and that the end of terrorist operations ought to prompt an 'imaginative' government response. In a speech in 1990, Brooke had added that the British government was not opposed in principle to a united Ireland, and that it 'has no selfish or strategic or economic interest in Northern Ireland'.

Brooke's comments had spawned political talks to which Sinn Fein, the IRA's political wing, was not invited because it would not publicly renounce violence. These talks failed to produce a political solution to the conflict. They were however enough to convince the leading lights in the republican movement, the Sinn Fein leader Gerry Adams and Martin McGuinness, that their strategy of 'bullet and ballot' might be about to bear fruit. The stepping-up of the IRA's campaign in Britain during the early 1990s may well have been designed to put pressure on the government at a time when republican leaders believed it was looking for a way out of Ireland.

Key security officials at Stormont, seat of the Northern Ireland government, and Knock, the Royal Ulster Constabulary HQ, had drawn opposite conclusions about the use of violence. Hugh Annesley, who had taken over as Chief Constable of the RUC in 1989, had mixed feelings about using intelligence from within the republican community to lay SAS ambushes. John Deverell, MI5's Director and Co-ordinator of Intelligence at Stormont, saw it as one of his principal tasks to brief the Secretary of State on what he saw as the deepening rift within the Provisionals about the tactics for ending their campaign. Annesley and Deverell were fascinated by intelligence reports suggesting that the IRA's seven-member Army Council had been split about whether to have a Christmas ceasefire in 1991. It was suggested by RUC Special Branch analysts that Adams had used his vote to bring about the brief halt to violence.

After an ambush by the Army's covert Special Forces unit near Coalisland in February 1992 in which four IRA men were killed, the policy for using soldiers from the twenty-strong SAS contingent based in Ulster was changed. During 1990–2 Army Special Forces had killed eleven republican terrorists. From Coalisland until the time of writing, more than three years later, the members of that unit, known by the cover name of Intelligence and Security Group, killed nobody. One senior SAS officer says that the change resulted from orders for 'non-lethal force' emanating from Stormont. The decision to remove the SAS from ambush duties was a repetition of a previous halt between December 1978 and December 1983. In 1992 ministers and senior police officers apparently believed that the further killing of IRA members would inflame republican opinion and damage the secret contacts going on with the leadership. The departure of Margaret Thatcher as Prime Minister late in 1991, together with her view that reason and goodwill were no substitute for force when dealing with the IRA, may also have been important for the change of climate concerning both peace talks and SAS operations.

Peter Brooke's political initiative had been accompanied by contacts between Michael Oatley, a senior MI6 officer, and the republican leadership. The MI6 officer had initially got to know republican figures during a posting to Stormont between 1973 and 1975 – a period during which Adams had secretly met British ministers for talks. Oatley's role in 1990 was puzzling, given that SIS had yielded to MI5 in Irish operations some years before. But it seems to have been justified within Whitehall because of the Foreign Office interest in negotiating solutions to the Irish question with the Dublin government and possibly because of Oatley's involvement in the earlier contacts. Sinn Fein later said that Oatley (although they did not name him) had met McGuinness in October 1990, after a break in contacts since the end of the 1981 IRA hunger strikes. McGuinness told a later press conference, 'He passed word to Sinn Fein that he was due for retirement and would like to meet me before he left and to prepare the way for a new British government representative.' McGuinness had been Chief of Staff, or commander, of the Provisional IRA during the 1981 events and Special Branch analysts believed he retained a place on the Army Council. Whether he or Oatley made the first move is unclear; following the later disclosure of these secret contacts, McGuinness evidently wanted to reassure supporters that republicans had not caved in.

Oatley retired early in 1991, passing the secret contacts on to his successor. The government used the communications channel to keep Sinn Fein and the IRA informed about the progress of the multi-party talks.

McGuinness's willingness to meet Oatley's successor was part of a broad republican strategy to bring the conflict to an end. The February 1992 Sinn Fein conference had launched a paper called *Towards a Lasting Peace*, setting out the movement's preconditions for ending the conflict as it sulked on the sidelines of Brooke's multi-party talks. In time, Adams developed his initiative with John Hume, who as leader of the non-violent Social Democratic and Labour Party had attended those talks. Hume and Adams were to produce a joint platform which compromised the traditional republican aim (still enshrined in its February 1992 paper) of a commitment by London and Dublin to end the partition of Ireland as a precondition for peace. Adams was also using a west Belfast priest as an intermediary to talk to the Irish government of Albert Reynolds. In time, the Sinn Fein leader convinced both Hume and Reynolds of his sincerity and willingness to compromise. Perhaps unsurprisingly, London remained unconvinced.

The British government was hamstrung by public ministerial commitments not to speak to Sinn Fein until the republicans had renounced their campaign of violence. Using SIS officers to brief McGuinness and discuss possible talks allowed them to maintain a deniable channel.

According to the official account, it was not until February 1993 that this most secret of the many channels between Sinn Fein and the outside world produced real results. In his later account of the clandestine contacts, Patrick Mayhew – who succeeded Brooke as Northern Ireland Secretary in April 1992 – said that a message was received from McGuinness on 22 February 1993 saying that 'the conflict is over, but we need your advice on how to bring it to a close. We wish to have an unannounced ceasefire in order to hold a dialogue leading to peace.' Mayhew subsequently admitted that the message was verbal rather than written, and Sinn Fein denied some of its specifics. The republican leaders were evidently fearful of how their own supporters might regard the revelation of secret contacts. According to Mayhew, their 22 February message had insisted on a secret ceasefire and continued, 'We cannot announce such a move as it will lead to confusion for the volunteers because the press will interpret it as a surrender.' Although McGuinness and Adams, not surprisingly, later denied using such language, they did concede that early in 1993 the idea of proper peace talks had been put forward by the government intermediary and that, in McGuinness's words, 'we began to take his proposal more seriously'.

What is clear is that both the government and the IRA feared their secret dialogue becoming public, and were well aware that the process Adams was embarked upon carried a risk of breaking apart the republican movement. The formation of the Provisional IRA itself, as well as the creation of the splinter groups the Irish National Liberation Army and the Irish People's Liberation Organisation, were evidence of the factional nature of republican politics and of the ability of political change to bring such in-fighting to a head. Fear of owning up to secret contacts was not the only thing that held Whitehall back. Intelligence assessments by the RUC Special Branch at Knock and by Deverell at Stormont underlined the possibility of hard-liners – IRA Active Service Units in places like east Tyrone and south Armagh – opposing Adams's moves and continuing to fight.

In addition to the multifaceted secret talks and the IRA operations in Britain, one other important matter weighed on the minds of the republican leadership: the growing lethalness of the campaign by loyalist terrorists. Between the beginning of 1993 and the end of June, loyalist groups had killed nineteen out of the thirty-seven victims of the violence in Ulster. The attack of 25 March on building workers at Castlerock near Londonderry was typical of the new wave of sectarian violence: four men had been machine-gunned by loyalists. Incidents such as Castlerock consolidated the pattern that had emerged since about 1990 of increased activity by Protestant groups, particularly by the largest of them, the Ulster Freedom Fighters or UFF (who used the political front-name Ulster Defence Association).

Throughout the 1980s the intelligence services had limited UFF effectiveness by penetrating the organization's entire leadership. A new generation of leaders had taken over by the early 1990s – partly as a result of arrests of key UFF men by detectives investigating leaks of security forces intelligence documents as part of the Stephens Inquiry – and they were determined to make the UFF more effective. Most feared amongst the new leaders was John Adair, a west Belfast terrorist who became commander of the UFF Brigade in that quarter of the city. Adair changed the pattern of sectarian violence: north Belfast had previously been the main killing ground for the sectarian death squads, and he himself had launched an increasing number of attacks from his base around the Shankill Road. Adair occasionally talked to journalists, one of whom wrote up the encounter, referring to him not by name but as Mad Dog. The same article suggested that his group had killed twenty people during the previous two years.

Adair's power base put him just a few hundred yards from the republican heartlands of west Belfast: the Falls Road and estates like Ballymurphy or Divis. Protestant attacks on the Falls deeply concerned Adams and other Sinn Fein leaders. They had always believed in the concept of the IRA as a non-sectarian force, even though only a tiny minority of its members were non-Catholics. They found themselves under increasing pressure from their supporters to retaliate more vigorously against the loyalists. The IRA and other republican groups made several attempts to assassinate Adair: he claimed to have survived six. The security forces were also taking more of an interest in Mad Dog. In March 1993 he and several accomplices cornered a plain-clothes member of 14 Intelligence Company, the Army's covert surveillance unit, near his house. The soldier shot his way out of the trap.

On 23 October 1993 the IRA Belfast Brigade thought it had a golden opportunity to dispose of Adair and several other key UFF players. They believed that a meeting was under way in an office used by the group over a fishmongers on the Shankill Road. Whereas previous attempts to kill Adair had involved firearms, this time two IRA men, Thomas Begley and Sean Kelly, were despatched with a powerful bomb. As Kelly waited outside, Begley took the package into the shop, probably with the intention of shouting a warning to the customers to leave. It did not go to plan: the bomb exploded, killing nine bystanders and Begley himself. Adair and the other UFF men were not even there. The judge who later gave Kelly nine life sentences called it 'one of the most appalling atrocities ever endured by the people of this province over the past quarter of a century'.

This botched operation caused consternation in the republican leadership and may well have played an important part in silencing IRA opponents of Adams's peace moves. One senior republican said the day after the Shankill bomb that it had been 'a complete disaster'. Alex Maskey, a Sinn Fein councillor, told the Belfast city council, 'It was a devastating human tragedy . . . every single death reinforces the need for a peace process and I would ask this council . . . to embrace the need for dialogue as a means of taking us out of this conflict.'

That conflict had, however, changed its character. The British Army was not killing republicans any more: 1993 made history as the first year of the Troubles in which no IRA members died at the hands of the security forces. But loyalists were killing Catholics in growing numbers, and the IRA did not know what to do about it. UFF retaliation for the Shankill Road bombing soon followed: seven people were cut down by gunmen in a pub at Greysteel on 30 October. RUC detectives eventually ended Adair's operations. They used concealed tape recorders to record him bragging about his activities, and gained sufficient evidence to get the UFF leader convicted of directing terrorist acts in September 1995. Adair received a sixteen-year sentence.

On 2 November 1993 the republican leadership sent another message to the British government. Its language reflected their desire to breathe new life into the secret contacts. 'We believe that the country could be at the point of no return,' they said, alluding to the sectarian assassinations. 'Please tell us as a matter of urgency when you will open up a dialogue in the event of a total end to hostilities.' This message was different in tone from previous ones. Its reference to a 'total end' rather than to an exploratory ceasefire met British demands; furthermore, there was no suggestion that this halt should remain 'unannounced', as there had been in the February communications.

Three days later the British responded, describing this republican message as being 'of the greatest importance and significance'. Although the government insisted that only a majority of the people of Northern Ireland could change its constitutional position, they held out some carrots to the IRA. The government would allow the IRA commitment to a *permanent* ceasefire to remain secret, and promised that talks with a republican delegation could begin within a few weeks of such a halt.

Within British intelligence there was still deep scepticism about Adams's ability to deliver. Deverell and Assistant Chief Constable Brian Fitzsimons, Head of the RUC Special Branch, both emphasized the possibility of splits in the organisation. They espoused the professional caution of the intelligence operator with a 'worst case' assessment. An article in the *Sunday Times* on 7 November 1993 pointed to the role of McGuinness and Gerry Kelly – believed to be a senior IRA figure – and quoted an 'intelligence source' as saying, 'They simply do not believe in peace with Westminster.' In fact, McGuinness was publicly as well as privately a key figure in the peace moves. Kelly would also be shown to have played an important part in them.

Kelly was variously described as Adjutant General of the IRA, OC Northern Command, or Sinn Fein/IRA liaison. Whichever post he actually held, it is likely that he was a member of the IRA Army Council (he was a convicted terrorist who had escaped from the Maze prison in 1983) and his role may have been to represent the tougher elements of the organization on the negotiating team.

On 16 November the Northern Ireland Secretary told the BBC, 'There have not been talks on behalf of the British government with Sinn Fein. Nobody has conducted talks with Sinn Fein.' Since the government had eleven days earlier sent a position paper to the republicans with detailed discussion of the arrangements for a meeting, it might be asked why Mayhew had painted himself into a corner over this issue. Was it because the received wisdom in the intelligence community was that Adams was probably incapable of delivering a deal? If this is true, the motive of the British government for continuing the contacts may have been cynical, essentially to string the IRA along and perhaps engineer a split.

Twelve days after Mayhew's denial the *Observer* broke the news that there had been secret contacts. It appears that a disgruntled official may have leaked a briefing paper to William McCrea, a Democratic Unionist MP of the 'no sell-out' school. The *Observer* then showed this paper to a government official who gave them the full story. The details published by the newspaper made the story undeniable. The government described Oatley and his successor's meetings as 'contacts' rather than negotiations. Ministers further suggested that some of the meetings between officials (in fact intelligence officers) and republicans had been unauthorized; if true, this is a disturbing instance of an intelligence agency operating without proper control. Senior officials had nevertheless been involved in leaking the story, and given Mayhew's earlier denial of the meetings, this may have been further evidence of the government's desire to use the secret talks to split the IRA.

At a press conference on 2 December Adams accused the government of underhand motives. He said they had acted 'in bad faith and had actively abused our contact with it in order to sow dissension and confusion'. Adams lambasted London, fearing perhaps the reaction of his own rank and file to the revelations, but nevertheless held out the prospect that the peace process could still be carried forward. He soon discovered there was little real dissension within the organization; a harsh discipline had built up within both IRA and Sinn Fein through the years of struggle. Now that the peace moves were in the open, the SDLP leader and the Irish premier increasingly found themselves in the position of trying to convince London that Sinn Fein was negotiating in good faith.

The 15 December joint declaration by the British and Irish governments contained a commitment to 'uphold the democratic wish of a greater number of the people of Northern Ireland', a kind of guarantee to the Protestants, and a pledge that parties renouncing violence 'are free to participate fully in democratic politics and to join in dialogue'.

With this attempt to cut the Gordian knot of Irish politics – to reassure the slim Protestant majority about their future while at the same time bringing the IRA campaign for a united Ireland to an end – the politics of the peace process moved on to a different plane. Sinn Fein was placed in a difficult position: rejecting the declaration meant rejecting the democratic principle in Northern Ireland. There followed a period of debate within Sinn Fein and the IRA, resulting in acceptance of the idea of an announced ceasefire to further the peace process. Whereas Hume and Reynolds apparently had little doubt that this would happen, British intelligence briefings questioned Adams's ability to deliver his entire organization into a permanent ceasefire. Fitzsimons, the Head of RUC Special Branch, and Deverell, MI5's Director and Co-ordinator of Intelligence at Stormont, simply could not take the Sinn Fein leader's remarks at face value. As debate within the IRA continued, bombs continued to explode in London and major MI5 operations were ready to produce impressive results.

In June 1994 an RAF Chinook helicopter carrying senior intelligence officials to an annual 'brainstorming' conference at an Army base in Scotland crashed. Fitzsimons, Deverell and Colonel Christopher Biles, head of Army intelligence in Ulster, were among the twenty-five victims. In an interview hours before the crash, the Head of Special Branch had told *Sunday Times* journalist Liam Clarke that Adams was trying to end the violence: 'However, he questioned Adams's ability to do so, and believed that a final decision to stop the killing would not be taken until the security forces had weakened the terrorist structure.'

When the IRA did announce that it would end hostilities on 31 August 1994, views of the kind expressed by Fitzsimons seem to have been responsible for John Major's apparent disbelief that any cessation would be permanent. Late that November the *Sunday Times*, continuing in its apparent role as the house journal of those in the intelligence community who were sceptical about the peace process, carried a story suggesting that a breakaway faction of 'more than fifty' IRA terrorists had given Adams an 'impossible deadline' of March 1995 to achieve Britain's 'total surrender'. Whether or not this ever happened, the month passed uneventfully. Despite the failure of its overall assessments at the political level, MI5 could take some comfort from successes on the ground.

As the IRA had stepped up its operations, so the likelihood of mistakes leading to the capture of its operatives had increased. There were three incidents of terrorists being stopped by suspicious policemen. On 8 June 1992 one constable was shot dead and another injured during a confrontation in North Yorkshire. The incident led to the arrest of Paul Magee, an IRA sniper who had been on the run since breaking out of Belfast's Crumlin Road prison in 1981. In March 1993 Magee was jailed for life. Michael O'Brien, another IRA man who had been with him, got eighteen years.

A similar night-time check by curious police resulted in the arrest on 14 November 1992 of Patrick Kelly, who was driving a lorry containing a bomb three times the size of the one that had devastated the City of London in April. Kelly was subsequently jailed for twenty-five years. There was a further incident in February 1993, when three IRA men were stopped by a policeman in Warrington. The constable was shot and injured, but the attack was foiled. One year later Patrick MacFhloinn, Dennis Kinsella and John Kinsella were jailed. In all three cases, the official version of events was probably accurate, since unarmed police would hardly have chosen to confront dangerous IRA men.

The police decision to release an enhanced video of two men behaving suspiciously near the Harrods department store prior to the bomb explosion there on 28 January 1993 is believed to have led them to Jan Taylor and Patrick Hayes, two Englishmen who had become part of the IRA campaign. They were found guilty of the Harrods attack and also of placing two large van bombs in London in late 1992. Although the timely discovery of one bomb at Canary Wharf in November and the other in Tottenham Court Road in December aroused suspicions that Taylor and Hayes might have been under surveillance for months, it seems that these convictions too resulted from effective criminal investigation by the police rather than by the changes to counter-terrorist arrangements that came into effect on 1 October 1992. The arrest of Vincent Wood, an Englishman, for possessing thirty-eight kilos of Semtex shortly after the new arrangements came into effect was also the result of a tip-off from the public.

T Branch officers had apparently not succeeded in penetrating any of the Active Service Units in Britain with agents. Instead, they were hoping to get intelligence from sources in Ireland about the arrival of a major terrorist or an arms shipment, and then to use their considerable resources to keep suspects or explosives under observation, for months if necessary, slowly to build up a picture of the IRA infrastructure. Such operations carried risks: what if the explosives under observation went astray and were used to kill people? What if the terrorists under observation planted bombs? The Security Service response to these challenges exploited the lessons learned in Ulster. Explosives or weapons discovered would have radio tracking devices placed in them to prevent them going astray. Under certain circumstances, those with experience of such operations suggest, T Branch was prepared to risk watching the bombs being planted, in the hope that the perpetrators would lead them to bigger fish, and to disguise this fact in later court hearings.

By early 1993 these operations were under way, involving dozens of surveillance teams from MI5's own A4 and from local Special Branch sections. In April 1993, for example, Gerard Mackin, an IRA suspect, was followed to within 200 yards of the large bomb that devastated the City. It later emerged that Mackin had been sent there by his employers, and that his presence near the blast seemed to have been an odd coincidence. Mackin left Britain, but was picked up again by surveillance when he returned in September – a measure of the effectiveness of intelligence-gathering. This new operation started producing results when on 1 October 1993 he and Derek Doherty, a fellow IRA man, picked up a gearbox packed with high explosive near London.

During the Mackin–Doherty trial in October 1994, the Security Service said that it had temporarily lost track of the two men as they planted bombs in London early the previous October; these had exploded without causing injury. The MI5 version, which echoed the line used by the police in the James Canning trial (that he had been out of view when planting a bomb in Soho in 1992) and in a subsequent Security Service case, seems to have owed much to a reluctance to admit in court that surveillance operatives had actually watched the bombs being planted – and were therefore placing their desire to keep the terrorists under continued surveillance ahead of the need to prevent the explosions.

The T Branch approach of blanket surveillance over long periods was to pay off with an operation in the Scottish town of Sauchie that also began in spring 1993. By early June, MI5's confidence in the guilt of Sauchie resident Hugh Jack was such that they had installed several surveillance cameras. It soon became clear that Jack's home was a kind of support base for IRA operatives in the north. Concealed video cameras monitored the entrance to his house and several lock-up garages nearby. Radio tracking devices were placed in his car and possibly in some of the explosives he was storing. MI5 technical officers manned an operations room at the nearby Alloa police station, monitoring this battery of surveillance technology.

As the summer wore on, IRA operatives began falling into MI5's trap. Robert Fryers, a burly Belfast man known to have served in the IRA's punishment squad, was soon spotted visiting Jack. Sean McNulty, a building worker with an English accent but of Irish descent, was also spotted in Sauchie. McNulty was part of an Active Service Unit that had bombed several oil and gas installations in north-east England during the spring of 1993. He was already under suspicion, apparently the subject of an MI5-led surveillance operation involving A4 and several Special Branches. McNulty was arrested on 21 June; fibres linking him with the depot blasts led to a twenty-five-year prison sentence in August 1994.

Watching the comings and goings at Sauchie involved scores,

perhaps hundreds, of police and Security Service members. At the subsequent trial, eighty-four operators from MI5 alone were put forward as witnesses. Each suspicious individual leaving the town might draw a retinue of tails. On 8 July 1993, for example, Fryers boarded the night sleeper from Glasgow to London, unaware that twelve MI5 watchers were on the train with him. This paid off, because Fryers was observed returning to Sauchie having picked up a car containing explosives. On 14 July Fryers was arrested by police carrying submachine guns as he walked across a north London street carrying a bomb. The difference between this result and the one in Gibraltar in 1988 showed how much MI5 had learned about counter-terrorism and the scale of the resources they needed to commit to it. Jack was arrested later, following a chase involving five carloads of armed police and MI5 officers. The two terrorists were convicted in January 1995.

During early 1994 MI5's surveillance led to perhaps its most important single catch, Feilim O'Haidmaill. According to later reports, this thirty-six-year-old holder of a philosophy doctorate was either the commander of the IRA in Britain or the quartermaster for the group of Active Service Units. Sources in Ireland appear to have tipped off MI5 about O'Haidmaill's journeys to England, and on 20 February 1994 he was arrested after collecting a car containing seventeen kilos of Semtex and other bomb-making materials. At his trial the softly-spoken terrorist said, 'I deeply regret being captured and I suppose congratulations are due to the security forces.'

Arrests made in the two years before MI5 took the lead in anti-IRA intelligence produced five convictions; arrests in the two years after produced fourteen. Of these, the convictions of Mackin, Doherty, Jack, Fryers, McNulty and O'Haidmaill could broadly be said to have resulted from the improved intelligence and surveillance procedures which MI5 had put forward as justification for its taking over the role. There had, of course, been disappointments: in three of the cases MI5 had watched the terrorists collecting explosives but IRA procedures had been sufficiently effective to protect the people who furnished them. In court, Public Interest Immunity Certificates were used to protect the methods used to keep track of these materials, and screens to hide the surveillance operatives.

Although some lawyers expressed concern at MI5's conduct of the court proceedings, within the counter-terrorist community there was a feeling that T Branch had delivered. Few doubted, however, that it had been the increase in resources which accompanied the changeover that had allowed operations on the scale of the Sauchie surveillance. William Taylor, the officer in overall charge of counter-terrorism at the Metropolitan Police at the time of the operation, says it vindicated police arguments for greater resources and does not accept that MI5 assumptions of leadership delivered dramatic results: 'I don't believe the outcome would have been any different, the people who were arrested would have been, whoever had the intelligence lead.' He does accept that the concentration of T Branch resources improved the security forces' knowledge about the IRA's use of forged documents, travel routes and methods of concealment.

Stella Rimington and other senior officers of her Service unsurprisingly argued in Whitehall that the increase in convictions was the result of MI5 leadership. There is little doubt that senior figures in the government and certain Conservative backbenchers shared their view rather than that of the police. For many Tories, the aura of quiet but tough efficiency surrounding the Service and its Director General had been enhanced.

With the IRA ceasefire, some senior policemen began to worry that the Security Service would now be searching for new territories to conquer. Their later operations against the Provisionals in Britain had been designed from the outset with prosecution in mind. Would the Service now follow the lead SIS had taken overseas and begin to look at other areas of domestic criminal intelligence-gathering such as drugs or organized crime?

The evolution of counter-terrorism within MI5 had meant that the Irish effort consumed more than half of the organization's resources. International counter-terrorism (G Branch) also took a substantial slice, leaving only about a quarter of resources to be shared between what had been the Cold War core, K Branch (Counter Espionage), and F Branch (Counter Subversion), which had been merged as D Branch.

According to officers, by the mid-1990s F Branch was devoting more resources to the far right in Britain than to the far left. Targeting the British National Party (BNP) was, however, subject to the same problems of definition as had been encountered with the Socialist Workers Party or the Campaign for Nuclear Disarmament. The DGSS said in her June 1994 TV lecture, 'The intention to undermine democracy is what "subversion" means to us. It does not include political dissent.' Far from urging the overthrow of Parliament, the

BNP actually contested elections. Certainly, Rimington and the others who moved into their new headquarters at Thames House in late 1994 did not consider surveillance of the far right to be any kind of saviour for the Service.

Ideas that MI5 might seek drugs and organized crime work had initially emerged at the time they took over the anti-IRA role. But denials by Rimington seemed to leave no room for manoeuvre. She said in her lecture, 'The work of the Service must be strictly limited to countering only threats to national security. We are not involved in countering drug trafficking or organised crime; and we would only become involved if they came to pose such a threat to this country.' Her remarks showed up the contradictions between different Whitehall definitions of security. If drugs or money-laundering were no threat to the UK, why was MI6 involved in combating them abroad? When asked by a reporter in November 1993 whether drug-running really was such a danger, Douglas Hurd had replied that MI6's targets, including drug traffickers, posed 'a very substantial threat to the state and its citizens. That is to say, if they succeeded, if they triumphed, our society would be undermined, and I think this is self-evident to the citizen.' Though not, it seems from her lecture, to the Director General of MI5.

Writing to the Labour Party's then Home Affairs spokesman and now leader Tony Blair in 1993, Kenneth Clarke, at that time Home Secretary, had tried to square the circle over these different interpretations of the narcotic menace. Clarke said that the problem was so serious in some countries that it threatened national security (implicitly justifying SIS interest in places like Colombia), but that 'I do not consider that there is any question that it amounts at present to a threat to the security of the United Kingdom.' He added that it was 'most unlikely indeed' that drugs would reach such a danger point. This appeared to provide the definitive reassurance that the police were looking for. However, the scars of the battle over the anti-IRA role remained; some senior Metropolitan Police officers argued that MI5 had denied its real objectives in that battle too.

Whatever MI5 bosses may or may not have said in 1993 in Whitehall corridors about their ambitions to tackle organized crime, it is clear that the situation had changed by the autumn of 1994. The IRA ceasefire had come into effect, heightening the Service's anxiety about what might be done with the additional personnel taken on to deal with the Provisionals. A paper written by officers in the Director

General's Secretariat at that time set out a philosophical basis for building on the anti-IRA successes. Referring to the arguments contained in this study, one officer says, 'You could argue in principle that the same sort of skills could be applied to strategic aspects of organized crime.'

David Bickford, the Service's Legal Adviser (as such he sat on the Board of Management), was an ardent advocate of the shift in priorities. In many ways it marked the final maturity of the strategy mapped out by Anthony Duff and Patrick Walker to turn the Service into a British FBI. Bickford says, 'Whereas law enforcement intelligence is good for ordinary crime because of its short-term dynamic, in organized crime the relationships are more long-term, as with espionage.'

Discreet but energetic Security Service lobbying of Home and Cabinet Office officials had shifted the ground by the spring of 1995. In May of that year Michael Howard, the Home Secretary, gave a written answer to an MP's question in which he suggested that if spare MI5 resources might be used to support the police, 'I would be ready to consider such proposals'. One senior policeman I spoke to criticized Bickford's forceful advocacy, denouncing him as a 'loose cannon' in Whitehall.

Michael Howard's announcement caused dismay among many senior members of the police, its National Criminal Intelligence Service (NCIS) and Customs and Excise. At the time, Richard Kellaway, the Chief Investigating Officer of Customs and Excise, suggested to me, 'I employ analysts, so does NCIS, rather than sack them; maybe MI5 analysts should come and work for us.' The argument that NCIS or Customs should simply poach redundant MI5 staff had many precedents, for example in the way MI6 took several proliferation experts from the Ministry of Defence in 1989–90, but it did not appeal to officials who had bought MI5's line that the organization's skills and approach were unique.

Whereas MI5's victory in counter-terrorism resulted in part from the fact that the police had failed to create an effective national squad, they were losing ground on organized crime despite the existence of NCIS, which had been set up specifically to deal with gangs operative across force boundaries. Some senior police concluded they could not win such Whitehall battles. William Taylor – who as Commissioner of the City of London Police was part of the Association of Chief Police Officers team which responded to MI5's initiative in the summer of 1995 – says, 'Stella [Rimington] is a Permanent Under

Secretary and as such meets regularly with colleagues under Robin Butler's chairmanship. That is a lever of power or influence. We don't have that lever. That is the price we pay for our constitutional independence.'

The elevation of Michael Heseltine to the post of Deputy Prime Minister that summer added weight to MI5's lobby. He was given the remit of pushing forward new government policies and had decided changes were needed to stop the spread of drugs and crime. Some police suggest Heseltine argued MI5 should be given the lead in a new counter-narcotics campaign. In the end, arguments by Taylor and other senior officers convinced the Home Office that the police should retain the lead in this area and that any use of MI5 against criminals would require amendments to the 1989 Security Service Act.

On Friday 13 October, John Major announced this change to the Conservative Party conference. Mr Major said in his speech that today a young person is more likely to be 'killed by a drug dealer than by an enemy missile'. MI5 had succeeded once more in redefining its role. To the Prime Minister and his Deputy, the use of the formerly secret police in this way was a good political weapon in taking a tough public stance on drug peddlers and gangs.

The October announcement was an important coup for the Director General of MI5, but it led to further struggles with Home Office and police colleagues about the legal changes that would be needed to bring about the new role. Throughout the latter part of 1995 and early 1996, Stella Rimington lobbied in the interests of her Service, inviting officials, journalists and MPs to dine with her at Thames House or visiting them with a similar message.

As this work was going on though, the spectre of Irish republican terrorism began to re-emerge. In a curious parallel to MI5's lobbying for new tasks, IRA frustration with the political rewards of its ceasefire manifested itself initially in a campaign against drug dealers. A wave of punishment beatings was followed by the killing of seven people whom the Provisionals claimed were dealers.

When the IRA exploded a bomb at Canary Wharf on 9 February 1996 killing two people, many were shocked. The *Guardian* said there had been an 'intelligence failure'. *The Times* claimed that, 'MI5 had warned the government a month ago to expect a renewal of violence.' Had the attack come as a surprise to the government or not?

It appears that any Security Service warning was vague and did not specify the likely date of any renewed bombing campaign and, in any case, it followed adverse Irish nationalist political reaction to British proposals for elections prior to any talks involving Sinn Fein, the IRA's political wing. Many commentators in Ireland had predicted that the British government's move might derail the peace process. On the other hand, someone present at one of Stella Rimington's talks to outsiders three weeks before the bombing notes that no indication was given that the ceasefire might be in danger or that Sinn Fein/IRA was in danger of splitting. With hindsight it is clear that the resumption of violence was not foreseen in any meaningful sense of the word by MI5.

As the IRA's new campaign unfolded it became apparent that violence was not returning to the early-1990s level. Republican leaders clearly wished to maintain a truce with loyalist terrorists in Ulster itself, where the preceding sectarian killing had caused such concern within the Catholic community. The IRA therefore initially refrained from attacking loyalists and, until 7 October 1996 when it set off two bombs inside Army headquarters at Lisburn, from strikes against security forces targets in the north of Ireland.

During the first year of resumed violence, the Provisionals managed three significant attacks: Canary Wharf and Manchester city centre together caused hundreds of millions of pounds' worth of damage to property, and the Lisburn attack represented an impressive breach of security and might have caused far more than a single death and over thirty injuries. In other respects, though, it soon became clear that the organization was not generating anything like the same level of violence as before the ceasefire. Many commentators regarded this as a deliberate policy of restraint designed to enhance rather than finish off Sinn Fein's chances of entering the all-party talks. There is ample evidence, however, to assume that the organization was going full out, particularly in England, but that its ability to generate violence had diminished.

Speculation about 'phoney war' – why the Provisionals were only generating roughly half the number of attacks compared with prior to the ceasefire – prompted the IRA itself to issue a statement in February 1997 that it was waging unrestrained operations. The Security Service and RUC Special Branch agreed that Active Service Units had been given full clearance to strike.

While the republicans found themselves struggling to pull off successful attacks, the police were making great inroads into their structure. Arrests in London in July and September 1996 resulted in twelve men being charged with terrorist offences: reports in Ireland suggested they included top figures in the England and Quartermasters' departments. In the Republic, a series of arms seizures followed the killing of a Gardai detective in an IRA 'fund-raising' robbery in June 1996.

A senior RUC figure says, 'there has been an incredible increase in the number of people giving information'. For some at least of those on the fringes of the republican community, or simply next-door neighbours who used to turn a blind eye, it would appear that anger at the dashed hopes of Ulster's ceasefire had become more significant in their calculations than the traditional aversion to informing. When I asked an MI5 officer whether there had also been an increase in the number of active Provisionals providing intelligence he was understandably reluctant to comment, but did say that counter-terrorist operations post-ceasefire were 'a different ballgame' because of changed attitudes in the wider community.

In the Republic, Belfast and London numerous bombs were defused before detonation – often a sign of tip-offs. In the operation resulting in the arrest of seven suspects in July 1996 in London there was evidence that the techniques perfected during the Alloa surveillance three years earlier had been carried to a higher level still. According to an MI5 officer the operation that produced this success involved hundreds of police and Security Service operatives over a period of months. Several locations where the suspects met to discuss operations were successfully bugged by MI5 technical officers.

The arrest of five men and seizure of ten tonnes of home-made explosives in London two months later also resulted from lengthy police/MI5 surveillance. The operation began with an informer tip-off passed on by the RUC about two lorries that were being sent across from Ireland.

There were also signs that the RUC and MI5 had better general intelligence about the Provisonals' intentions than they had before the resumption of violence. Two bombs on railway lines in northern England in March 1997 had been preceded by public and secret warnings of imminent violence. MI5 had also correctly forecast that the campaign would not be halted for the UK General Election.

The IRA bomb at Canary Wharf underlined once more the perils of trying to run intelligence services in the post-Cold War world. Until the bomb went off the Security Service had been looking for new tasks for people whose jobs were under threat. The IRA ceasefire had undoubtedly been the main spur in MI5's quest for a role against organized crime. Despite its failure to predict the renewed bombing, there were in the events of February 1996 to February 1997 signs of a changed balance of power between the IRA and the counter-terrorist forces arrayed against it. Changing public attitudes and a substantial increase in the resources arrayed against the Provisionals played important roles. It is hard to ignore, however, that the plan of rebuilding begun in 1985 by Anthony Duff, perhaps the only really far-sighted manager in the intelligence services during this era, also played its part in securing this dividend.

Conclusion

More than anything else, British intelligence is a system for repackaging information gathered by the USA. Most intelligence relates to foreign or defence policy, most of that intelligence is sigint, and the vast majority of sigint processed at Cheltenham has been obtained from the USA. Of course, MI5 with its domestic focus is an important exception, disseminating a largely home-grown product. Equally, MI6 retains respectable networks of agents in some parts of the world. But the volume of material circulating in Whitehall that has been gathered by the UK–USA eavesdropping partners is of a completely different order: interviewees have suggested that it accounts for 80 to 90 per cent of the raw reports flowing through the Joint Intelligence Committee machine.

British dependence on the USA increased markedly during the Cold War. Although the Government Code and Cipher School at Bletchley Park was prodigiously successful during the Second World War, the growing cost of interception and code-breaking in the satellite age has relegated GCHQ to the second division. There can be no doubt that the US National Security Agency has techniques, resources and daring quite unmatched in the world, having been responsible for most of the West's genuine strategic intelligence coups of the last decade, including bugging Saddam Hussein during the Gulf War, tapping Soviet military land lines, and packing the Chinese embassy in Australia with audio and video monitoring equipment. The appeal of sharing the product of such an organization is obvious.

In the 1990s, to borrow an analogy from manufacturing industry, the British intelligence community may make some distinctive sports cars – SIS could perhaps be represented by Morgan, the Security Service by TVR – but the volume production is in the hands of a concern where a British management adds a few distinctive components, notably the bonnet emblem, to a vehicle made up largely of US components. Fortunately for the intelligence mandarins, theirs is not an open market, and even the ministers or officials who have access to this product usually receive it in a form where it has been blended with other information so as to disguise its origin. There are good professional reasons why agent runners or eavesdroppers are preoccupied with safeguarding what they term 'sources and methods', but equally such secrecy helps their masters to keep to themselves the actual return on the country's £1 billion annual spending on intelligence.

Although Britain's gathering of secret information about the wider world may be largely dependent on a foreign power, it does retain a system for analysing what that information might mean for national interests. For this reason, much of my book has focused on the Joint Intelligence Committee in Whitehall's Cabinet Office and its teams of experts, the Current Intelligence Groups. The Defence Intelligence Staff in the old War Office also plays a role in extracting the most significant elements from the great flow of allied information. If one were to ask the chiefs of the secret bureaucracy, 'What did *you* do in the Cold War?' they would be most likely to answer, 'Analyse.'

Much of the intelligence effort of the Cold War years was devoted to 'bean counting': working out where the Warsaw Pact's weapons were and how effective they might be. Regarding such matters as whereabouts on the outskirts of Tula the 106th Guards Airborne Division might be found, or whether the Sukhoi Su-27 had yet been deployed at an air base in Byelorussia, Britain's intelligence assessment was based on US material and gave an accurate picture. However, Whitehall analysts shied away from some of the exaggerations made by the Pentagon because of its obsession, embodied in the 1980s by the *Soviet Military Power* pamphlets, with using alleged Soviet weapons developments to justify almost all of its own procurement. On both sides of the Atlantic, however, the estimating of numbers proved least reliable where the most destructive weapons were concerned: nuclear and chemical warheads.

Pentagon experts were always uncertain about the size of the Soviet nuclear and chemical stockpiles because of the difficulties satellites had in gauging the activities of warhead plants or the contents of nerve gas storage bunkers. British analysts produced slightly different estimates for nuclear warhead stocks, and their figures for chemical weapons were one of the few instances of them publicizing a national estimate quite different from that of the USA. On chemical weapons, the British were hopelessly wrong: the suggested

300,000 tonnes of nerve gas in fact probably never exceeded 35,000. On nuclear weapons, the record was less dismal, but still showed an almost twofold margin of error: an actual stockpile in excess of 45,000 compared with Whitehall estimates of 25,000.

Also, the British were often at fault in assessing deployed nuclear missile systems. The USA failed to detect the deployment of eighteen SS-23 missile launchers to East Germany, only discovering their oversight when Moscow revealed exactly how many weapons it had in this category after the signing of the 1987 Intermediate Nuclear Forces treaty. The Pentagon had believed that about forty of the weapons were deployed in the western Soviet Union, British DIS analysts believed it was 'nearer twelve', but the real total (in Germany and the USSR) turned out to be eighty-two. Veterans of British military intelligence are candid enough to admit now that they never once located nuclear warheads being moved in East Germany. Oversights of this kind may have been inevitable because of the limitations of technology or surveillance, but given the power of the weapons concerned, they could have been catastrophic in the event of war.

Although assessments of the critical aspects of Soviet military power were either sketchy or wrong, they were highly influential in Whitehall. Multi-billion-pound defence procurement programmes were driven by them, and conservative analysts of Soviet Bloc affairs consistently stated that these military 'facts' gave reason to doubt the words of Kremlin leaders. Michael Herman, the one-time head of GCHQ's J Division which dealt with the Soviet Bloc, noted, 'Western intelligence has claimed a special responsibility to lead thinking rather than to follow it.'

By placing the endless counting of tanks or frigates at the centre of their world, Whitehall's intelligence analysts provided a textbook example of how an obsession with detail can obscure the overall picture. Reporting on the missiles coming off the production lines helped to flesh out the pessimistic reports handed to ministers; indeed, figures such as these were essential to the people who doubted Mikhail Gorbachev's sincerity, because they were among the few indicators that appeared to confirm their view that 'nothing has changed'. Any ordinary visitor to the Soviet Union in the mid-1980s quickly realized that military production was about the only area of the economy which still worked.

By 1989 the CIA was beginning to be aware of the dismal state of the Soviet civilian economy, but remained convinced that the political system was still viable. British assessments were even more resistant to change: right up to the 1991 coup, just a few months before Gorbachev stood down from office, several senior figures argued that the Cold War had not ended and that the Soviet leader still had a long-term plan for world domination. Morton Abramowitz, the US Assistant Secretary of State for intelligence matters, noted that it was 'hard to be to the right' of his British colleagues.

While the JIC and DIS proved even more reluctant than the CIA to reassess their traditional view of Soviet power, all three failed to devote sufficient attention to the economic and nationalist grievances that would rip the Soviet Union apart. Many of the people in Downing Street or elsewhere who were privy to the best of British intelligence 'take' were therefore profoundly disappointed. The former Prime Minister's Private Secretary notes that the Soviet assessments were a 'colossal failure' of intelligence analysis and political judgement.

Intelligence became an industry geared up to producing annual 'threat reports' until long after the Soviet system had sunk to its knees economically. The Sovbloc Current Intelligence Group and JIC found the end of that system as hard to contemplate as the proverbial turkeys voting for Christmas. Men such as Anthony Duff and Lieutenant-General Derek Boorman who doubted this pessimistic groupthink were steamrollered by Whitehall's received wisdom. Perhaps the end of the Cold War, and the fact that no area of foreign policy now gives rise to quite the same vested interests as the former Soviet Union did, offers some hope for renewal?

It seems not. Today the real problem for the secret world is that the focus once provided by high defence spending and superpower arms control has vanished with the Warsaw Pact and the Soviet Union. The USA has made deep cuts in its intelligence activities, and has switched much of what remains to targets that are of little or no interest to Britain, such as Japanese trading practices or the deployments of the North Korean army. The global fibre-optic telecommunications revolution and the spread of strong cryptography threaten the flow of signals intelligence. The mandarins of the secret world are worrying about the 'know-nothing' syndrome: the likelihood of being able to offer few insights into emerging problems.

It has been apparent since Iraq's invasion of Kuwait in 1990 that military or intelligence bureaucracies simply cannot maintain sizeable cadres of staff expert in every possible flash-point around the world. As political change became unfrozen in the Middle East or

Africa because of the end of superpower confrontation, the spies began to look increasingly accident-prone: no sources in Baghdad in 1990, no good sigint on North Korea, ignorance about the Oslo talks on Middle East peace, and so on.

For years, Britain has been able to use US intelligence to make up for its under-investment in the home-grown product. Whereas it is accepted in Washington that spending on intelligence should equal about 10 per cent of the defence budget, in Britain the proportion falls well below this. In 1995, for example, UK defence spending was around £24 billion, compared with only £900 million on GCHQ, MI5 and MI6. The difference is explained principally by the cost of using space, the satellites that are the USA's global eyes and ears.

Britain might, in theory, have gone the same way. France's leaders concluded that the only way to cope with the uncertainty of the post-Cold War world was to spend more on intelligence; they knew that their information-gathering agencies could not remain in the first rank without buying their own satellites. Programmes to develop photographic, radar imaging and sigint craft were started. Israel, a small state but one usually ranked as a leading player in the secret world, appears to have come to the same conclusion, and had by 1995 launched at least three 'spy in the sky' payloads.

The notion of Britain becoming a player in the same league lasted only from 1983 to 1987, in the shape of the ZIRCON project. Ultimately, Whitehall's spending decisions are too much concerned with finding the path of least resistance for GCHQ to have contemplated what might have been a doubling or trebling of its budget; instead, they decided to write the USA a very large cheque.

Even those true believers in intelligence, Thatcher and Cradock, were unwilling to fund the expansion of British intelligence into space. To them, such spending was quite pointless as long as the USA was being so helpful.

The decision to pay the US National Security Agency around £500 million arose from the preoccupation of GCHQ management and Whitehall mandarins with 'doing our bit' for the UK–USA partnership, a mantra familiar to every permanent secretary who has sat in on the agencies' spending round. Impressing the USA thus emerges as one of the principal justifications for the national espionage effort, even though it is utterly subjective and impossible to measure. It may also be largely unnecessary.

It is apparent from talking to US espionage chiefs that Britain's value to them is primarily geographical: its location as a ground station for NSA's sigint satellites and for the positioning of one or two listening posts able to eavesdrop on European allies as well as the Middle East. The quality of British intelligence analysis and the existence of SIS agent networks (notably those in European states and the Middle East) are cited as important but secondary factors.

Lieutenant-General William Odom, the former Director of NSA, puts the UK in the same category of usefulness as Australia, the other main sigint satellite downlink point and operator of eavesdropping posts in the Pacific region. If the USA regards Britain and Australia as being of equal importance as intelligence partners (which it does both *de jure* under the UK–USA Treaty and *de facto* in the quality of material it provides them), then 'impressing the USA' is hardly a valid reason for having a national intelligence effort several times the size of Australia: SIS employs around 2,000 people, but its Antipodean equivalent, the Australian Secret Intelligence Service, only 300.

What then is the justification for maintaining the current establishment? The Security Service has benefited enormously from the unique arrangement whereby it defines the threats to national security and is therefore 'self-tasking'. Anthony Duff exploited this during his period as Director General, backing his analysis of the decline of Soviet communism – which was being largely ignored in the wider forum of the JIC – with a switch of resources inside his own organization to counter-terrorism. This trend was continued by his successors Patrick Walker and Stella Rimington, with the result that by the early 1990s MI5 had converted itself into a national anti-terrorist force able to increase its staff and budget when all the other secret agencies were facing cuts.

In matters of overseas espionage, it is clear that the current spending arrangements are the result of a delicate balance between consumers and producers. If SIS, DIS or GCHQ now find themselves spread thinly over too many regions or subjects, the blame lies largely with Whitehall for its confusion over what national priorities should be.

At the Foreign Office, senior figures still claim that Britain's 'global interests' justify its permanent seat on the United Nations Security Council, and argue for an intelligence effort to back up their worldwide diplomatic network. At the Treasury, particularly under the chancellorship of Kenneth Clarke, there has been a 'little England' approach: they argue that Britain's security policy should reflect its status as a middle-ranking European power. At the Ministry of

Defence, the official doctrine is that the nation will not involve itself in any future war independently and will instead take part in a coalition. So what is the future to be? A global mission, foreign military adventures only in US-led coalitions (as in the Gulf), or membership of a European security family? In each case, the implications for the espionage world are quite different.

Foreign Office officials, so important both to the Joint Intelligence Committee set-up and as customers, apparently reserve the right to set global objectives and at the same time to deride the blandness of the information collected. Perhaps it is time for the Foreign Office to shift to a policy that focuses on Europe and its periphery (including Russia and the Middle East). This would allow resources to be focused on the questions that most directly concern politicians and the public: the possibility of extreme nationalists taking over in Moscow, instability in the Balkans, or the quest by Middle East dictators for weapons of mass destruction – as well as missiles that might allow them to strike at Britain. Operations aimed at the Far East, the Americas and sub-Saharan Africa could be run down.

A focus on Europe and its periphery could be accompanied by a return to traditional definitions of national security. The proliferation of weapons of mass destruction and terrorism aimed at British subjects fit this definition: targeting drug smugglers or money launderers does not. It helps if the nation or group supposedly threatening national security is explicitly aiming to do so – for example, terrorists – rather than simply engaged in a criminal enterprise to make money. The argument that narcotics pose a threat to national security because they kill people should be resisted, for it could ultimately lead to MI6 or MI5 being put on the trail of industrial polluters or the carriers of infectious diseases.

The Security Service and SIS are trained to run agents in the most hostile environments: Russian counter-intelligence retains substantial resources, the IRA has killed dozens of its own people on suspicion of informing. For this reason, intelligence officers skilled in tradecraft and counter-surveillance are over-qualified for running agents in criminal gangs. These two espionage agencies also retain systems for protecting their own secrets – such as highly secure data storage and the extensive vetting of personnel – that are geared to withstanding the assaults of foreign states. The combination of the offensive capability of these agencies with the cost of the measures they take to protect themselves means that they cannot deliver information on criminals with the same efficiency as police information-gathering agencies. The National Criminal Intelligence Service, for example, has 500 staff and in 1995 cost £25 million, or roughly £50,000 for each employee. The Security Service has 2,000 staff and spent about £150 million in the same year, or £75,000 per employee.

Notwithstanding these arguments, the government announced in October 1995 that the Security Service was to join the fight against organized crime (SIS had been involved at the international level since 1988). This was a volte face: until early 1995 the government had said that the change was most unlikely to happen. So enthusiastic were the managers of MI5 and their Special Branch associates about the counter-terrorist mission that they failed to see the coming IRA ceasefire, and in so doing imitated their overseas espionage colleagues who had been unable accurately to gauge the changes in Moscow. The IRA ceasefire was preceded by a series of MI5 and RUC Special Branch assessments suggesting that the republican leadership would be incapable of carrying its hard-liners along with such a move. Once the ceasefire became reality, the organization began an energetic struggle to use its expanded staff against gangsters. The organization does not seem to have given the government specific warnings about the resumption of IRA bombing in February 1996. Counter-terrorism remains the Service's core mission, but MI5's Board of Management has the comfort of knowing that the task of creating an opening for the organization as fighters of organized crime has been achieved.

MI5 has pursued its claim to the new mission by emphasizing, in Whitehall-speak, its 'skills and approach'. This strategy proved successful in the struggle to gain control of anti-IRA operations in Britain, and appears to be based on the simple proposition that MI5 officers are cleverer than their police counterparts. Even if this is true, the solution probably lies in changing police recruitment procedures rather than in applying to the problem an organization skilled at processing information rather than gathering evidence.

The perils of switching to a more aggressive use of intelligence agencies in the pursuit of economic information have been shown by recent events. Three CIA officers were expelled from France in 1995, and another from Germany in 1997. So far SIS has not embraced this kind of mission on the same scale as its American cousin or the French themselves. The dangers are clear, though: they are job preservation schemes which can undermine close relationships between allies. In short, aggressive economic information-gathering is more trouble than it is worth.

The absence of British equivalents of the Drug Enforcement Administration (DEA) or the Federal Bureau of Investigation is not in itself an argument for unleashing MI6 and MI5 on drug traffickers. The challenges posed by drug dealers need to be resolved by those schooled in the law, perhaps by expanding the National Criminal Intelligence Service, perhaps by establishing an organization similar to the DEA. The intelligence services should remain the prime practitioners of military and political espionage.

If any IRA ceasefire lasts or if the level of Provisionals' violence reduces in the long term, ministers and officials need to recognize that the time could come when considerable cuts might be made in the Security Service. Its main function of counter-terrorism – with cadres dealing with counter-espionage and with those subversive groups which might plot to seize power – may remain, but those holding the purse-strings need to ask whether national security is under the kind of threat today which justifies a staff several times that which the MI5 had on the eve of the Second World War.

If the agencies collecting secret information could be smaller and more focused, what of the way in which the information is analysed? Members of the intelligence community take pride in the system by which all agencies agree to a common JIC view (as opposed to the US system of competing assessments) and in the small size of the staff at the Cabinet Office that compiles these reports. The Assessment Staff's 'small is beautiful' philosophy – just thirty people run the operation – has clear advantages over the US approach, where hundreds of CIA and National Security Council staffers are needed to perform much the same role. The JIC's Current Intelligence Groups can produce papers reflecting the view of all of the agencies remarkably quickly.

The JIC system appears to work best when it is based on papers compiled by these Current Intelligence Groups and on *ad hoc* minutes by the Chairman to the Prime Minister. The Thursday meeting of the JIC itself, which dozens may attend, is an unwieldy forum, and many of those involved with the meetings apparently feel that churning out the JIC's collective wisdom in the form of the Red Book is a pointless exercise. Intelligence becomes sanitized to the point of blandness, and the views expressed represent an interdepartmental lowest common denominator.

Whitehall's system of analysis is crucially dependent on the personality of the JIC Chairman. Cradock responded to what he apparently regarded as the impossible task of being the government's foremost oracle by turning into a professional pessimist. This, coupled with his innate *gravitas*, led to him being held in awe by many in government on both sides of the Atlantic. He is remembered by ministers and officials alike with greater respect than, for example, his successor Rodric Braithwaite, whose only mistakes seem to have been scepticism about certain types of intelligence and a less apocalyptic style than his predecessor.

Cradock perhaps thought that more people would remember him for being right over Moscow's biological weapons programme or Saddam Hussein's intentions regarding Kuwait than for his memos about imminent war between India and Pakistan or chemical weapons in the basement of the Iraqi embassy in London. Most importantly, Cradock maintained the toughest line on Gorbachev, which even brought him into conflict with a Prime Minister of Thatcher's convictions.

Did it matter that the JIC went along with such a negative view of Gorbachev during his early years? The Prime Minister and Foreign Minister undoubtedly spent much of the time in their meetings with Gorbachev and Shevardnadze lambasting them on the issues that the intelligence community considered important: chemical weapons and KGB operations against Britain. Clearly, Thatcher had domestic political reasons for keeping defence spending high, though she was also on a crusade to curb public spending. It is interesting to speculate whether an intelligence chief who believed in the momentous import of the Kremlin changes could have convinced her that billions might be saved from the defence budget.

Had the Prime Minister's undoubted influence with both superpowers been used instead to accelerate moves towards disarmament and to seek openings for British trade, the financial dividends could well have considerable – enough, perhaps, to have paid the bill for the intelligence services for many years to come.

According to Geoffrey Howe, the job of the JIC machine will become tougher in future because 'the multiplication of risks means that good intelligence remains as important as ever but its assessment becomes ever more difficult. It's harder to reach conclusions.' The hierarchical system of government does, however, make it hard for those with a fresh view to make themselves heard. There is a need somewhere within the Cabinet Office system for a professional devil's advocate who will be privy to the raw information but who questions Whitehall's received wisdoms.

Anthony Duff, who found himself in a minority on the JIC for taking a charitable view of Gorbachev, says, 'In theory, the JIC accommodates the dissenting voice by saying, "On the one hand this, on the other hand that," and generally does not identify the voice – unlike the US National Intelligence Estimates, which does do that in the footnotes. Being a British committee, the JIC may fall into the trap of seeking words to accommodate all points of view. One has to be constantly alert for this danger; it's right to give ministers one piece of paper, but strongly dissenting views need to be reflected.'

Under John Major, MI5, GCHQ and MI6 have been placed on a statutory footing. At the same time, Parliament has gained limited oversight and independent commissioners have the right to delve into operations. It would be a shame if these important moves proved sufficient to satisfy Parliament's appetite.

The current legislation on the intelligence services is flawed. Anthony Duff: 'It is not as perfect as I would wish it to be . . . the committee of parliamentarians is tasked to oversee the intelligence and security services. Where this is not adequate is that they report to the Prime Minister – they ought to be reporting to Parliament like a normal select committee.' While former heads of MI5 express these views, few MPs, it seems, are ready to pressure the government into taking accountability the last mile. Some form of scandal involving the agencies may be necessary to convince them that a system which allows the Prime Minister to determine what is said to the committee and which of its observations are passed on to Parliament – and which also deflects scrutiny from the mountains of reports passed on by the USA – should be changed.

The publication of the first edition of this book underlined, in a small way, one of these systemic problems. The UK's decision to invest hundreds of millions in American spy satellites revealed by it was news to all Members of Parliament except the handful on the Intelligence Service Committee. They had been told about it but, I was informed, were unable to say anything about it to their colleagues. In this way the Intelligence Services Committee is prevented from passing on potentially embarrassing information unless the Prime Minister authorizes it.

Managers at GCHQ and MI6 have decided that they can now

stand firm against further calls for openness. They apparently feel that mystery is good for recruitment. At the same time, few people with any insight into the intelligence world can fail to see the hypocrisy inherent in mounting overseas operations in the interests of one international law (for example, the Biological Weapons Convention that SIS was able to show the Soviet Union had broken) while flouting all kinds of others (those dealing with diplomatic immunity as well as national statutes against espionage). A mantle of secrecy is also useful in cloaking management errors, be they in the buying of new computers or the treatment of staff.

One of the benefits of the end of the Cold War must surely be that the mystery which surrounded intelligence work in the era of such fictional heroes as Smiley can be stripped away. In fact there is little hope that spies will accept the need for more openness either within the government or *vis-à-vis* the public. One MI6 officer, something of a dissident in favouring further reforms, notes, 'If ministers realized how much power they have, things could be very different, they could kick the machinery into action.' The system continues to be run, though, as a highly expensive, secret news service in which the number of elected people briefed with high-grade material can be counted on the fingers of one hand. Little wonder that someone appointed as Defence or Foreign Secretary may have little idea about the potential of MI6 or GCHQ, if the only intelligence they may have seen in their ministerial career up to that point are the sanitized essays contained in the weekly Red Book.

There is no doubt that the agencies are capable of some impressive successes: Gordievsky, GCHQ's intercepts of Chinese military intentions after the Tiananmen massacre and the MI5 record against IRA bombers in Britain from 1992–4. But on most matters at most times what they have delivered is, like the average newspaper, a warmed-over selection of facts gathered by others, gossip and received opinions. It is clearly unreasonable to expect them to possess the gift of perfect prophecy, and those who claim Britain's organizations are still world-class frequently point out that intelligence successes must, by their very nature, remain secret, whereas failures become public. But if ministers or key officials are not told about these successes, or are told in a form so sanitized that the information does not attract their attention, then the entire multi-million-pound exercise is a waste of time.

During the Gulf War, intelligence analysts in the UK were not prepared to share much of what they knew with the officers actually commanding the forces in the Middle East. The report by Lord Justice Scott into the arms to Iraq affair showed that the agencies did a thorough job of infiltrating Saddam's military procurement network and had a good idea of what he was buying, but that MI6 waited far too long to tell ministers about it. When Customs investigators seized the supergun and raided various firms, MI6 and MI5 would not tell them that key executives in these firms were their agents. Army generals, government ministers and Customs officers are all people within the 'ring of secrecy', who ought to have the right information. In the post-Cold War world the agencies that collect or analyse intelligence must be prepared to take greater risks with their sources, act faster and tell people more or risk becoming obsolete.

One reason often given in Whitehall for the tight dissemination of signals intelligence product has been the desire not to damage the relationship with the US. As a result of past decisions – most importantly the one in 1987 not to develop a UK intelligence satellite – the government has created enormous difficulties for the future.

A huge sum has been paid to the NSA for questionable results. Early in 1995, GCHQ used its stake in the US satellite constellation to change the orbit of one eavesdropping craft in order to give a better coverage of Bosnia. Senior GCHQ managers 'were really excited by this', according to one senior intelligence officer, who revealed to me that the results were 'highly disappointing'. An enormously sophisticated satellite designed to pick up Russian signals is of less use against a communications system like that of the Serbs and is of increasingly limited value as nations install more fibre-optic lines. What is worse, Britain has helped to pay for a system which may have been used to spy on its own officers: it is reasonably clear that the US intercepted communications by Lieutenant General Rose in 1984. If that was not enough, the product of the part UK-financed system can be removed by the Americans from the jurisdiction of the Parliamentary committee set up to oversee the security and intelligence services under the terms of the 1994 law, which placed MI6 and GCHQ on a statutory basis.

GCHQ and the NSA remain 'joined at the hip' in many other ways; Menwith Hill in north Yorkshire, for example, is a vital US base. While these arrangements maintain British access to a great deal of Washington's intelligence, there is evidence that the Americans are no longer as reluctant to spy on the UK as they used to be and that they use their own and GCHQ stations to eavesdrop on European allies.

While the sigint relationship remains a transatlantic one, MI5 are increasingly integrated in European counter-terrorist arrangements and MI6 officers question whether they should start targeting the Americans. France and Germany meanwhile are establishing European intelligence structures which may one day have impressive satellite as well as other capabilities. Britain watches this process from the sidelines.

In so many areas there is case for radical reform of the British espionage system: in most international crises it can tell ministers no more than the newspapers can; it remains outside effective Parliamentary scrutiny; its efforts are spread across too many targets around the world; it links the country closely to an American 'take' on the world while business as well as diplomacy are centred on Europe. New thinking is needed, beginning with a Cabinet blueprint rationalizing and prioritizing overseas interests. This might then be used to change the Joint Intelligence Committee system and the agencies. Dynamic people, probably outsiders, would be needed to do to DIS, MI6 and GCHQ what Anthony Duff did to MI5 from 1985–7.

How likely is any of this to happen? Given the culture of 'need to know', the apparent unwillingness of politicians to retreat from a world role and the heavy hand of the mandarins of the Cabinet Office, it seems more likely that ingrained habits will remain, and that the process of gradual cuts to the agencies (except possibly MI5) will continue. Under these circumstances, reports marked UK Eyes Alpha will increasingly become a devalued currency in Whitehall.

Glossary

Agent	Supplier of intelligence under the control of a government agency
Armalite	American-made assault rifle
Assessments Staff	Body of around thirty civil servants which analyses intelligence in Whitehall's Cabinet Office
Asset	Supplier of intelligence
ASU	Active Service Unit – a terrorist cell, generally of two to six people
ASIO	Australian Security Intelligence Organization – the Australian equivalent of MI5
ATU	Anti-Terrorist Unit of the Metropolitan Police
BDA	Bomb Damage Assessment – the term for estimating the effectiveness of airstrikes
Blue Book	Weekly digest of signals intelligence reports
BND	Bundesnachrichtendienst (Federal Intelligence Service – Germany's foreign espionage arm
BRIXMIS	British Military Mission to the headquarters of the Soviet Army in the former East Germany
CDI	Chief of Defence Intelligence, the head of DIS (*see below*)
Centcom	Central Command – the US Army headquarters dealing with operations in the Middle East

Century House	Headquarters of the Secret Intelligence Service (MI6) until 1994
CIA	Central Intelligence Agency – the foreign espionage arm of the USA
CIG	Current Intelligence Group – a group of experts on a particular region or topic chaired by somebody from the Assessments Staff (*see above*)
CNN	Cable News Network – US television station
Cocom	Co-ordinating Committee – a body set up by Western nations to restrict the flow of technology to the former Eastern Bloc
Comint	Communications Intelligence – information gathered by intercepting communications
CX	Secret Intelligence Service agent reports
Delta Force	US special operations commando unit
DES	Data Encryption Standard – a yardstick for the encoding of business information
DCI	Director of Central Intelligence – head of the CIA (*see above*)
Deep Cover	Operations in which an intelligence officer uses extensive measures to disguise his/her identity and mission
DIA	Defense Intelligence Agency – the information-gathering arm of the US armed forces
Defense Support Programme	US satellite system designed to detect the launch of ballistic missiles
DGSS	Director General Security Service – head of MI5
DGSE	Direction Générale du Surveillance de L'Exterieure – France's overseas espionage arm
DIS	Defence Intelligence Staff – UK Ministry of Defence's information arm

DST	Direction Surveillance de Territoire – France's domestic espionage arm
DTI	Department of Trade and Industry of the UK government
DWIS	Defence Weekly Intelligence Summary – classified publication of DIS (*see above*)
Fibre Optics	Glass strands used to transmit information in the form of light
GCHQ	Government Communications Headquarters – the UK's signals intelligence organization
Geostationary	Type of orbit in which the forward speed of a satellite exactly matches the rotation of the earth, also called a geosynchronous orbit
glasnost	Russian for 'transparency' or 'openness' – the policy embraced by Mikhail Gorbachev in the late 1980s
GRU	Glavnoye Rezvedatelnoye Upravleniye – the main intelligence directorate first of the Soviet then of the Russian General Staff
Hizbollah	Party of God – Shia Islamic guerilla group
Illegals	Intelligence officers living long-term in a target country under a false identity
Imaging Craft	A satellite capable of producing pictures using cameras or radar
INF	Intermediate Nuclear Forces – the term for nuclear missiles deployed in Europe with a range in excess of 500km, but not intercontinental range
INLA	Irish National Liberation Army – republican terrorist group
INR	Intelligence and Research – arm of the US State Department
JIC	Joint Intelligence Committee – the UK's top forum for analysing intelligence and setting tasks for the agencies which collect it

JFHQ	Joint Force Headquarters – military command centre involving all three armed services
JNA	Jugoslovenska Narodna Armija – Yugoslav People's Army
King Charles Street	Headquarters of the UK Foreign and Commonwealth Office
KGB	Komitet Gosudarstvenoi Bezopasnosti (Committee for State Security) – the Soviet Union's intelligence organization
Light Cover	Operations in which an intelligence officer travels abroad as a diplomat or military officer under his/her own name
MBR	Ministerstvo Bezopasnosti Russiy (Russian Ministry of Security) – post 1991 Russia's internal security organization
MI5	Security Service – the UK organization countering espionage, subversion, terrorism and serious crime at home
MI6	Secret Intelligence Service – the UK's foreign espionage arm
Mobiles and Statics	surveillance units of MI5 operating in different modes
Mossad	Israeli foreign espionage arm
MPSB	Metropolitan Police Special Branch, detectives dealing with terrorism and other forms of politically motivated crime
Mujahedeen	Holy warriors – the term used by Afghan guerrillas opposing the Soviet occupation of 1979–89
National Security Council	US intelligence analysis organization
NCIS	National Criminal Intelligence Service – information-gathering organization established by the police to work throughout the UK

NSA	National Security Agency – US signals intelligence organization
OEIC	Overseas Economic Intelligence Committee – Cabinet Office body which assesses information on economic trends
OPEC	Organization of Petroleum-Exporting Countries – the international oil producers' association
Perestroika	Russian for 'reconstruction' – the policy pursued by Mikhail Gorbachev
PGP	Pretty Good Privacy – a type of encryption software
PSIS	Permanent Secretaries' Intelligence Services committee – a group of senior Whitehall civil servants who oversee espionage agencies' budgets and tasks
Psyops	Psychological Operations – measures designed to change the mind of an enemy
Red Book	Weekly survey of intelligence; papers agreed at weekly meetings of the JIC (*see above*) and circulated within government
REU	Restricted Enforcement Unit – a committee set up under the DTI (*see above*) in 1987 to control exports of military or militarily useful goods
Rezident	Russian term for the senior intelligence officer in a foreign station
Rezidentura	Russian term for a station gathering intelligence abroad
Saceur	Supreme Allied Commander Europe – the top Nato general in Europe
SAS	Special Air Service – British Army special forces unit
SBS	Special Boat Service – Royal Marine special forces unit
Scud	Type of ballistic missile originally designed in the Soviet Union and widely exported

Shabak	Sherut ha Bitachon ha Klali (General Security Service) – the Israeli domestic intelligence arm
SIS	Secret Intelligence Service or MI6 – the UK overseas espionage organization
Sigint	Signals Intelligence – electronic eavesdropping
Source	Someone who provides information
Sovbloc	Soviet Bloc controllerate within SIS (*see above*)
Special Forces	Troops trained to operate in small groups, often behind enemy lines
Spetsnaz	Spetsialnoye Naznacheniye – Special Designation or Special Forces (*see above*) of the Soviet Union until 1991, then of the Russian Federation
START	Strategic Arms Reduction Talks – US/Soviet treaty aimed at cutting long-range nuclear weapons
Star Wars/ Strategic Defense Initiative	US programme to provide defence against ballistic missiles
SVR	Sluzhba Vneshnoi Razvedki – overseas intelligence service; the Russian foreign espionage arm post 1991
Tradecraft	Skills used by spies or their controllers to avoid detection
Unprofor	United Nations Protection Force – deployed in Bosnia-Herzegovina
Walk-in	A person who offers to provide information

Index